McDougal Littell

Grammar for Writing

McDougal Littell
A HOUGHTON MIFFLIN COMPANY

McDougal Littell

Grammar for Writing

- GRAMMAR
- USAGE
- MECHANICS

McDougal Littell
A HOUGHTON MIFFLIN COMPANY

ISBN 13: 978-0-618-56618-1   ISBN 10: 0-618-56618-X

Printed in the United States of America.

Acknowledgments begin on page 377.

3 4 5 6 7 8 9–DCI–12 11 10 09 08

Contents Overview

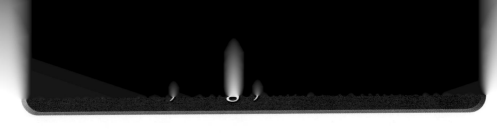

3 Pronouns

8 Sentence Structure

Quick-Fix Editing Machine

Special Features

Grammar Across the Curriculum

Grammar in Literature

Quick-Fix Editing Machine

Student Resources

Grammar, Usage, and Mechanics

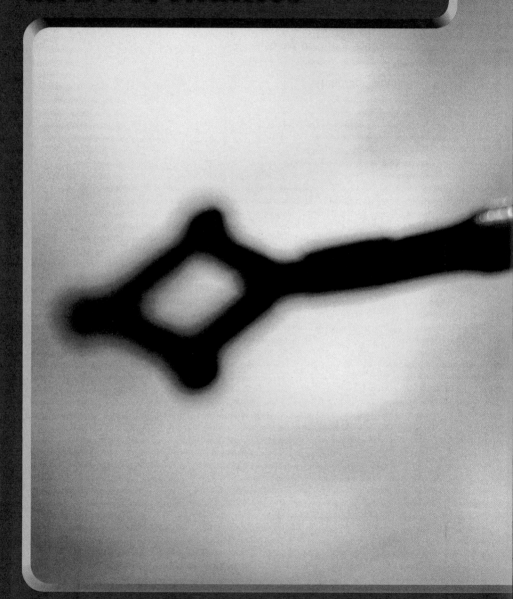

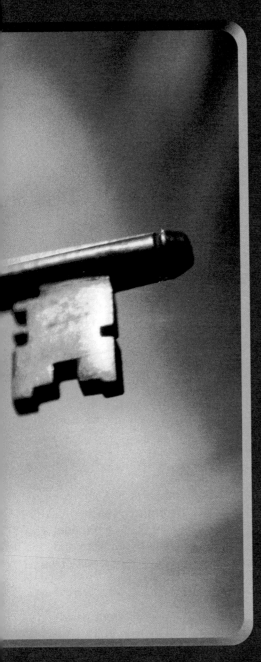

The Key to Clear Communication

If you don't have the key to a house, you can't
enter. Grammar is the key to the house of
language. By learning proper grammar and
usage, you'll have the keys to unlock your
imagination in words.

The Sentence and Its Parts

Theme: Cities and Towns

Parts of a Whole

This postcard shows photographs of several parts of San Francisco. How are the neighborhoods different from each other? How are they parts of a whole? Just as cities are made up of neighborhoods, sentences are composed of subjects and predicates. These basic parts can appear in different kinds of sentences that add variety to writing.

Write Away: Picture This

If you were asked to create a postcard showing different parts of your city or town, what pictures would you include in it? Write a paragraph explaining your choices. Save your paragraph in your 🗀 **Working Portfolio.**

Diagnostic Test: What Do You Know?

Choose the letter of the term that correctly identifies each underlined item in the paragraph below.

> Most <u>Americans</u> live in urban areas. Cities offer <u>people</u> a wide
> (1)   (2)
> variety of activities. They also <u>provide</u> many job opportunities.
> (3)
> <u>Offices and factories</u> are often located in cities. Yet rural life has
> (4)
> <u>advantages</u>. Small towns <u>can seem</u> friendlier. <u>People</u> usually know
> (5)   (6)   (7)
> their neighbors. <u>There is more open space, the pace is slower.</u> <u>What
> (8)
> kind of place should you live in?</u> <u>Let your heart be your guide.</u>
> (9)   (10)

1. A. simple subject
   B. simple predicate
   C. complete subject
   D. complete predicate

2. A. predicate noun
   B. predicate adjective
   C. direct object
   D. indirect object

3. A. simple subject
   B. simple predicate
   C. complete subject
   D. complete predicate

4. A. direct object
   B. simple predicate
   C. compound subject
   D. compound verb

5. A. predicate noun
   B. predicate adjective
   C. direct object
   D. indirect object

6. A. verb phrase
   B. helping verb
   C. main verb
   D. compound subject

7. A. simple subject
   B. simple predicate
   C. compound subject
   D. compound verb

8. A. fragment
   B. run-on sentence
   C. exclamatory sentence
   D. interrogative sentence

9. A. fragment
   B. run-on sentence
   C. exclamatory sentence
   D. interrogative sentence

10. A. imperative sentence
    B. exclamatory sentence
    C. fragment
    D. declarative sentence

SENTENCE PARTS

LESSON 1

Complete Subjects and Predicates

❶ Here's the Idea

In order to share ideas and information successfully, you need to use complete sentences.

▶ **A sentence is a group of words that expresses a complete thought.**

Here is a group of words.

cities   central   suburbs   around   develop

The words cannot get a message across unless they have a structure. Here is a sentence built from the same words. Notice that the sentence communicates a complete idea.

Suburbs develop around central cities.

▶ **Every complete sentence has two basic parts: a subject and a predicate.**

1. The **complete subject** includes all the words that tell whom or what the sentence is about.

   COMPLETE SUBJECT

   Metropolitan areas include suburbs.

2. The **complete predicate** includes the verb and all the words that complete the verb's meaning.

   COMPLETE PREDICATE

   Metropolitan areas **include suburbs.**

Here's How Finding Complete Subjects and Predicates

Metropolitan areas include suburbs.

1. **To find the complete subject, ask who or what does something (or is something).**

   What includes suburbs? **Metropolitan areas**

2. **To find the complete predicate, ask what the subject does (or is).**

   What do metropolitan areas do? include suburbs

---

❷ Why It Matters in Writing

Writers often use isolated words and phrases when jotting down ideas and information. For example, when writing about Tokyo, you might jot down "metropolitan population more than 30 million" and "highways, public transportation strained." To turn these notes into thoughts that you can share with others, you must use complete sentences.

STUDENT MODEL

> Tokyo is a very crowded city. More than 30 million people live in the metropolitan area. Commuters often jam the highways. The public transportation system is also strained.

❸ Practice and Apply

CONCEPT CHECK: Complete Subjects and Predicates

In separate columns on a sheet of paper, write the complete subject and complete predicate of these sentences.

Urban Sprawl
1. Species of plants and animals are disappearing near cities.
2. Urban sprawl harms their habitats.
3. Growing families want bigger houses and yards.
4. Many of them move from dense central cities into suburbs.
5. Real-estate developers need land for new housing.
6. Some projects take over forests and woodlands.
7. New policies limit growth in some areas.
8. State and local governments buy undeveloped land.
9. Some cities encourage development on old industrial sites.
10. Every reclaimed acre saves about seven acres of unspoiled land.

➡ For a SELF-CHECK and more practice, see the EXERCISE BANK, p. 312.

SENTENCE PARTS

Simple Subjects

❶ Here's the Idea

You have learned that one basic part of a sentence is the complete subject. Now you will learn about the key part of the complete subject.

▶ **The simple subject is the main word or words in the complete subject.** Descriptive words are not part of the simple subject.

COMPLETE SUBJECT

Some small towns hold town meetings.

⬆ SIMPLE SUBJECT

Adult residents vote directly on community issues.
⬆ SIMPLE SUBJECT

When a proper name is used as a subject, all parts of the name make up the simple subject.

New England is the birthplace of town meetings.
SIMPLE SUBJECT

❷ Why It Matters in Writing

The simple subject is one of the key words in a sentence. Make sure that you have chosen a precise one so that readers will know whom or what the sentence is about.

STUDENT MODEL

DRAFT

Democracy is simple in some parts of New England. **People** make decisions at town meetings instead of electing officials to make them. **This** helps ordinary people feel in charge.

REVISION

Democracy is simple in some parts of New England. **Voters** make decisions at town meetings instead of electing officials to make them. This **system** helps ordinary people feel in charge.

❸ Practice and Apply

A. CONCEPT CHECK: Simple Subject

On a separate sheet of paper, write the simple subject of each sentence. Remember, descriptive words are not part of the simple subject.

Example: Many large universities have urban planning programs.
Simple subject: universities

City Planning
1. The Industrial Revolution transformed old cities.
2. Healthy new industries attracted people from the countryside.
3. Most workers had to live in overcrowded, filthy slums.
4. Some leaders recognized the need for improvements.
5. Early planners focused on preventing disease.
6. City officials passed laws to improve sanitary conditions.
7. Urban reformers also tackled problems in housing and education.
8. These groundbreaking efforts led to the urban planning movement.
9. Any modern city can experience rapid change.
10. A good plan allows a city to meet this challenge.

➡ For a SELF-CHECK and more practice, see the EXERCISE BANK, p. 312.

B. REVISING: Using Specific Subjects

Read the following passage. Then replace the underlined words with more specific subjects.

Bettles Field is a small town in Alaska. The <u>number of people</u> is only 51. <u>Those who come from other places</u> usually must take a plane to get there. The <u>degree of coldness</u> can plunge to 70 degrees below zero in winter. Some <u>24-hour periods</u> have only three hours of sunlight. The <u>ones who live there</u> often schedule town dinners to keep their spirits up.

LESSON 3 **Simple Predicates, or Verbs**

❶ Here's the Idea

You have learned about the simple subject of a sentence. You also need to know about the simple predicate.

▶ **The simple predicate, or verb, is the main word or words in the complete predicate.**

COMPLETE PREDICATE

Many Mexicans celebrate Cinco de Mayo.

SIMPLE PREDICATE

The holiday commemorates a famous battle.
SIMPLE PREDICATE

Verb

▶ **A verb is a word used to express an action, a condition, or a state of being.** A **linking verb** tells what the subject *is.* An **action verb** tells what the subject *does,* even when the action cannot be seen.

The Mexicans fought a French army. (action you can see)

They wanted independence. (action you cannot see)

Cinco de Mayo is very popular in Mexico City. (linking)

❷ Why It Matters in Writing

People sometimes drop verbs from sentences when they write quickly. Watch out for missing verbs when you revise.

STUDENT MODEL

Gilroy, California, ^*is* the Garlic Capital of the World. Every

year the town hosts a three-day garlic festival. The festival

organizers ^*build* a huge flaming model of a garlic bulb.

CHAPTER I

❸ Practice and Apply

A. CONCEPT CHECK: Simple Predicates, or Verbs

On a separate sheet of paper, write the simple predicate, or verb, of each sentence.

A Small-Town Festival
1. Stahlstown, Pennsylvania, is the home of an old-time ritual.
2. Residents hold a flax-scutching festival every year.
3. This festival preserves the skills of their ancestors.
4. Pioneer settlers created fabric from flax plants.
5. First they dried the plants.
6. Then they separated the plant fibers.
7. Scutching is the name for the separation process.
8. The settlers spun the scutched flax into thread.
9. They wove the thread into linen fabric.
10. The resourceful pioneers made clothing from this fabric.

➜ For a SELF-CHECK and more practice, see the EXERCISE BANK, p. 313.

B. WRITING: Communicating Information

Use the following information to write a five-sentence paragraph about Atlanta. Underline the verb in each sentence. Include at least three different verbs in your paragraph.

    Example: the Jimmy Carter Library
                 Atlanta <u>contains</u> the Jimmy Carter Library.

Facts About Atlanta
• the capital of Georgia
• in the foothills of the Blue Ridge Mountains
• about 3 million people in the metropolitan area
• the birthplace of Martin Luther King, Jr.
• host of the 1996 Summer Olympic Games

SENTENCE PARTS

Verb Phrases

❶ Here's the Idea

The simple predicate, or verb, may consist of two or more words. These words are called a verb phrase.

▶ **A verb phrase is made up of a main verb and one or more helping verbs.**

VERB PHRASE

We can imagine the city of the future.

HELPING VERB ⬈   ⬉ MAIN VERB

Main Verbs and Helping Verbs

A **main verb** can stand by itself as the simple predicate of a sentence.

Technology changes cities. (action)
              MAIN VERB

The changes are rapid. (linking)
              MAIN VERB

Helping verbs help main verbs express action or show time.

VERB PHRASE

Technology will change cities.
HELPING VERB ⬈   ⬉ MAIN VERB

The changes will be occurring rapidly.

City dwellers should have been preparing for change.

Notice that sometimes the main verb changes form when it is used with helping verbs. For more on these changes, see pages 100–104.

Common Helping Verbs	
Forms of *be*	is, am, are, was, were, be, been
Forms of *do*	do, does, did
Forms of *have*	has, have, had
Others	may, might, can, should, could, would, shall, will

❷ Why It Matters in Writing

Writers often use verb phrases to show time. Notice how the verb phrases convey past, present, and future time in the following paragraph.

PROFESSIONAL MODEL

This year, a team of students from New Morning School in Plymouth, Michigan, designed a city of the future. Residents of Terrania will travel on computer-guided hover shuttles. This system can reduce traffic and pollution.

PAST

PRESENT

FUTURE

—Randy Vickers

❸ Practice and Apply

CONCEPT CHECK: Verb Phrases

Write the verb phrase in each sentence below.

Pollution Problems

1. Modern industries have allowed cities and towns to flourish.
2. However, they can cause serious problems as well.
3. Chemical wastes from factories can poison our environment.
4. Pollution is endangering animals and plants.
5. Automobiles have been polluting the air for decades.
6. Industries and individuals can prevent pollution.
7. The Environmental Protection Agency was created in 1970.
8. It has been overseeing federal action against pollution since then.
9. Laws have tightened standards for pollutants like carbon monoxide.
10. Such laws should have a substantial effect in the future.

➡ **For a SELF-CHECK and more practice, see the EXERCISE BANK, p. 313.**

LESSON 5

Compound Sentence Parts

❶ Here's the Idea

Sentences can have **compound subjects** and **compound verbs**.

▶ **A compound subject is made up of two or more subjects that share the same verb.** The subjects are joined by a conjunction, or connecting word, such as *and, or,* or *but.*

COMPOUND SUBJECT

Tornadoes and hurricanes are dangerous.

SUBJECT ➦   ↖ SUBJECT

A flood or an earthquake can devastate a city.

▶ **A compound verb is made up of two or more verbs that have the same subject.** The verbs are joined by a conjunction such as *and, or,* or *but.*

COMPOUND VERB

The swollen river rose and crested.

VERB ➦   VERB ➦

Rescue workers located and evacuated residents.

❷ Why It Matters in Writing

Sometimes two sentences contain similar information. You can use compound subjects and verbs to combine such sentences and avoid repetition in your writing.

STUDENT MODEL

In 1964 the Good Friday earthquake struck ^*and devastated* Anchorage, Alaska. ~~It devastated the city.~~ ˅*and the tidal wave that followed it* The earthquake ^caused damage as far south as California. ~~The tidal wave that followed it~~ ~~also caused damage~~.

❸ Practice and Apply

A. CONCEPT CHECK: Compound Sentence Parts

On a separate sheet of paper, write the compound subject or the compound verb for each sentence.

The Alaska Gold Rush

1. Juneau and other Alaskan cities owe their existence to the gold rush.
2. Joseph Juneau and Richard Harris discovered gold in southeastern Alaska in 1880.
3. This area and the nearby Yukon region proved rich in gold deposits.
4. Professional prospectors and amateurs soon flooded into Alaska.
5. Some of these adventurers survived and profited.
6. Others froze or starved in the harsh environment.
7. Jack London and Robert Service wrote about the prospectors' hardships.
8. Their writings preserve and glorify this exciting period.
9. Tourism and government are the big industries in Juneau today.
10. However, stories of the gold rush still excite and captivate residents.

➡ **For a SELF-CHECK and more practice, see the EXERCISE BANK, p. 313.**

For a SELF-CHECK and more practice, see the EXERCISE BANK, p. 313.

B. REVISING: Combining Sentences

Luisa tried to write this note on a postcard, but she ran out of space. Make it more compact by using compound subjects and verbs to combine sentences.

Dear Ahmed,

 Jeff is having a great time in Seattle. So am I. The parks are great. The restaurants are great, too. Yesterday we swam at a beach along Puget Sound. We also sunbathed. The water surrounding the city makes it beautiful. So do the mountains.

Love,

Luisa

SENTENCE PARTS

The Sentence and Its Parts **15**

LESSON 6

Kinds of Sentences

❶ Here's the Idea

▶ **A sentence can be used to make a statement, to ask a question, to make a request or give a command, or to show strong feelings.**

Four Kinds of Sentences

	What It Does	Examples
Declarative **.**	Makes a statement; always ends with a period	I went to Honolulu last week. My hotel was on Waikiki Beach.
Interrogative **?**	Asks a question; always ends with a question mark	What did you do there? Did you surf?
Imperative **. or !**	Tells or asks someone to do something; usually ends with a period but may end with an exclamation point	Show me your photographs. Take me with you next time!
Exclamatory **!**	Shows strong feeling; always ends with an exclamation point	What a lucky person you are! That beach looks gorgeous!

❷ Why It Matters in Writing

Writers use the different kinds of sentences in dialogue to imitate how people speak. Notice which sentences in this dialogue express Henry's anxiety during his stay in London.

LITERARY MODEL

Henry. When will they be back?   INTERROGATIVE
Servant. In a month, they said.   EXCLAMATORY
Henry. A month! This is awful! Tell me how   IMPERATIVE
to get word to them. It's of great importance.   DECLARATIVE

—from Mark Twain, *The Million-Pound Bank Note,*
dramatized by Walter Hackett

❸ Practice and Apply

A. CONCEPT CHECK: Kinds of Sentences

Identify each of the following sentences as declarative (D), interrogative (INT), exclamatory (E), or imperative (IMP).

Cherry Blossom Time

1. Do you know whose idea it was to plant cherry trees in Washington, D.C.?
2. Writer and photographer Eliza Scidmore came up with the idea.
3. Scidmore admired the flowering cherry trees she saw in Japan.
4. The city government had recently dredged the Potomac River and piled the dirt along the river.
5. Wouldn't blooming trees hide that sight nicely?
6. The city of Tokyo gave Washington 3,020 cherry trees in 1912.
7. Come to the Cherry Blossom Festival next spring and see them for yourself.
8. You would love Washington in the spring!
9. Look at the trees' reflections in the Tidal Basin.
10. The delicate pink blossoms look beautiful!

➡ **For a SELF-CHECK and more practice, see the EXERCISE BANK, p. 314.**

B. WRITING: Describing a Photograph

The famous gateway arches in Mombasa, Kenya, are shaped like giant elephant tusks. Write a declarative, interrogative, imperative, and exclamatory sentence about what you see in this photograph.

Subjects in Unusual Order

❶ Here's the Idea

In most declarative sentences, subjects come before verbs. In some kinds of sentences, however, subjects can come between verb parts, follow verbs, or not appear at all.

Questions

▶ **In a question, the subject usually comes after the verb or between parts of the verb phrase.**

↰VERB PHRASE↱
Are you walking to the Brooklyn Bridge?
↳ SUBJECT

Is it **far away? When** will you arrive **there?**

To find the subject, turn the question into a statement. Then ask who or what is or does something.

Can I go **with you?**

I can go **with you.** (Who can go? *I*)

Commands

▶ **The subject of a command, or an imperative sentence, is usually *you.*** Often, *you* doesn't appear in the sentence because it is implied.

(You) Put **on your comfortable shoes.**
↳ IMPLIED SUBJECT

(You) Meet **me in the lobby.**

Inverted Sentences

In an inverted sentence, the subject comes after the verb. Writers use inverted sentences to emphasize particular words or ideas.

Inverted Subject and Verb	
Normal	The **bridge** extends across the East River.
Inverted	Across the East River extends the **bridge**.
Normal	Its **towers** are reflected in the water.
Inverted	Reflected in the water are its **towers**.

Sentences Beginning with *Here* or *There*

▶ **In some sentences beginning with *here* or *there*, subjects follow verbs.** To find the subject in such a sentence, look for the verb and ask the question *who* or *what*.

WHAT IS?

There is the world-famous bridge.
VERB   SUBJECT

WHAT COMES?

Here comes the bus to Brooklyn.
VERB   SUBJECT

❷ Why It Matters in Writing

Inverting the word order enables you to add variety to your sentences. Notice how the changes in the revision below make it more interesting to read.

STUDENT MODEL

DRAFT

    We have walked all the way to the tip of Manhattan. The Brooklyn Bridge stands before us. Brooklyn lies beyond the river.

REVISION

    We have walked all the way to the tip of Manhattan. **Before us stands the Brooklyn Bridge. Beyond the river lies Brooklyn.**

SENTENCE PARTS

➌ Practice and Apply

A. CONCEPT CHECK: Subjects in Unusual Order

In separate columns on a sheet of paper, write the simple subject and the verb (or verb phrase) of each sentence below.

Coney Island: King of Amusement Parks

1. Have you heard of Coney Island?
2. On the edge of Brooklyn lies this famous amusement park.
3. Among its attractions are many rides.
4. Test your courage on the old-fashioned wooden roller coaster.
5. There is a ride worth taking.
6. Do you like games of skill?
7. Then walk down the midway at Coney Island.
8. On both sides are games like the ring toss.
9. There are not too many winners in those games.
10. Here is a map of the amusement park.

➡ For a SELF-CHECK and more practice, see the EXERCISE BANK, p. 314.

B. REVISING: Adding Variety

Rewrite the following sentences according to the instructions given in parentheses.

1. You would like to learn more about Brooklyn. (Change the sentence to a question.)
2. Your chance has arrived. (Rewrite the sentence to begin with *Here is*)
3. You come on a walking tour of the borough. (Change the sentence to a command.)
4. Many fascinating neighborhoods are scattered throughout Brooklyn. (Begin the sentence with *Scattered throughout* and place the subject after the helping verb.)
5. You meet your guide on the Brooklyn side of the bridge. (Change the sentence to a command.)

In your 🗀 **Working Portfolio,** find the paragraph that you wrote for the **Write Away** on page 4. Add variety to the sentences by changing the positions of some of their subjects.

Complements: Subject Complements

❶ Here's the Idea

A complement is a word or a group of words that completes the meaning of a verb. Two kinds of complements are **subject complements** and **objects of verbs**.

▶ **A subject complement is a word or group of words that follows a linking verb and renames or describes the subject.** A linking verb links the subject with a noun or an adjective that tells more about the subject.

LINKING VERB ↘
Pennsylvania is **the Keystone State.**
SUBJECT ↗   ↖ COMPLEMENT

Common Linking Verbs	
Forms of *be*	am, is, are, was, were, being, been
Other linking verbs	appear, feel, look, sound, seem, smell, taste, grow, become

Predicate Nouns and Predicate Adjectives

Both nouns and adjectives can serve as subject complements.

▶ **A predicate noun follows a linking verb and defines or renames the subject.**

DEFINES
Philadelphia is **the largest city in Pennsylvania.**
SUBJECT ↗   ↖ PREDICATE NOUN

RENAMES
The capital of Pennsylvania is **Harrisburg.**

▶ **A predicate adjective follows a linking verb and describes a quality of the subject.**

DESCRIBES
Philadelphia cheesesteaks taste **great.**
SUBJECT ↗   ↖ PREDICATE ADJECTIVE

DESCRIBES
The Liberty Bell is **historic.**

❷ Why It Matters in Writing

Subject complements can provide important information and vivid details about your subjects.

PROFESSIONAL MODEL

The town of Hershey smells delicious. A huge candy factory is the source of this pleasurable sensation. Tourists seem happy just to breathe in the air.

PREDICATE NOUN

PREDICATE ADJECTIVES

—Rachel Robinson

❸ Practice and Apply

A. CONCEPT CHECK: Subject Complements

Find the subject complement in each sentence and identify it as a predicate noun (PN) or a predicate adjective (PA).

By Any Other Name
1. Chicago is the Windy City.
2. This nickname is a reference to loud and windy promoters.
3. Denver is the Mile-High City.
4. It is high above sea level.
5. Paris became the City of Light long ago.
6. It looks so beautiful at night.
7. Molde, Norway, is the Town of Roses.
8. Its rose gardens smell fragrant.
9. Tin Can Island is the nickname for Niuafo'ou, Tonga.
10. Tin cans are the containers that islanders used for exchanging letters with passing ships.

➜ For a SELF-CHECK and more practice, see the EXERCISE BANK, p. 315.

B. REVISING: Replacing Subject Complements

Find each subject complement below and replace it with a synonym. Identify your replacement as a predicate noun or predicate adjective.

Los Angeles seems glamorous. It has become the heart of the entertainment industry. The presence of movie stars is a delight for tourists.

Complements: Objects of Verbs

❶ Here's the Idea

In addition to subject complements, there are objects of verbs. Action verbs often need complements called direct objects and indirect objects to complete their meaning.

Direct Objects

▶ **A direct object is a word or group of words that names the receiver of the action.** A direct object answers the questions *what* or *whom*.

RIDE WHAT?

Many Beijing residents ride bicycles.
DIRECT OBJECT

New Yorkers take the subway. (take what? *subway*)

Indirect Objects

▶ **An indirect object is a word or group of words that tells to whom or what (or for whom or what) an action is performed.** An indirect object usually comes between a verb and a direct object.

TO WHOM?

Mass transit offers people easy commutes.
INDIRECT OBJECT   DIRECT OBJECT

Gondolas give Venetians romantic rides.

Verbs that are often followed by indirect objects include *bring, give, hand, lend, make, offer, send, show, teach, tell, write,* and *ask.*

> **Here's How** Finding Direct and Indirect Objects
>
> **The conductor hands us our change.**
> 1. Find the action verb in the sentence. *hands*
> 2. To find the **direct object**, ask, Hands what? *change*
> 3. To find the **indirect object**, ask, Hands to or for whom? *us*

❷ Why It Matters in Writing

Direct objects and indirect objects are important when you are describing the effects of actions.

LITERARY MODEL

Grady Bishop had just been hired as a driver for Metro Bus Service. When he put on the gray uniform and boarded his bus, nothing mattered, not his obesity, not his poor education, not growing up the eleventh child of the town drunk. Driving gave him power. And power mattered.

DIRECT OBJECTS

INDIRECT OBJECT

—"The Woman in the Snow," retold by
Patricia C. McKissack

❸ Practice and Apply

CONCEPT CHECK: Objects of Verbs

For each sentence below, write each object and identify it as either a direct object (DO) or an indirect object (IO).

Easy Riding
1. The interstate highway system offers American cities a connection with each other.
2. State governments began building the system in the 1950s.
3. The federal government gave the states funds for their portions of the interstate highway system.
4. Builders poured concrete by the ton during the project.
5. They moved enough soil to cover Connecticut.
6. The project gave many towns an economic boost.
7. The system now reaches all areas of the country.
8. Astronauts can even see it from space.
9. It brought Americans increased mobility.
10. Drivers can cross the country without stopping for a traffic light.

➜ For a SELF-CHECK and more practice, see the EXERCISE BANK, p. 315.

Fragments and Run-Ons

❶ Here's the Idea

Sentence fragments and run-on sentences are writing errors that can make your writing difficult to understand.

Sentence Fragments

▶ **A sentence fragment is a part of a sentence that is written as if it were a complete sentence.** A sentence fragment is missing a subject, a predicate, or both.

FRAGMENTS

Ghost towns usually around deserted mines and oil fields. (missing a predicate)

Abandoned **them after the mines or fields were exhausted.** (missing a subject)

Numerous in the western states. (missing both)

To make a complete sentence, add a subject, a predicate, or both.

REVISION

Ghost towns usually can be found **around deserted mines and oil fields. Residents** abandoned **them after the mines or fields were exhausted. Such towns** are **numerous in the western states.**

For more help, see the Quick-Fix Editing Machine, p. 290.

SENTENCE PARTS

Run-On Sentences

▶ **A run-on sentence consists of two or more sentences written as though they were a single sentence.**

RUN-ON

Most ghost towns are **in ruins, some** have been restored **to their original condition.**

REVISION

Most ghost towns are **in ruins. Some** have been restored **to their original condition.**

REVISION

Most ghost towns are **in ruins, but some** have been restored **to their original condition.**

For more help, see the Quick-Fix Editing Machine, p. 291.

When combining two sentences with a conjunction, insert a comma before the conjunction.

❷ Why It Matters in Writing

Fragments and run-on sentences can confuse and frustrate readers. Fixing these problems will make your writing clearer.

STUDENT MODEL

DRAFT

The town of Garnet flourished for a while. During the second half of the 19th century. One thousand people lived there in 1898, seven years later the population was only 200. Now a ghost town.

REVISION

The town of Garnet flourished **during the second half of the 19th century.** One thousand people lived there in 1898, **but** seven years later the population was only 200. **Garnet is** now a ghost town.

❸ Practice and Apply

A. CONCEPT CHECK: Sentence Fragments and Run-Ons

On a separate sheet of paper, identify each of the following sentences as a fragment (F), a run-on (RO), or a complete sentence (CS).

Ink, Arkansas

1. A tiny village in Arkansas had no name, residents walked to the next town for their mail.
2. Tired of walking such a distance.
3. They wanted their own post office.
4. The U.S. Postal Service replied to the residents, it sent them questionnaires.
5. Asked what name the village wanted.
6. Every family in town received a questionnaire, the instructions said, "Please write in ink."
7. The residents did just that.
8. Wrote in the word "Ink" for the name of their town.
9. Now Ink, Arkansas, has a name and a post office.
10. Just 12 miles from Pencil Bluff, Arkansas.

➜ **For a SELF-CHECK and more practice, see the EXERCISE BANK, p. 316.**

B. REVISING: Frustrating Fragments and Ridiculous Run-Ons

A friend of yours is going to Montana. You have dashed off a note with suggestions on visiting ghost towns. Complaining that it is confusing, she hands back the note. Correct the fragments and run-on sentences so that your note is easier to understand.

Suggestions for Visiting Ghost Towns

    You will need comfortable shoes. Be careful as you. Many of the buildings are badly deteriorated, there may be old mine shafts you can fall into. Rattlesnakes another danger. Never remove any items from a ghost town, leave them for other visitors to enjoy.

Grammar in Literature

Using Different Types of Sentences

When you write for school or for fun, you can use different types of sentences to create dialogue. Using different types of sentences makes dialogue more interesting and realistic. Notice the types of sentences author Amy Tan uses in the dialogue from "Rules of the Game."

from

RULES of the GAME

BY AMY TAN

"Let me! Let me! I begged between games ...

IMPERATIVE SENTENCES

Vincent explained the rules, pointing to each piece. "You have sixteen pieces and so do I. One king and queen, two bishops, two knights, two castles, and eight pawns. The pawns can only move forward one step,

DECLARATIVE SENTENCE

except on the first move. Then they can move two. But they can only take men by moving crossways like this, except in the beginning, when you can move ahead and take another pawn."

"Why?" I asked as I moved my pawn. "Why can't they move more steps?"

INTERROGATIVE SENTENCES

Chinese Girl, Emil Orlik. Oil on canvas. Christie's Images/SuperStock.

CHAPTER 1

Practice and Apply

WRITING: Using Different Types of Sentences

Some of the rules for the board game checkers are listed below. Create a dialogue between two people about the game. You might have a sister explain the rules to her sister, a friend explain the rules to another friend, or one stranger explain the rules to another stranger. Be sure to use different types of sentences. Save your dialogue in your 🗀 **Working Portfolio.**

SENTENCE PARTS

Rules for Checkers

The object of the game is to capture all of your opponent's pieces.

1. The first player moves a black piece diagonally toward the red pieces.

2. The second player moves a red piece diagonally toward the black pieces.

3. The pieces can only be moved diagonally on the black squares.

4. Players can only move the pieces forward, toward the opponent's starting place.

5. To capture a piece, a player must "jump" diagonally, from one square, over the opponent's piece, landing on the closest empty square.

6. When a player captures a piece, that piece is removed from the board.

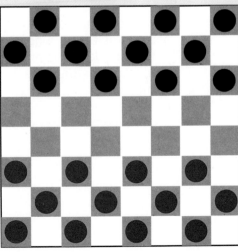

Mixed Review

A. Subjects, Predicates, and Compound Sentence Parts Read the passage, and then write the answers to the questions below it.

Riding Underground

(1) A subway is an underground railway. **(2)** Electricity powers the trains. **(3)** Subways are very convenient in crowded urban areas. **(4)** Some large cities have built extensive subway systems. **(5)** They must plan and construct those systems carefully. **(6)** Cost and efficiency are the main concerns. **(7)** There are several different methods for building subway tunnels. **(8)** Construction crews often tear apart and rebuild streets over subway lines. **(9)** Can you imagine the traffic problems such construction would create? **(10)** However, the benefits will outweigh any inconvenience.

1. What is the simple subject of sentence 1?
2. What kind of sentence is sentence 2?
3. What is the simple predicate of sentence 3?
4. What is the main verb in sentence 4?
5. What is the compound part of sentence 5?
6. What is the compound part of sentence 6?
7. What is the simple subject of sentence 7?
8. What is the complete subject of sentence 8?
9. What kind of sentence is sentence 9?
10. What is the complete predicate in sentence 10?

B. Complements Identify each underlined word as a predicate adjective (PA), a predicate noun (PN), a direct object (DO), or an indirect object (IO).

1. Concord is a <u>town</u> in Massachusetts.
2. The town is <u>famous</u>.
3. American revolutionaries encountered British <u>soldiers</u> there.
4. The revolutionaries gave the <u>British</u> a good fight.
5. Concord was also the <u>home</u> of several important writers.
6. Trenton, New Jersey, is another <u>site</u> of a Revolutionary War battle.
7. George Washington crossed the <u>Delaware River</u> near the city.
8. This maneuver was <u>daring</u>.
9. His troops handed the <u>enemy</u> a major defeat.
10. Trenton was the nation's <u>capital</u> for a brief period.

Choose the letter of the term that correctly identifies each underlined part of this passage.

Cities <u>are home to a variety of wildlife</u>. Pigeons <u>have thrived</u> in
               (1)   (2)
cities. They build <u>nests</u> on ledges. Squirrels are hardy <u>acrobats</u>.
               (3)   (4)
<u>Many people appreciate their playful behavior, others consider</u>
                      (5)
<u>them pests</u>. <u>More exotic forms of wildlife</u> are appearing in cities.
                   (6)
<u>Los Angeles, New York, and other cities</u> attract coyotes. These
                 (7)
creatures <u>hunt and scavenge</u> for food. <u>One coyote in New York</u>
              (8)   (9)
enjoyed shrimp lo mein and spaghetti! <u>What would you do if you</u>
                                       (10)
<u>saw a coyote in your neighborhood?</u>

1. A. simple subject
   B. complete subject
   C. simple predicate
   D. complete predicate

2. A. main verb
   B. helping verb
   C. verb phrase
   D. compound verb

3. A. simple predicate
   B. complete predicate
   C. direct object
   D. indirect object

4. A. predicate adjective
   B. predicate noun
   C. direct object
   D. indirect object

5. A. compound subject
   B. compound verb
   C. fragment
   D. run-on sentence

6. A. complete subject
   B. simple subject
   C. complete predicate
   D. compound subject

7. A. compound subject
   B. compound verb
   C. complement
   D. predicate noun

8. A. compound subject
   B. compound verb
   C. complement
   D. predicate noun

9. A. declarative sentence
   B. interrogative sentence
   C. exclamatory sentence
   D. imperative sentence

10. A. declarative sentence
    B. interrogative sentence
    C. exclamatory sentence
    D. imperative sentence

SENTENCE PARTS

Student Help Desk

The Sentence at a Glance

A sentence has two parts: a complete subject and a complete predicate.

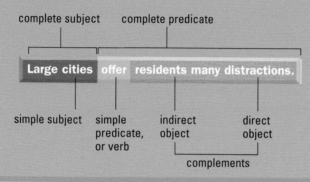

complete subject   complete predicate

Large cities offer **residents many distractions.**

simple subject   simple   indirect   direct
                  predicate,   object   object
                  or verb

complements

Subjects and Predicates   Central City

Term or Concept	Example	How to Find It
Complete subject	**Most cities** have a downtown area.	Ask who or what is or does something.
Simple subject	**cities**	Find the key word(s) in the complete subject.
Complete predicate	Skyscrapers *tower over pedestrians.*	Ask what the subject is or does.
Simple predicate	*tower*	Find the verb(s) or verb phrase(s).

Complements   Outer Neighborhoods

	Term or Concept	Example	What It Does
Linking verbs	Predicate noun	This is my **neighborhood.**	Renames or defines the subject
Linking verbs	Predicate adjective	It is **peaceful.**	Describes the subject
Action verbs	Direct object	I ride my **bike** downtown.	Completes the verb's action
Action verbs	Indirect object	A map shows **me** the route.	Tells to whom/what or for whom/what the action is done

Kinds of Sentences   Seeking Variety

Declarative sentence	I'm going to the museum.
Interrogative sentence	Will it be interesting**?**
Imperative sentence	**(You)** Come with me.
Exclamatory sentence	The show is fascinating**!**

The Bottom Line

Checklist for Editing Sentences

Have I . . .

____ made sure that each sentence has a subject and a predicate?

____ corrected any fragments or run-on sentences?

____ combined any sentences with similar ideas by using compound subjects or verbs?

____ used different kinds of sentences and different orders of sentence parts for variety?

____ used complements to make the meanings of sentences clear?

Nouns

Theme: Stars and Planets

Naming It

For thousands of years, astronomers have been giving names to stars, planets, constellations, and other objects in the sky. How many different ones can you list? All of these names are nouns. Nouns allow us to communicate our ideas about places that are far away from our planet. Without nouns, you might say that we would be lost in space—unable to talk or write about the world around us.

Write Away: Travel Plans

Write about a planet you would like to visit. Why does it interest you? What would you like to learn about it? Save your work in your 🗀 **Working Portfolio.**

Diagnostic Test: What Do You Know?

For each underlined item, choose the letter of the term that correctly identifies it.

> The first <u>telescopes</u> were built about 1608 by lens makers in the
> (1)
> <u>Netherlands</u>. An Italian scientist, <u>Galileo Galilei</u>, used this new
> (2)   (3)
> <u>invention</u> to observe heavenly <u>bodies</u>. Galileo's telescope had little
> (4)   (5)
> power by today's standards. However, this remarkable <u>instrument</u>
> (6)
> allowed Galileo to make important discoveries about the <u>solar</u>
> (7)
> <u>system</u>. Over the <u>centuries</u>, our knowledge of the universe has
> (8)
> been greatly expanded by <u>astronomers'</u> observations through
> (9)
> telescopes. We now know that the stars, planets, and galaxies we
> see as <u>pinpoints</u> of light may be many light-years away.
> (10)

1. A. proper noun
   B. common noun
   C. collective noun
   D. compound noun

2. A. predicate noun
   B. proper noun
   C. collective noun
   D. possessive noun

3. A. noun as direct object
   B. noun as indirect object
   C. noun as appositive
   D. noun as object of preposition

4. A. noun as subject
   B. noun as direct object
   C. noun as indirect object
   D. noun as object of preposition

5. A. concrete noun
   B. abstract noun
   C. proper noun
   D. compound noun

6. A. noun as object of preposition
   B. noun as subject
   C. noun as direct object
   D. noun as indirect object

7. A. proper noun
   B. collective noun
   C. compound noun
   D. abstract noun

8. A. noun as indirect object
   B. noun as direct object
   C. noun as subject
   D. noun as object of preposition

9. A. collective noun
   B. singular noun
   C. compound noun
   D. possessive noun

10. A. possessive noun
    B. collective noun
    C. singular noun
    D. compound noun

NOUNS

Kinds of Nouns

❶ Here's the Idea

▶ **A noun is a word that names a person, place, thing, or idea.** There are several ways to classify nouns.

PERSONS
astronaut
James B. Irwin

PLACES
landing site
moon

THINGS
flag
lunar module

IDEAS
patriotism
achievement

Common and Proper Nouns

A **common noun** is a general name for a person, place, thing, or idea. Common nouns are usually not capitalized.

A **proper noun** is the name of a particular person, place, thing, or idea. Proper nouns are always capitalized.

Common	astronaut	planet	mission
Proper	Sally Ride	Jupiter	*Apollo 11*

Concrete and Abstract Nouns

A **concrete noun** names a thing that can be seen, heard, smelled, touched, or tasted. Examples include *sunlight, explosion, fuel, rocks, moon,* and *ice.*

The **astronauts collected rocks from the moon.**

An **abstract noun** names an idea, feeling, quality, or characteristic. Examples include *exploration, excitement, lightness,* and *courage.*

They felt great excitement as they explored.

Every noun is either common or proper and also concrete or abstract. For example, *planet* is common and concrete. *Mars* is proper and concrete.

Collective Nouns

A **collective noun** is a word that names a group of people or things. Examples include *community, audience, panel, crowd, class, government,* and *staff.*

A panel of scientists presented their findings.

Some collective nouns name specific groups of animals or sometimes people. Examples include *pack, herd,* and *colony.*

They hope to establish a colony on the moon.

❷ Why It Matters in Writing

Without concrete common and proper nouns, writing is often too vague. Notice how the highlighted concrete nouns in the following description help make it specific.

PROFESSIONAL MODEL

Early on the morning of July 20, 1969, I was circling the moon with Neil Armstrong and Buzz Aldrin in our spacecraft *Columbia.* We had just awakened from a short sleep and were sucking lukewarm coffee out of plastic tubes and munching on bacon which had been squeezed into little cubes, like lumps of sugar.

— Michael Collins, *Flying to the Moon: An Astronaut's Story*

PROPER NOUNS

COMMON NOUNS

❸ Practice and Apply

A. CONCEPT CHECK: Kinds of Nouns

Write the nouns in these sentences, identifying each as common or proper. Then identify three collective nouns.

Dining in Orbit
1. The first astronauts squeezed food from tubes.
2. Astronauts in the Space Shuttle Program eat from a tray with forks and spoons.
3. They use straws to drink beverages from sealed pouches.
4. NASA employs a team of dietitians to make sure the astronauts eat properly.
5. Before the flight, each astronaut chooses food from a large group of items.
6. There is a supply of snacks available to the crew.
7. Yet most astronauts crave certain favorite foods.
8. Shannon Lucid missed her favorite candy during her six-month mission.
9. Astronauts cannot gain weight in space.
10. The extra fat will show up on their return to Earth.

➡ **For a SELF-CHECK and more practice, see the EXERCISE BANK, p. 316.**

B. WRITING: Using Nouns

Read the following biographical facts about Mae Jemison. Then write a paragraph about her, using common and proper nouns.

Mae Jemison
Born: October 17, 1956
Birthplace: Decatur, Alabama
Family: one of three children of Charlie and Dorothy Jemison; father, a maintenance worker; mother, a teacher
Education:
- Stanford University, Palo Alto, California, 1977 Bachelor of Science in Chemical Engineering
- Cornell University, Ithaca, New York, 1981 Doctor of Medicine

Achievement: first African-American female astronaut
Advice to Students: encourages students to pursue careers in science and engineering

Singular and Plural Nouns

❶ Here's the Idea

▶ **A singular noun names one person, place, thing, or idea. A plural noun names more than one person, place, thing, or idea.**

> **One astronomer saw a star.** (singular nouns)
>
> **The astronomers saw many stars.** (plural nouns)

One of the hardest things about plural nouns is spelling them correctly. Use these rules in the Quick-Fix Spelling Machine.

QUICK-FIX SPELLING MACHINE: PLURALS OF NOUNS

	SINGULAR	RULE	PLURAL
❶	star planet	Add -s to most nouns.	stars planets
❷	gas dish	Add -es to a noun that ends in s, sh, ch, x, or z.	gases dishes
❸	radio	Add -s to most nouns that end in o.	radios
	hero	Add -es to a few nouns that end in o.	heroes
❹	galaxy	For most nouns ending in y, change the y to an i and add -es.	galaxies
	ray	When a vowel comes before the y, just add -s.	rays
❺	half life	For most nouns ending in f or fe, change the f to v and add -es or -s.	halves lives
	belief	Just add -s to a few nouns that end in f or fe.	beliefs
❻	sheep species	For some nouns, keep the same spelling.	sheep species

NOUNS

► **The plurals of some nouns are formed in irregular ways.**

Singular	man	child	foot	mouse
Plural	men	children	feet	mice

❷ Why It Matters in Writing

Writing plural nouns can be tricky. Note the various ways plural nouns are spelled in the model.

PROFESSIONAL MODEL

When you look up at the night sky, the **stars** seem like tiny **points** of light. Yet many of them are much larger than the sun. All **varieties** of life on Earth depend on the heat and light of a star that is no different from **billions** of other stars in the billions of **galaxies** in the universe.

—Gerald Ng

❸ Practice and Apply

A. CONCEPT CHECK: Singular and Plural Nouns

Rewrite the nouns in parentheses in their plural forms.

The Exciting Lives of Stars
1. Stars are made of hydrogen, helium, and small (quantity) of other elements.
2. They create enormous (amount) of energy when their hydrogen atoms join together and change into helium.
3. Like human (being), stars go through a life cycle.
4. Stars fall into (category), mainly based on their size.
5. Many stars shrink as they age into smaller (body) known as white dwarfs.
6. Other stars, called supergiants, may end their (life) in explosions called supernovas.
7. (Astronomer) believe our sun is a middle-aged star.
8. Most of the sun's surface consists of (wave) of energy.
9. There are also dark (patch) on its surface, called sunspots.

10. The sun's powerful (ray) can damage your eyes.

➡ **For a SELF-CHECK and more practice, see the EXERCISE BANK, p. 317.**

For a SELF-CHECK and more practice, see the EXERCISE BANK, p. 317.

B. PROOFREADING: Spelling Plural Nouns

Ten plural nouns in the following passage are misspelled. Find them, and write the correct spellings.

Twinkle, Twinkle

Ancient observers thought stars were the flickering torchs of the gods. These old beliefs are poetic. However, the real reason stars twinkle is that their light must pass through Earth's atmosphere. Moving air currentes and dust cause starlight to bend. Our ancestores may not have understood why stars twinkle. However, they could enjoy seeing thousands of them while watching their flocks of sheeps. During our lifes artificial lighting has brightened the night sky over citys. Rayes from streetlights and neon signs of factorys obscure our view. Today pollution interferes with our searchs of the night skys.

C. WRITING: Comparing Photographs

One of Many

Astronomers estimate that there are 100 billion galaxies in the universe. Look at the pictures of two galaxies below. Write a paragraph comparing their shapes. Underline the plural nouns in your comparison. Be sure you spell plural nouns correctly.

LESSON 3 Possessive Nouns

❶ Here's the Idea

▶ **The possessive form of a noun shows ownership or relationship.**

Rudy's teacher discussed the Martian atmosphere.
RELATIONSHIP

Inez could see Mars through her **father's telescope.**
OWNERSHIP

You may use possessive nouns in place of longer phrases.

Mars's
We saw photos of ~~the~~ moons ~~of Mars.~~

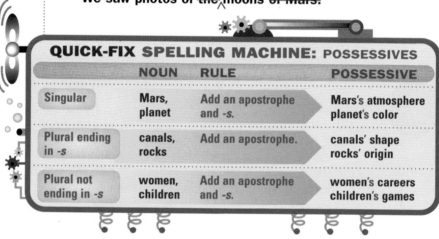

QUICK-FIX SPELLING MACHINE: POSSESSIVES

	NOUN	RULE	POSSESSIVE
Singular	Mars, planet	Add an apostrophe and -s.	Mars's atmosphere planet's color
Plural ending in -s	canals, rocks	Add an apostrophe.	canals' shape rocks' origin
Plural not ending in -s	women, children	Add an apostrophe and -s.	women's careers children's games

❷ Why It Matters in Writing

Possessive nouns can make your writing less wordy and easier to understand. Be sure not to make spelling errors by putting apostrophes in the wrong places.

STUDENT MODEL

REVISION

A radio show about a Martian landing grabbed the _nation's_
attention ~~of the nation~~ in 1938. _The show's_ ~~Listeners of the show~~
believing the invasion was real, panicked.

❸ Practice and Apply

A. CONCEPT CHECK: Possessive Nouns

Write the possessive form of each noun in parentheses. Then label each possessive noun singular or plural.

Astronomy: The Early Years
1. (Astronomy) history dates back 5,000 years to Babylon.
2. The (Babylonians) calendar was based on their observations of the stars and planets.
3. (Men) and (women) lives were governed by the stars.
4. Ancient (Egypt) builders may have used the stars to guide their placement of the pyramids.
5. The Greek philosopher Aristotle claimed that Earth was the (solar system) center.
6. He used the (sun) movement across the sky as proof.
7. His theory was accepted for more than a thousand (years) time.
8. The Polish astronomer Copernicus pointed out (Aristotle) errors in the 1500s.
9. He showed that (Earth) rotation makes it seem as if the sun revolves around it.
10. All of the (planets) orbits are actually centered around the sun.

➜ For a SELF-CHECK and more practice, see the EXERCISE BANK, p. 317.

B. REVISING: Labeling a Science Display

Use possessive nouns to make these phrases short enough to fit as photo captions.

Example: The Moons of Jupiter

Answer: Jupiter's Moons

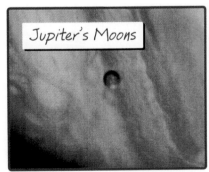

1. Soil Samples from the Mission
2. The Rings of Saturn
3. The Cabin in the Spacecraft
4. The Atmosphere of Venus
5. The Fuel Tanks of the Rocket Boosters

Compound Nouns

LESSON 4

❶ Here's the Idea

▶ **A compound noun is made of two or more words used together as a single noun.** The parts of a compound noun may be written as

- a single word: **liftoff, spacecraft**
- two or more separate words: **rocket engine, peanut butter**
- a hyphenated word: **light-year**

Plural Compound Nouns

QUICK-FIX SPELLING MACHINE: COMPOUND NOUNS			
	SINGULAR	**RULE**	**PLURAL**
One word	liftoff	Add *-s* to most words.	liftoffs
	wristwatch	Add *-es* to words that end in *ch, sh, s, x,* or *z*.	wristwatches
Two or more words or hyphenated words	rocket engine mother-in-law	Make the main noun plural. The main noun is the noun that is modified.	rocket engines mothers-in-law

❷ Why It Matters in Writing

Many spelling errors in writing involve compound nouns. Note how these are spelled correctly in the following model.

LITERARY MODEL

My father . . . was not impressed by the growing enthusiasm for parachute-jumping as a sport. Young **daredevils** like my brother could call it "**sky-diving**" if they wanted to, but the aviation pioneers referred to it disgustedly as "jumping out of a perfectly good **airplane**."

—Reeve Lindbergh, "Flying"

❸ Practice and Apply

A. CONCEPT CHECK: Compound Nouns

Write each compound noun in the sentences, and label it singular or plural.

Telescopes

1. The world's most powerful optical telescope is located on the volcanic mountaintop of Mauna Kea in Hawaii.
2. Mauna Kea's remote location can cause headaches and forgetfulness for workers not used to the lack of oxygen at more than 13,000 feet above sea level.
3. Gary Puniwai, who is very much the commander in chief at the Keck I telescope site, keeps a notebook as a memory backup.
4. Melted snow can also freeze on a telescope dome and cause a shutdown.
5. Astronomers do not have to work at this rugged outpost.
6. They can radio their instructions to workers from a communication hookup in a warm village 50 miles away.
7. Radio telescopes were another breakthrough for astronomers.
8. These telescopes collect radio waves from objects light-years away and turn them into computer images.
9. Astronomers can sit in a comfortable workplace as they analyze the images with sophisticated software.
10. Astronomers hope spacecraft will provide even better telescopes to help solve the mysteries of the universe.

➜ **For a SELF-CHECK and more practice, see the EXERCISE BANK, p. 318.**

B. REVISING: Plural Compound Nouns

Write the plural for each singular compound noun in parentheses.

On dark nights in the countryside, you can usually see the stars. Sirius is the brightest. It is 8.6 (light-year) away. You and your friends can set your (wristwatch) for midnight. Wear your (sweatsuit) and (windbreaker). Bring your (flashlight), your (notebook), and maybe some (leftover) from dinner, and see if you can find it.

LESSON 5 — Nouns as Subjects and Complements

❶ Here's the Idea

▶ **A noun can be the subject of a sentence or it can work as a complement.**

Nouns as Subjects

A **subject** tells whom or what a sentence is about. Nouns are often subjects, as this description shows.

> **PROFESSIONAL MODEL**
>
> **Comets** are made of ice, dust, and gas.
> **Astronomers** often describe them as dirty snowballs.
> The **tails** only appear when comets come near the sun.
>
> —Helen Witowski

Nouns as Complements

A **complement** is a word that completes the meaning of the verb. Three kinds of complements are *predicate nouns, direct objects,* and *indirect objects.*

Nouns as Complements		
Predicate noun	Renames or defines the subject after a linking verb	Carolyn Shoemaker is an **astronomer.**
Direct object	Names the receiver of the action of the verb	She has discovered many **comets.**
Indirect object	Tells *to whom or what* or *for whom or what* an action is done	One of her discoveries gave **astronomers** a thrill.

CHAPTER 2

❷ Why It Matters in Writing

Specific complements are needed in your writing, particularly in informative writing. Notice how the nouns acting as complements complete the meaning and add information.

Jupiter is the **king** of planets, bigger than all the others put together. In 1994 a comet named Shoemaker-Levy 9 hit the **planet** with enormous force. The Hubble Space Telescope sent **astronomers** spectacular photographs of the collision.

PREDICATE NOUN

DIRECT OBJECTS

INDIRECT OBJECT

❸ Practice and Apply

CONCEPT CHECK: Nouns as Subjects and Complements

Identify each underlined noun as a subject or a complement.

Target Earth
1. <u>Comets</u> orbit the <u>sun</u> just as planets do.
2. However, their <u>orbits</u> are not very predictable.
3. A small <u>comet</u> gave <u>human beings</u> a <u>scare</u> in 1908.
4. The <u>comet</u> destroyed a <u>forest</u> when it crashed into Siberia.
5. <u>People</u> felt its <u>impact</u> hundreds of miles away.
6. <u>Asteroids</u> are another potential <u>danger</u> to us.
7. These rocky <u>objects</u> can be as wide as 600 miles.
8. Sometimes their <u>orbits</u> bring them very close to Earth.
9. An <u>asteroid</u> could destroy all <u>life</u> on our planet if it crashed here.
10. Such a <u>collision</u> may have killed off the <u>dinosaurs</u> about 65 million years ago.

➡ **For a SELF-CHECK and more practice, see the EXERCISE BANK, p. 318.**

Further label each complement as *predicate noun, direct object,* or *indirect object.*

Nouns in Phrases

LESSON 6

❶ Here's the Idea

Nouns often appear in prepositional phrases and appositive phrases. Such phrases add information to a sentence.

Nouns as Objects of Prepositions

An **object of a preposition** is the noun or pronoun that follows the preposition. Nouns often appear in sentences as objects of prepositions.

Mount Wilson is an observatory in California.

PREPOSITION ⬈   ⬉ OBJECT OF PREPOSITION

Edwin Hubble made many discoveries at the famous observatory.

Nouns as Appositives

An **appositive** is a noun or pronoun that identifies or renames another noun or pronoun. An **appositive phrase** is made up of an appositive and its modifiers.

APPOSITIVE PHRASE

The Milky Way, our galaxy, is one of many.

⬆ APPOSITIVE

Edwin Hubble, the famous astronomer, proved this.

Hubble showed that the Milky Way, a galaxy with billions of stars, is only one of many galaxies in the universe.

Note that you should use commas before and after the appositive phrase if the information isn't essential to understanding the preceding noun or pronoun.

Cosmology, the study of the universe, owes a great debt to Hubble.

❷ Why It Matters in Writing

The use of nouns in prepositional phrases and appositives can provide the specific details you need to support the statements you make in explanatory writing.

STUDENT MODEL

> Henrietta Leavitt, an astronomer, discovered the way to measure how far away stars are from our planet. Her observations provided Edwin Hubble with a method for finding other galaxies.

APPOSITIVE

OBJECT OF PREPOSITION

❸ Practice and Apply

CONCEPT CHECK: Nouns in Phrases

Identify each underlined noun as an object of a preposition or an appositive.

Working Overtime in Space

1. Shannon Lucid, an experienced <u>astronaut</u>, was chosen for a joint American-Russian space mission in 1996.
2. She spent a year in Russia preparing for her duties on *Mir*, a Russian <u>space station</u>.
3. She flew to *Mir* on a <u>space shuttle</u>.
4. Two Russians aboard *Mir* showered her with <u>greetings</u>.
5. Lucid grew used to eating Russian foods such as borscht, a beet <u>soup</u>.
6. She did experiments to see how plants grow in <u>space</u>.
7. Her mission was supposed to last for four <u>months</u>.
8. Her return was delayed by seven <u>weeks</u>.
9. Lucid's 188 days in space set a record for <u>Americans</u>.
10. She was delighted to return to Houston, her home <u>city</u>.

➡ For a SELF-CHECK and more practice, see the EXERCISE BANK, p. 319.

For each sentence, write the phrase in which the object of a preposition or the appositive is found.

Grammar in Physical Education

Using Specific Nouns

For a physical education class, some students have gathered information about physical requirements for astronauts. They plan to use this information to create a brochure encouraging all students to become competent swimmers. Notice the specific nouns the students have used in their notes.

All **candidates** for the astronaut **corps** must pass a swimming **test** before they receive physical **training** at the **Johnson Space Center** near **Houston, Texas**.

Candidates must swim a total of 75 **meters**, or about 225 **feet**. During the **test** they must wear **tennis shoes** and a flight **suit**, a one-piece **garment** that combines **pants** with a long-sleeved **shirt**.

Swimmers may swim the **sidestroke, breaststroke,** or **freestyle**. For the final **requirement** of the **test**, they must tread **water** for 10 **minutes**.

Only when astronaut **candidates** have successfully passed this swimming **test** can they go on to learn more advanced **skills**. The next **steps** in their physical **training** are to become scuba-qualified and to complete military water-survival **training**.

As part of her training, astronaut Eileen M. Collins attended water-survival training school. Here she is shown in a parachute dropping into water.

National Aeronautics and Space Administration

CHAPTER 2

Practice and Apply

A. DRAFTING: Plan a Brochure

Create a brochure encouraging students to learn to swim. The following steps will help you plan your brochure.

1. Make a list of reasons for learning to swim. Use specific nouns to name the reasons. (Exercise and enjoyment are two possible reasons.)
2. Use specific nouns to name careers that require swimming.
3. Provide information about the swimming test that astronaut candidates must pass.
4. Provide information about where in your town or school students can learn to swim. Use specific nouns to name people or places students should contact.
5. Write a slogan for the cover of your brochure. Use a very specific noun in your slogan. (Swim for Success is a possible slogan.)

B. WRITING: Create a Brochure

1. Turn an $8\frac{1}{2}$ by 11 inch sheet of paper horizontally. Fold it into thirds.
2. On your first panel, place your slogan (and an illustration if you wish).
3. Provide reasons for being a competent swimmer on another panel. You might want to list all the occupations that require swimming along with the reasons, or you may choose to devote one panel to this information.
4. Describe the swimming test given to astronaut candidates. Use the information to convince students of the importance of swimming. (You may decide to use two panels for the text about astronauts.)
5. Provide information about where students can learn to swim.

Be sure to use specific nouns on your brochure. Save your brochure in your ⬒ **Writing Portfolio.**

NOUNS

Mixed Review

A. Plurals, Possessives, and Compounds Read the following help-wanted ad and correct ten errors in spelling. Remember an error in placing an apostrophe is a spelling error.

Sectio|

Astronauts' Wanted

Must be strong enough to lift rocksamples. Should have knowledge of nine planet's orbites and nearby galaxys. Preference will be given to applicants' who can pilot a space craft. People of all age's and ethnic backgrounds welcome. Send application to NASAs department of human resources.

B. Nouns and Their Jobs In each group of sentences, the same underlined noun is used in different ways. Label each noun as subject, direct object, indirect object, predicate noun, object of a preposition, or appositive.

Group 1
1. <u>Saturn</u> is the second largest planet in the solar system.
2. At least eighteen moons orbit <u>Saturn</u>.
3. The sun's rays give <u>Saturn</u> its bright appearance.
4. The planet <u>Saturn</u> is encircled by thousands of rings.
5. The rings around <u>Saturn</u> are made of water, ice, and rock.

Group 2
6. The seventh planet from the sun is <u>Uranus</u>.
7. The atmosphere of <u>Uranus</u> is so thick that we cannot see the planet's surface.
8. The astronomer William Herschel discovered <u>Uranus</u> in 1781.
9. Another astronomer gave <u>Uranus</u> its name.
10. <u>Uranus</u> has rings that are less noticeable than Saturn's rings.

For each underlined item, choose the letter of the term that correctly identifies it.

> Lunar eclipses occur when <u>Earth's</u> shadow falls on the moon.
> (1)
> They give the <u>moon</u> a beautiful reddish <u>glow</u>. Solar <u>eclipses</u> occur
> (2) (3) (4)
> when the moon comes between the sun and Earth. The moon
> blocks out the sun, and <u>daylight</u> fades dramatically. Many ancient
> (5)
> peoples believed eclipses were signs of evil. The ancient <u>Chinese</u>
> (6)
> feared a dragon was devouring the sun during solar eclipses. They
> would make <u>noise</u> to scare away the dragon. Emperors hired
> (7)
> astronomers to predict <u>eclipses</u>' arrivals. Two Chinese <u>astronomers</u>
> (8) (9)
> failed to predict an eclipse in 2136 B.C. The emperor, <u>Chung K'ang</u>,
> (10)
> had them executed.

1. A. common noun
   B. possessive noun
   C. compound noun
   D. plural noun

2. A. noun as subject
   B. noun as direct object
   C. noun as indirect object
   D. noun as predicate noun

3. A. compound noun
   B. possessive noun
   C. common noun
   D. collective noun

4. A. possessive noun
   B. compound noun
   C. plural noun
   D. proper noun

5. A. proper noun
   B. plural noun
   C. possessive noun
   D. compound noun

6. A. noun as direct object
   B. noun as indirect object
   C. noun as predicate noun
   D. noun as subject

7. A. noun as predicate noun
   B. noun as direct object
   C. noun as indirect object
   D. noun as object of preposition

8. A. singular noun
   B. possessive noun
   C. predicate noun
   D. compound noun

9. A. noun as subject
   B. noun as predicate noun
   C. noun as object of preposition
   D. noun as direct object

10. A. noun as object of preposition
    B. noun as appositive
    C. noun as predicate noun
    D. noun as indirect object

NOUNS

Student Help Desk

Nouns at a Glance

A noun names a person, place, thing, or idea. There are several ways to classify nouns.

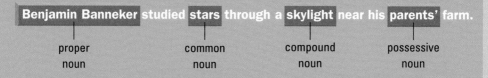

Benjamin Banneker studied stars through a skylight near his parents' farm.

| proper noun | common noun | compound noun | possessive noun |

QUICK-FIX SPELLING MACHINE: PLURALS OF NOUNS

SINGULAR	RULE	PLURAL
① comet	Add -s to most nouns.	comets
② crash	Add -es to a noun that ends in s, sh, ch, x, or z.	crashes
③ photo	Add -s to most nouns that end in o.	photos
echo	Add -es to a few nouns that end in o.	echoes
④ discovery	For most nouns ending in y, change the y to an i and add -es.	discoveries
way	When a vowel comes before the y, just add -s.	ways
⑤ wharf	For most nouns ending in f or fe, change the f to v and add -es or -s.	wharves
reef	Just add -s to a few nouns that end in f or fe.	reefs
⑥ salmon	For some nouns, keep the same spelling.	salmon

Classifying Nouns · Classifying Your Collection

Possessives of Nouns

Relationship	Ownership
Linus's brother	Tim's automobile

Collective Nouns

Collective Noun	Group
colony	colony of ants or badgers
flock	flock of birds or sheep
herd	herd of cattle or elephants

More Noun Types

Concrete	Abstract
rock	love

Nouns and Their Jobs

Nouns as . . .	Example
Subject	**Saturn** was spectacular.
Predicate noun	The student astronomer was our **guide.**
Direct object	We studied the **planet** with a powerful telescope.
Indirect object	The scientists gave **Saturn** a long look.
Object of preposition	The rings of **Saturn** are colorful.
Appositive	The planet **Saturn** is the sixth from the sun.

The Bottom Line

Checklist for Nouns

Have I . . .

____ chosen precise nouns?

____ spelled plural nouns correctly?

____ spelled possessive nouns correctly?

____ used nouns to provide specific details in explanatory writing?

____ used possessive nouns to show ownership or relationship?

____ spelled compound nouns correctly?

Pronouns

Theme: Survival

Hanging On

Imagine this conversation without the words *you, me, who, we,* and *which*. These words are called **pronouns**. They take the place of other nouns or pronouns. Be careful, though. If you don't use pronouns correctly, your meaning may not survive.

Write Away: Survival Instincts
Humans, like all living species, have a strong survival instinct. Every day, people survive injury, illness, natural disaster, and plain old tough times. Write a paragraph describing the survival of someone you know. Place the paragraph in your **Working Portfolio.**

Choose the letter of the best revision for each underlined word or group of words.

At age eighteen, Daniel Huffman was a football star planning to play football in college. But <u>they</u> had a problem. <u>His</u> grandmother,
(1)   (2)
Shirlee Allison, was dying. She needed a kidney transplant. <u>Would someone donate his</u> kidney? <u>Whom would help?</u> <u>His grandmother</u>
(3)   (4)   (5)
<u>and him</u> discussed it. Huffman decided that he <u>himself</u> would give
(6)
her a kidney, even though that meant he would never play college ball. Right after the transplant, Allison began to regain her health. <u>Daniel had made herself</u> a very lucky person. "That was happiness
(7)
for <u>me</u>," said Daniel. <u>It was him</u> who then received a full
(8)   (9)
scholarship to Florida State and an appointment as athletic trainer for <u>it's football team</u>.
(10)

1. A. he
   B. she
   C. someone
   D. Correct as is

2. A. Their
   B. Her
   C. They're
   D. Correct as is

3. A. Would someone donate their
   B. Would someone donate his or her
   C. Would someone donate her
   D. Correct as is

4. A. Who would help?
   B. Whose would help?
   C. Who would help who?
   D. Correct as is

5. A. Him and his grandmother
   B. Him and her
   C. His grandmother and he
   D. Correct as is

6. A. hisself
   B. himselves
   C. themselves
   D. Correct as is

7. A. Daniel had made her
   B. Daniel had made him
   C. Daniel had made she
   D. Correct as is

8. A. I
   B. us
   C. myself
   D. Correct as is

9. A. It was his
   B. It was he
   C. It was himself
   D. Correct as is

10. A. their football team
    B. his football team
    C. its football team
    D. Correct as is

What Is a Pronoun?

❶ Here's the Idea

▶ **A pronoun is a word that is used in place of a noun or another pronoun.** Like a noun, a pronoun can refer to a person, place, thing, or idea. The word that a pronoun refers to is called its **antecedent.**

REFERS TO

Maria was lost. She didn't panic.

REFERS TO

She checked the flashlight. It still worked.

Personal Pronouns

▶ **Pronouns such as *we, I, she, them,* and *it* are called personal pronouns.** Personal pronouns have a variety of forms to indicate different **persons, numbers,** and **cases.**

Person and Number There are first-person, second-person, and third-person personal pronouns, each having both singular and plural forms.

Singular	Plural
I shivered.	**We lit a fire.**
You slept.	**You all fell asleep.**
She saw a light.	**They ran toward it.**

Case Each personal pronoun forms has three cases: subject, object, and possessive. Which form to use depends on the pronoun's function in a sentence.

Subject: **She took a deep breath.**

Object: **Jerry told her about the problem.**

Possessive: **I like your story better than mine.**

The chart on the next page shows all the forms of the personal pronouns.

CHAPTER 3

LESSON 1

Personal Pronouns			
	Subject	**Object**	**Possessive**
Singular			
First person	I	me	my, mine
Second person	you	you	your, yours
Third person	he, she, it	him, her, it	his, her, hers, its
Plural			
First person	we	us	our, ours
Second person	you	you	your, yours
Third person	they	them	their, theirs

❷ Why It Matters in Writing

Pronouns often are used to make writing flow smoothly from sentence to sentence. Notice how some of the pronouns in this paragraph connect one sentence to the sentence before it.

STUDENT MODEL

My friend Jan and I barely survived last summer. **We** were sailing with **her** family off the coast of Florida when a storm came up. **It** capsized our boat. Fortunately, we had life jackets, which saved our lives.

We refers to *My friend Jan and I.*

Her refers to *Jan.*

It refers to *storm.*

❸ Practice and Apply

A. CONCEPT CHECK: What Is a Pronoun?

List the personal pronoun(s) in each sentence.

Wilderness Survival
1. Hannah Nyala is known for her tracking expertise.
2. She has found many lost hikers before they got into real trouble.
3. She wrote a book called *Point Last Seen*.
4. She learned some of her skills in the Mojave and Kalahari deserts.

5. Other experts remind us to plan ahead for danger.
6. To them, a first-aid kit is a necessity.
7. They advise us to find out before we go whether the water is safe to drink.
8. We are also advised to conserve our energy.
9. We are told to find shelter and avoid becoming too hot or too cold.
10. They say that all hikers should carry plenty of water with them.

➜ **For a SELF-CHECK and more practice, see the EXERCISE BANK, p. 319.**

Name the antecedents for the personal pronouns in sentences 1–4 and 6.

B. REVISING: Substituting Pronouns for Nouns

Rewrite this student's draft of a science report. Change the underlined nouns to pronouns to connect the sentences smoothly.

> Experts say we will run out of natural resources some day. **(1)** Experts point out that Americans use nearly 25 percent of the world's resources, but **(2)** Americans make up only four percent of the world's population. This overuse is not fair, environmentalists say.
> **(3)** Environmentalists say that **(4)** this overuse is leading to a shortage of resources and too much pollution.

C. WRITING: Dialogue

Based on the photograph below, write a short dialogue between two people who are hiking. Use pronouns to make the dialogue sound natural.

Example:

Speaker 1: Do **you** see that moose?

Speaker 2: Yes, **I** do. In fact, **I** see a mother moose and **her** calf.

Speaker 1: **I** can't see the calf. Shall **we** get closer to **them?**

Subject Pronouns

❶ Here's the Idea

▶ **A subject pronoun is used as the subject of a sentence or as a predicate pronoun after a linking verb.**

Subject Pronouns	
Singular	**Plural**
I	we
you	you
he, she, it	they

Pronouns as Subjects

Use a subject pronoun when the pronoun is a subject or part of a compound subject.

> **The Apollo program was a great success.**

> **It got us to the moon.** (*It,* referring to *The Apollo program,* is the subject of the sentence.)

A pronoun can be part of a compound subject.

> **You and I both think we should go on to Mars.**

Predicate Pronouns

A predicate pronoun follows a linking verb and identifies the subject. Use the subject case for predicate pronouns.

> *IDENTIFIES*
>
> **The greatest astronauts were they.**
>   ↑ SUBJECT   ↑ PREDICATE PRONOUN

> *IDENTIFIES*
>
> **The biggest supporters were she and I.**

> *IDENTIFIES*
>
> **The first astronaut on Mars will be I.**

Remember, the most common linking verbs are forms of the verb *be,* including *is, am, are, was, were, has been, have been, can be, will be, could be,* and *should be.*

❷ Why It Matters in Writing

It's sometimes difficult to know which pronoun forms to use in writing because many people use them incorrectly in speech. Always double-check the pronouns in your writing, and make sure you've used the correct forms.

STUDENT MODEL

Neil Armstrong commanded Apollo 11, the first mission to reach the moon. Buzz Aldrin and ~~him~~ *he* spent hours on the moon. They were trailblazers.

❸ Practice and Apply

CONCEPT CHECK: Subject Pronouns

Write the correct form of the pronoun(s) to complete each sentence.

Apollo 13: A Close Call

1. Some big fans of space exploration are Sam and (I, me).
2. (We, Us) learned that in April 1970, the Apollo 13 astronauts almost didn't make it back to Earth.
3. (They, Them) never did land on the moon.
4. Two hundred thousand miles from home, (they, them) heard an explosion.
5. Jim Lovell was the mission commander; it was (he, him) who radioed the message "Houston, we've had a problem."
6. Then (he, him), Jack Swigert, and Fred Haise were forced to abandon the main ship for the lunar module.
7. The tiny module was designed to keep two people alive for just two days, but (they, them) were four days from Earth.
8. (They, Them) finally splashed down in the Pacific Ocean four days later, having overcome crisis after crisis.
9. (We, Us) watched the movie about their dangerous journey.
10. It was (they, them) who won our respect and admiration.

→ For a SELF-CHECK and more practice, see the EXERCISE BANK, p. 320.

LESSON 3 Object Pronouns

❶ Here's the Idea

▶ **An object pronoun is used as a direct object, an indirect object, or an object of a preposition.**

Object Pronouns	
Singular	**Plural**
me	us
you	you
him, her, it	them

Direct Object The pronoun receives the action of a verb and answers the question *whom or what.*

SCARE WHOM?

Bad storms scare me.
                    ↑ DIRECT OBJECT

Do you like them? (like what? *them*)

Indirect Object The pronoun tells to whom or what or for whom or what an action is performed.

TO WHOM?   ↙ DIRECT OBJECT
Give me an explanation of how hurricanes form.
        ↑ INDIRECT OBJECT

I told him the story of Hurricane Floyd.

Object of a Preposition The pronoun follows a preposition (such as *to, from, for, against, by,* or *about*).

When he sees big storms, he runs from them.
                              PREPOSITION ↗   ↖ OBJECT

The storm is coming straight at us.

Always use object pronouns after the preposition *between.*

It's a contest between him and me. (NOT between he and I.)

❷ Why It Matters in Writing

People commonly misuse subject and object pronouns in conversation, especially *I* and *me*. Pay attention to your use of these words when they are part of compound subjects or objects.

My mother and ~~me~~ listened to a radio program about Hurricane Floyd.

❸ Practice and Apply

MIXED REVIEW: Subject and Object Pronouns

Write the correct pronoun(s) for each sentence. Label each pronoun *subject* or *object*.

Hurricane Floyd

1. Hurricane Floyd ravaged the East Coast in 1999; the extent of the damage horrified my friends and (I, me).
2. My brother and (I, me) read that Floyd was 600 miles across and had winds of 155 miles an hour.
3. Gerald Keeth is a U.S. sailor; the hurricane gave (he, him) the scare of his life.
4. "The bad weather started pounding (we, us) Tuesday night," he wrote.
5. "(We, Us) launched our life raft in . . . 55-foot seas with 60-knot winds."
6. The raft accidentally left (he, him) and two others behind.
7. (They, Them) had only life jackets and an emergency locator beacon.
8. "I could hear each wave from behind (I, me) like a freight train coming."
9. Then a helicopter rescued (they, them).
10. "Rescue swimmer Shad Hernandez put a harness on each of (we, us), and (we, us) were hauled into the helicopter."

➜ **For a SELF-CHECK and more practice, see the EXERCISE BANK, p. 320.**

Tell how each pronoun functions in the sentence.

Possessive Pronouns

LESSON 4

① Here's the Idea

▶ **A possessive pronoun is a personal pronoun used to show ownership or relationship.**

Possessive Pronouns	
Singular	**Plural**
my, mine	our, ours
your, yours	your, yours
her, hers, his, its	their, theirs

The possessive pronouns *my, your, her, his, its, our,* and *their* come before nouns.

The dog pricked up its little ears.

It saw the boy and heard his loud cry for help.

RELATIONSHIP

The owner and his best friend came to the rescue.

The possessive pronouns *mine, ours, yours, his, hers, its,* and *theirs* can stand alone in a sentence.

This cat is mine. That cat is his.

Is the striped cat yours? No, mine is all black.

What color is his? Hers hasn't come home yet.

Possessive Pronouns and Contractions

Some possessive pronouns sound like contractions (*its/it's, your/you're, their/they're*). Because these pairs sound alike, writers often confuse possessive pronouns and contractions.

Remember, a possessive pronoun *never* has an apostrophe. A contraction, however, *always* has an apostrophe. The apostrophe shows where a letter or letters have been left out in a combination of two words. Look on the next page to see how this works.

QUICK-FIX SPELLING MACHINE

POSSESSIVE PRONOUNS		CONTRACTIONS	
its	Its paws are muddy.	it's	It's been a long day.
your	Your dog is nice.	you're	You're all right.
their	Their dog is smart.	they're	They're proud of her.

② Why It Matters in Writing

Proofread your work carefully to see that you haven't confused contractions and possessive pronouns. Remember that the spell-checker on a computer won't catch these mistakes.

STUDENT MODEL

Many Alpine travelers owe ~~they're~~ *their* survival to the trusty St. Bernard dog. This dog was first used in the 1600s by a group of monks at the St. Bernard monastery in the Swiss Alps. The dog's intelligence and ~~it's~~ *its* keen sense of smell enable it to find lost travelers or warn them of dangerous footing. Even today, the monks of St. Bernard and ~~they're~~ *their* dogs rescue many travelers every winter.

❸ Practice and Apply

A. CONCEPT CHECK: Possessive Pronouns

Write the correct pronoun or contraction for each sentence.

Bustopher, the Rescue Cat

1. Has (your, you're) pet ever saved a life?
2. David and Marjorie Giles can say yes; a woman survived an accident because of (their, they're) cat.
3. One morning in Dobbins, California, Bustopher was in (its, it's) yard.
4. Birds were calling, but amidst (their, they're) songs David Giles heard a peculiar noise.
5. Then he noticed Bustopher; (its, it's) front paw was pointing.
6. There is a steep drop-off to a canyon beyond the Gileses' lawn; (its, it's) not far away.
7. When Giles walked over to the drop-off, he heard the noise again; (its, it's) source was in the canyon.
8. He looked and saw (they're, their) neighbor, an 84-year-old woman who had fallen and broken her hip.
9. "(Your, You're) going to be all right," Giles assured her.
10. (Its, It's) amazing how animals can help people to survive.

➜ For a SELF-CHECK and more exercises, see the EXERCISE BANK, p. 321.

B. PROOFREADING: Using Possessive Pronouns

Correct the possessive pronoun errors in the paragraph below. If a sentence contains no error, write *Correct*.

Marie Murphy was paralyzed, and she used an iron lung to help her breathe. **(1)** It's mechanism breathed for her at night, while she and her family slept. **(2)** One night she awoke and realized that they're electricity had gone out— she could no longer hear the machine's electrical hum. **(3)** You're probably wondering what someone who couldn't move or breathe would do. **(4)** Its remarkable, but she had just enough breath to whisper to her dog, Rosie, whose barking woke Murphy's family. **(5)** Their quick response, putting the iron lung on batteries, saved her life.

LESSON 5

Reflexive and Intensive Pronouns

❶ Here's the Idea

A pronoun that ends in *self* or *selves* is either a **reflexive** or an **intensive** pronoun.

Reflexive and Intensive Pronouns		
myself	yourself	herself, himself, itself
ourselves	yourselves	themselves

Reflexive Pronouns

▶ **A reflexive pronoun refers to the subject and directs the action of the verb back to the subject.** Reflexive pronouns are necessary to the meaning of a sentence.

REFLECTS

The Carson family tried to lift themselves out of poverty.

REFLECTS

Ben Carson dedicated himself to becoming a doctor.

Notice that if you drop the reflexive pronoun, the sentence no longer makes sense. (*Ben Carson dedicated to becoming a doctor.*)

Intensive Pronouns

▶ **An intensive pronoun emphasizes a noun or another pronoun within the same sentence.** Intensive pronouns are not necessary to the meaning of the sentence.

You yourself have overcome many hardships.

Dr. Carson himself has survived great poverty.

Notice that when you drop the intensive pronoun, the sentence still makes sense. (*Dr. Carson has survived great poverty.*)

Avoid the use of *hisself* and *theirselves,* which are grammatically incorrect. Use *himself* and *themselves* instead.

❷ Why It Matters in Writing

You can use an intensive pronoun to stress a point. In the following model, the writer used the pronoun *himself* to emphasize that Ben Carson knew something just as well as the other students knew it.

PROFESSIONAL MODEL

When Ben Carson was in fifth grade, his classmates considered him the dumbest kid in the class. They teased him, but he didn't seem to mind. He **himself** knew that he couldn't read very well.

❸ Practice and Apply

CONCEPT CHECK: Intensive and Reflexive Pronouns

Write the reflexive or intensive pronoun in each sentence. Then identify it as reflexive (R) or intensive (I).

Beyond Survival to Success
1. By fifth grade, Ben Carson considered himself the dumbest kid in his class.
2. His mother was raising Ben and his brother herself.
3. When she saw his report card, she decided that she herself would give him extra homework assignments: two book reports every week.
4. She also told her sons to limit themselves to only two TV shows each week.
5. Ben outdid himself.
6. He learned to love reading and then to love learning itself.
7. He promised himself he would rise to the top of his class.
8. Carson went on to become a first-rate doctor, surprising even himself with some of his successful cases.
9. He has performed many operations that other doctors feared to try themselves.
10. He himself likes the challenge of difficult surgery.

➡ **For a SELF-CHECK and more practice, see the EXERCISE BANK, p. 322.**

LESSON 6 Interrogatives and Demonstratives

❶ Here's the Idea

Interrogative Pronouns

▶ **An interrogative pronoun is used to introduce a question.** The interrogative pronouns are *who, whom, what, which,* and *whose.*

> **Who** used up all the water?
>
> **Whose** cup is this?

Using *Who* and *Whom*

▶ ***Who* is always used as a subject or a predicate pronoun.**

> Subject: **Who called the power company?**
>
> Predicate pronoun: **The electrician is who?**

▶ ***Whom* is always used as an object.**

> Direct object: **Whom did you call?**
>
> Indirect object: **You gave whom my number?**
>
> Object of preposition: **To whom did you speak?**

Here's How Choosing *Who* or *Whom* in a Question

(Who, Whom) will you see?

1. Rewrite the question as a statement.
   You will see (who, whom).

2. Decide if the pronoun is used as a subject or an object. Choose the correct form. The pronoun in the sentence above is an object.
   You will see whom.

3. Use the correct form in the question.
   Whom will you see?

Don't confuse *whose* with *who's. Who's* is a contraction that means *who is.* ("Who's missing?") *Whose* is an interrogative pronoun. ("Whose book is gone?")

Demonstrative Pronouns

▶ **A demonstrative pronoun points out a person, place, thing, or idea.**

The demonstrative pronouns—*this, that, these,* and *those*—are used alone in sentences as shown below.

Singular

That is a circuit breaker.

This is our emergency shelter.

Plural

Those are electrical appliances.

These are bottles of water.

Never use *here* or *there* with a demonstrative pronoun. The pronoun already tells which one or ones. *This* and *these* point out people or things that are near, or *here*. *That* and *those* point out people or things that are far away, or *there*.

This ~~here~~ is a dead refrigerator.

That ~~there~~ is five pounds of rotting food.

❷ Why It Matters in Writing

In dialogue, questions can show a character's mood, such as curiosity, shock, or anger. The author in this model uses interrogative pronouns in questions to show Sammy's confusion.

> **PROFESSIONAL MODEL**
>
> "**What** just happened?" Sammy cried.
> "The lights went out. We must have lost power," said Gilberto. There was a knock at the door.
> "**Who**'s there?" Sammy called out.
> "It's your neighbor." Sammy's heart began to beat fast.
> "**Which** neighbor? I don't have any neighbors!" he said.

❸ Practice and Apply

A. CONCEPT CHECK: Interrogatives and Demonstratives

Choose the correct word in parentheses.

Urban Emergency

1. (What, Whose) would you do if a natural disaster like an earthquake or blizzard struck close to home?
2. (That, Those) is a good question.
3. (These, That) is a situation in which you might not have access to water, food, or electricity for days.
4. To (who, whom) should you turn for advice?
5. The Federal Emergency Management Agency (FEMA) has a plan. (This, That) is its most important advice: store lots of clean water ahead of time.
6. (What, Who) do you need to purify your water?
7. (What, Whom) does FEMA recommend? They advise a two-week supply of water for each person.
8. For food, you'll need a manual can opener and a camp stove or grill. Make sure you have (these, this).
9. (Who, Whom) will be responsible for your family's emergency plan?
10. (Whose, Who's) most organized and knowledgeable? You should choose that person.

➜ For a SELF-CHECK and more practice, see the EXERCISE BANK, p. 322.

B. WRITING: Using Demonstrative Pronouns

You are a TV reporter showing your audience some things they should have on hand for emergencies. Write a one-paragraph script naming the necessary items and explaining why they are necessary. Use four demonstrative pronouns in your paragraph and underline them.

Pronoun-Antecedent Agreement

❶ Here's the Idea

▶ **The antecedent is the noun or pronoun that a pronoun replaces or refers to.** The antecedent and the pronoun can be in the same sentence or in different sentences.

REFERS TO

The Hopi people made their homes in the desert.
↑ ANTECEDENT   ↑ PRONOUN

REFERS TO

The Hopi settled what is now Arizona. They have been here for more than ten centuries.

Pronouns must agree with their antecedents in number, person, and gender.

Agreement in Number

▶ **Use a singular pronoun to refer to a singular antecedent.**

REFERS TO

Hopi culture, in all its forms, is alive and well.

▶ **Use a plural pronoun to refer to a plural antecedent.**

REFERS TO

Traditional members keep cattle on their farms.

Agreement in Person

▶ **The pronoun must agree in person with the antecedent.**

3RD PERSON

Tribal elders tell the myths of their people.

1ST PERSON

We like to listen to our grandparents' stories.

Avoid switching from one person to another in the same sentence or paragraph.

Incorrect

Visitors realize you can learn from other cultures.

(*Visitors* is third person; *you* is second person.)

Correct

Visitors realize they can learn from other cultures.

(*Visitors* and *they* are both third person.)

Agreement in Gender

▶ **The gender of a pronoun must be the same as the gender of its antecedent.**

Personal pronouns have three gender forms: masculine (*he, his, him*), feminine (*she, her, hers*), and neuter (*it, its*).

Derrick Davis performs his hoop dances.

Laurel Mansfield teaches her students at Hopi High.

Don't use only masculine or only feminine pronouns when you mean to refer to both genders.

DRAFT:

Each dancer has his favorite moves.

(The dancer could be male or female.)

There are two ways to make this sentence more accurate.

1. Use the phrase *his or her*.

Each dancer has his or her favorite moves.

2. Rewrite the sentence using a plural antecedent and a plural pronoun. Be careful! Other words in the sentence, especially verbs, may also need to be made plural.

The dancers have their favorite moves.

❷ Why It Matters in Writing

For many years, people used the pronoun *he* to refer to nouns or pronouns of unclear gender. This custom is changing. Often, the problem can be fixed by changing the subject to the plural form.

~~The~~ Native American artist~~s~~ ~~is~~ *are* becoming better known.

They are
~~He is~~ working with traditional ideas in new materials.

❸ Practice and Apply

A. CONCEPT CHECK: Pronoun-Antecedent Agreement

Write the pronouns in these sentences, along with their antecedents.

> **Old Cultures Survive in a New World**
> **1.** Native cultures have faced great threats to their survival.
> **2.** For years, Native Americans were pushed to adopt a white, industrial way of life. They have had to fight to hold on to their own cultural and spiritual traditions.
> **3.** Rose Robinson was a member of the Hopi tribe. She founded the Native American Journalists' Association.
> **4.** Robinson monitored and resisted nuclear-waste dumping in her tribal lands.
> **5.** Raymond Cross is a lawyer for the Mandan, Arikara, and Hidatsa nations. He sued the government for flooding tribal land with a dam. He won $150 million for the tribes.
> **6.** Other tribes have gone to court to get back the rights to their land, minerals, and other valuable resources.
> **7.** Native languages are another important issue; speaking them helps people keep their heritages alive.
> **8.** Each person follows his or her own spiritual path based on respect for nature.
> **9.** Native arts and crafts continue to celebrate both function and beauty; they also earn income.
> **10.** Self-determination is the right of a group to make decisions about its future. It is becoming a reality for Native American nations.

➡ For a SELF-CHECK and more practice, see the EXERCISE BANK, p. 323.

Write the number, person, and gender of each pronoun.

B. REVISING: Correcting Errors in Agreement

The paragraph below contains four errors in pronoun-antecedent agreement. Rewrite the paragraph, correcting the errors.

> Lance Polingyouma works at a Native American learning center, where he teaches tourists about the customs of his or her people, the Hopi. The tourists hope to expand her knowledge of the Hopi culture. Lance often asks his elders for his advice about how to explain the Hopi ways. If a tourist asks a question, Lance wants to give him a thorough answer.

Indefinite-Pronoun Agreement

CHAPTER 3

❶ Here's the Idea

▶ **An indefinite pronoun does not refer to a specific person, place, thing, or idea.**

Indefinite pronouns often do not have antecedents.

Nothing lasts forever.

Anyone can make a time capsule.

▶ **Some indefinite pronouns are always singular, some are always plural, and some can be either singular or plural.**

Indefinite Pronouns			
Singular		**Plural**	**Singular or Plural**
another	much	both	all
anybody	neither	few	any
anyone	nobody	many	most
anything	no one	several	none
each	nothing		some
either	one		
everybody	somebody		
everyone	someone		
everything	something		

Pronouns containing *one, thing,* or *body* are always singular.

Singular Indefinite Pronouns

▶ **Use a singular personal pronoun to refer to a singular indefinite pronoun.**

REFERS TO

Everyone added his or her favorite item to the capsule.
(*Everyone* could be male or female.)

REFERS TO

One of the girls put her soccer ball in the box.

Plural Indefinite Pronouns

▶ **Use a plural personal pronoun to refer to a plural indefinite pronoun.**

REFERS TO

Many contributed **their** favorite CDs or video games.

REFERS TO

Few realized that **their** electronics may become completely outdated.

Singular or Plural Indefinite Pronouns

▶ **Some indefinite pronouns can be singular or plural.** The phrase that follows the indefinite pronoun will often tell you whether it is singular or plural.

Some of the time capsule **looks** like **it** is very old.
- SINGULAR INDEFINITE PRONOUN
- SINGULAR NOUN
- SINGULAR PERSONAL PRONOUN

Some of the time capsules **list their** contents outside.
- PLURAL INDEFINITE PRONOUN
- PLURAL NOUN
- PLURAL PERSONAL PRONOUN

❷ Why It Matters in Writing

You can use indefinite pronouns in your writing when you want to show how a whole group of people is acting or feeling.

LITERARY MODEL

She heard the irritability in their voices, knew that soon **someone** would refuse to go on. . . . **No one** commented. **No one** asked any questions.

—Ann Petry, *Harriet Tubman: Conductor on the Underground Railroad*

❸ Practice and Apply

A. CONCEPT CHECK: Indefinite-Pronoun Agreement

Choose the pronoun that agrees with the indefinite-pronoun antecedent.

A Message to the Future

1. Everyone likes to think that (he or she, they) will leave a mark on the world.
2. We all want to create something, and we hope (it, they) will outlive us.
3. Some take an unusual approach; for (him or her, them), a time capsule is the answer.
4. Anyone who assembles a time capsule hopes that (he or she, they) can send a message to the future.
5. Each of the people who planned the time capsule at the New York World's Fair in 1939 had (his or her, their) opinion about what should go into it.
6. What did all of those experts finally agree on? (He or she, They) put nineteen items in the capsule.
7. Most of the items would be familiar to us today. (They, It) included an alarm clock, a safety pin, and a dollar bill.
8. However, none of the people knew at the time that (his or her, their) slide rules would become outdated in just a few decades.
9. One of California's tar pits acts as a time capsule because (it, they) contains people's throwaways.
10. Although time capsules often remain sealed for decades, few are meant to keep (their, its) treasures hidden for as long as the Crypt of Civilization. Completed in 1940, it is meant to last until the year 8113!

➜ For a SELF-CHECK and more practice, see the EXERCISE BANK, p. 324.

B. WRITING: Using Correct Indefinite-Pronoun Agreement

Write a paragraph describing what you would choose to put in a time capsule and why. Use at least one singular indefinite pronoun, one plural indefinite pronoun, and one indefinite pronoun that could be singular or plural. Underline all of the indefinite pronouns.

Pronoun Problems

❶ Here's the Idea

We and *Us* with Nouns

The pronoun *we* or *us* is sometimes followed by a noun that identifies the pronoun (*we students*, *us students*).

▶ **Use *we* when the pronoun is a subject or a predicate pronoun. Use *us* when the pronoun is an object.**

We humans don't always appreciate trees.
⬑ SUBJECT

Trees can feed and shelter us humans.
⬑ OBJECT OF VERB

> **Here's How** Choosing *We* or *Us*
>
> **Some trees depend on (us, we) humans for survival.**
>
> **1.** Drop the identifying noun from the sentence.
>
> **Some trees depend on (us, we) for survival.**
>
> **2.** Decide whether the pronoun is used as a subject or an object. In this sentence, the pronoun is the object of the preposition *on*.
>
> **Some trees depend on us for survival.**
>
> **3.** Use the correct pronoun with the noun.
>
> **Some trees depend on us humans for survival.**

Unclear Reference

▶ **Be sure that each personal pronoun refers clearly to only one person, place, or thing.** If there is any chance your reader will be confused about whom or what you are talking about, use a noun instead of a pronoun.

Confusing

Sara and Anne want to become tree farmers. She works after school at an orchard. (Who works? Sara or Anne?)

Clear

Sara and Anne want to become tree farmers. Anne works after school at an orchard.

❷ Why It Matters in Writing

Readers get frustrated and may give up if your writing is too confusing. To get your ideas across, you must be clear about who is doing what. This is especially important when there is more than one noun that a pronoun could be replacing.

> **STUDENT MODEL**
>
> Until a century ago, humans competed with animals in the
> eastern United States. ~~They~~ *Animals* needed the nuts to get through
> hard winters. Farmers saw them as a cash crop.

❸ Practice and Apply

A. CONCEPT CHECK: Pronoun Problems

Choose the correct noun or pronoun from the words in parentheses.

The Majestic Chestnut Tree

1. For decades, (we, us) carpenters used the wood from chestnut trees to build houses and furniture.
2. Chestnuts were a nutritious food for both (we, us) country dwellers and wildlife. The trees provided bushels of them.
3. Then in 1904, a fungus began killing (them, the trees).
4. Now scientists are crossbreeding American chestnut trees with Chinese chestnut trees. (They, Chinese chestnut trees) resist the blight.
5. (They, Scientists) hope the new hybrid trees will survive for centuries.

➡ **For a SELF-CHECK and more practice, see the EXERCISE BANK, p. 324.**

B. REVISING: Correcting Pronoun Errors

Correct the five pronoun errors in the following paragraph.

If Trees Could Talk . . .
Us chestnut trees are very generous. We give you boards for building and nuts for eating and even flowers in the spring. They make fine furniture. They taste sweet and crunchy. However, a fungus is killing us. What do we ask you to do for we trees in return? Just help us fight it.

More Pronoun Problems

❶ Here's the Idea

Using Pronouns in Compound

Pronouns sometimes cause difficulty when they are parts of compound subjects and compound objects.

▶ **Use the subject pronoun *I, she, he, we,* or *they* in a compound subject or with a predicate noun or pronoun.**

Greg and she decided to learn more about Sacajawea.

The researchers are Polly and I.

▶ **Use the object pronoun *me, her, him, us,* or *them* in a compound object.**

Her story has always fascinated Polly and me.

The research was divided between Greg and her.

 To choose the correct case of a pronoun in a compound part, read the sentence with only the pronoun in the compound part. Mentally screen out the other pronoun or other noun. Then choose the correct case.

My grandmother told the story to ~~Ron and~~ me.

Phrases That Interfere

Sometimes a group of words comes between a noun and a pronoun that refers to it. Don't be confused by the words in between.

REFERS TO

Sacajawea, ~~who guided Lewis and Clark,~~ never lost her way. (*Her* agrees with *Sacajawea* and not with *Lewis* and *Clark.*)

REFERS TO

About 40 men started ~~up the Missouri River~~ on their voyage. (*Their* agrees with *men* and not with *Missouri River.*)

❷ Why It Matters in Writing

Many people think it sounds better to use *I* rather than *me* in a compound object. This isn't true—use *me* as part of a compound object.

STUDENT MODEL

> When our friends go camping, they always like to take
>
> along my sister and ~~I.~~ *me.* She and I have a lot of experience.

❸ Practice and Apply

A. CONCEPT CHECK: More Pronoun Problems

Write the correct word to complete each sentence. Choose from those given in parentheses.

Sacajawea, Young Explorer

1. Meriwether Lewis is a favorite topic for Polly and (I, me).
2. In 1803, President Jefferson sent (he, him) and William Clark to explore thousands of miles of wilderness.
3. Lewis and Clark met Sacajawea, a young Shoshone woman, in 1804; (they, she) hired her as a guide.
4. They had first hired her husband, Toussaint Charbonneau, as an interpreter. Both Sacajawea and (he, him) translated their conversations with Native Americans.
5. Lewis, Clark, a band of soldiers, and (she, her) headed west when she was around 17.
6. She survived near starvation and illness as (she, they) accompanied the explorers.
7. Greg, Polly, and (I, me) learned that she was very important to the expedition.
8. The baby on Sacajawea's back made (her, it) much less threatening to Native Americans than the white soldiers alone would have been.
9. At one point, she, Lewis, and Clark visited (her, their) people's summer home.
10. The expedition, short on food and medicines, was able to restock (its, their) supplies from her tribe's stores.

➡ For a SELF-CHECK and more practice, see the EXERCISE BANK, p. 325.

B. PROOFREADING: Correct Use of Pronouns

Rewrite the passage below, correcting the pronoun errors.

Sacajawea: Explorer and Survivor

Polly and me read Lewis and Clark's journals. Sacajawea and them met at Fort Mandan, near present-day Bismarck, North Dakota. Several months later, Lewis described how their supplies were washed overboard as he traveled by boat. Sacajawea's quick thinking saved journals, instruments, and medicines.

Sacajawea introduced Lewis and Clark to their tribe, the Shoshone, in the summer of 1805. Lewis had left she, Clark, and most of the other men behind while he scouted ahead, looking for the Shoshone villages. Finally, he met a Shoshone leader named Cameahwait. When Clark and Sacajawea rejoined Lewis, she recognized Cameahwait; he was her brother! Now Lewis and him could be friends.

C. WRITING: Using Pronouns Correctly

The map shows milestones in Sacajawea's journey. Working with a partner, use it and the information in exercises A and B to write a paragraph, explaining in your own words what she survived and accomplished.

Underline the pronouns you use. Proofread your work to be sure you have used the pronouns correctly.

Example: No one could have guessed how hard the journey would be.

Sacajawea's Journey West with Lewis and Clark, 1805
Shown on a current map of the western United States

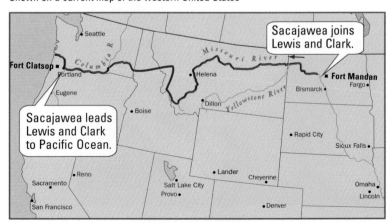

Grammar in Literature

Using Personal Pronouns Effectively

When you write, you have a choice about pronouns. You might choose to use first-person pronouns—like *I, me, we* and *us*—or you might find it better to use third-person pronouns—including *he, she, him, her, they, them*. First-person pronouns show a close relationship between writer and reader. In the passage below, the late actor Christopher Reeve used first-person pronouns to reveal his reactions to a horse-riding accident that left him paralyzed.

from

Still Me

by Christopher Reeve

[T]he chief radiologist ... showed me that the damage to my spinal cord was only one centimeter wide, and said that if I had landed with my head twisted only a fraction further to the left, I would have been killed instantly. If I had landed with my head slightly more to the right, I probably would have sustained a bruise and been up on my feet within a few weeks. I just happened to hit the rail at an angle that turned me into a C2 vent-dependent quadriplegic. The irony of it hit me very hard, although I kept my emotions to myself. I knew there was no point dwelling on it. But now I knew on a visceral level how fragile our existence is.

> **FIRST PERSON** pronouns create a sense of closeness. You are there with Reeve, reading his innermost thoughts.

> What effect does Reeve produce by using the pronoun *our?* How would the last sentence change if the pronoun were omitted?

Christopher Reeve with his wife after his injury left him paralyzed.

Practice and Apply

WRITING: Using Pronouns

The following passage is from a news story about Reeve's accident. Read the passage; then follow the directions below.

"He was in the middle of the pack . . . , and he was pretty excited about it," says Lisa Reid, [who] witnessed his May 27 ride. "The horse was coming into the fence beautifully. The rhythm was fine and Chris was fine, and they were going at a good pace." But then, Reid says, . . . "The horse put his front feet over the fence, but his hind feet never left the ground.". . . "Chris is such a big man. He was going forward, his head over the top of the horse's head. He had committed his upper body to the jump. But the horse . . . backed off the jump. . . . Reeve kept moving, pitching forward over the horse's neck." To Reid it appeared that Reeve first hit his head on the rail fence, then landed on the turf on his forehead.

—**"Fallen Rider,"** *People Weekly,* **June 12, 1995**

1. The passage is written from an observer's point of view. What pronouns does the observer use?
2. Imagine that Reeve himself wrote the report, and revise the passage, using first-person pronouns like *I* and *me.*
3. Compare your revision with the original. Which version is more personal and immediate? Why?

Save your revision in your 🗀 **Working Portfolio.**

A. Pronouns Write the pronoun that correctly completes the sentence. Choose the correct pronoun from those in parentheses.

1. E. L. Konigsburg tells an unusual survival story in (her, its) book *From the Mixed-Up Files of Mrs. Basil E. Frankweiler.*
2. It's the story of Claudia Kincaid; (she, herself) ran away to live in the Metropolitan Museum of Art.
3. (She, Her) and her brother Jamie lived there for a week.
4. They slept in an antique bed and took (their, they're) baths in a fountain.
5. The fountain had coins all over (it's, its) base.
6. (These, This) is where both of the children collected (their, his or her) lunch money.
7. There was a new statue; (its, it's) origin was a mystery to everyone.
8. Claudia and Jamie decided to solve the mystery (theirselves, themselves).
9. They contacted Mrs. Basil E. Frankweiler. That statue had come from (her, his) private collection.
10. (Who, Whom) made the statue? You'll have to read the book (yourself, itself)!

B. Pronoun Use This student report about the novel *Island of the Blue Dolphins* contains nine errors in pronoun usage. Rewrite the passage to correct the errors.

STUDENT MODEL

What if my brother and me were abandoned by my entire community on our island home? How would us castoffs survive? What would we do with ourself?

In *Island of the Blue Dolphins,* by Scott O'Dell, the heroine was left behind with her brother, who was soon killed by wild dogs. It was her who remained on the island for eighteen years. She tamed one of the island dogs herself and named it Rontu; it's friendship was invaluable to her.

Few of the people I know would take such good care of himself or herself if left alone on an island. Even these who know the wilderness might not have the mental strength to last alone for such a long time. O'Dell's heroine showed great skill, courage, and patience. Whom else would be so strong?

Choose the correct replacement for each underlined word in the passage, or indicate if it is correct as is.

<u>Who</u> is Thomas Eisner? <u>Him</u> and his wife Maria are
(1)   (2)
entomologists, or insect experts. <u>Their</u> concerned about the survival
(3)
of endangered insects. <u>Himself</u> and writer Diane Ackerman explored
(4)
insect life in Florida. Ackerman describes what she learned in <u>her</u>
(5)
book *The Rarest of the Rare: Vanishing Animals, Timeless Worlds.* It

was <u>him</u> who proved that some insects contain medicines that can
(6)
cure human diseases. <u>That</u> has encouraged drug companies to help
(7)
protect the rain forests for insect research. Eisner has also testified

before members of the U.S. Senate, asking <u>them</u> to reauthorize the
(8)
Endangered Species Act. Eisner reminded the Senate that <u>us</u>
(9)
humans share the planet with many other species. In helping them

survive, we may ultimately help <u>themselves</u>.
(10)

---

1. A. Whom
   B. Which
   C. Whose
   D. Correct as is

2. A. Himself
   B. He
   C. His
   D. Correct as is

3. A. There
   B. They're
   C. Them are
   D. Correct as is

4. A. Him
   B. Them
   C. He
   D. Correct as is

5. A. his
   B. their
   C. hers
   D. Correct as is

6. A. he
   B. himself
   C. his
   D. Correct as is

7. A. These
   B. His discovery
   C. This
   D. Correct as is

8. A. it
   B. those
   C. they
   D. Correct as is

9. A. our
   B. my
   C. we
   D. Correct as is

10. A. ourselves
    B. we
    C. humans
    D. Correct as is

Student Help Desk

Pronouns at a Glance

Subject Case

I	we
you	you
he	they
she	
it	

Use this case when
- the pronoun is a **subject**
- the pronoun is a **predicate pronoun**

Object Case

me	us
you	you
him	them
her	
it	

Use this case when
- the pronoun is the **direct object**
- the pronoun is the **indirect object**
- the pronoun is the **object of a preposition**

Possessive Case

my/mine	our/ours
your/yours	your/yours
his	their/theirs
her/hers	
its	

Use this case for
- pronouns that show **ownership or relationship**

Pronoun-Antecedent Agreement
We'll Do Our Best

A pronoun should agree with its antecedent in number, person, and gender.

A singular antecedent takes a singular pronoun.

Marisella is saving **her** candles for a power outage. (**singular**)

A plural antecedent takes a plural pronoun.

The **Garcias** have boarded up **their** house against the hurricane. (**plural**)

Avoid incorrect gender reference.

Everyone has **his or her** favorite precautions.
We all have **our** favorite precautions.

Types of Pronouns
Everything in Its Place

Intensive & Reflexive	Interrogative	Demonstrative	Indefinite
myself	who	this	someone
yourself	whom	that	anyone
herself	what	these	each
himself	which	those	several
itself	whose		many
ourselves			all
yourselves			most
themselves			none

For a full list of indefinite pronouns, see page 76.

Pronoun Problems   A Clear-cut Case

We: Subject/Predicate Pronoun	**We** Californians have survived many natural disasters.
Us: Object	So many natural disasters have struck **us** Californians.
Who: Subject/Predicate Pronoun	**Who** has ever survived a tornado?
Whom: Object of verb or preposition	To **whom** will we turn for advice?

The Bottom Line

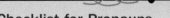

Checklist for Pronouns

Have I . . .

____ used the subject case for pronouns that are subjects and predicate pronouns?

____ used the object case for pronouns that are objects of verbs or prepositions?

____ used the possessive case to show ownership or relationship?

____ used *who* and *whom* correctly?

____ made sure that pronouns agree with their antecedents in number, person, and gender?

____ used the correct cases in compound subjects and objects?

PRONOUNS

Verbs

Theme: Great Rides
Three Thrilling Minutes

How does it feel to speed through the air on a roller coaster? Does your skin tingle? Does your stomach churn? Do your ears pop? Verbs help you recreate how real-life experiences feel, look, sound, smell, and taste. What verbs do you think the passenger in this picture would use to recreate his real-life experience on a roller coaster?

Write Away: Want a Ride?
Write a paragraph describing the most thrilling ride you can imagine. It could be a roller coaster ride, a train trip through a wild animal preserve, or a drive along a twisting mountain road. Put the paragraph in your 📁 **Working Portfolio.**

Choose the best way to rewrite each underlined word or group of words.

Amazing things <u>happen</u> on roller coasters. In 1949, a West
(1)
Virginian coal miner <u>ride</u> the Cyclone at Coney Island. For six
(2)
years before, the miner <u>will be</u> mute. After the ride, he <u>speaks</u>
(3) (4)
again. He <u>said</u>, "I feel sick." While this man found his voice on a
(5)
roller coaster, other people <u>are losing</u> things. In 1994, workers at
(6)
an amusement park in England <u>have drained</u> a pool beneath two
(7)
roller coasters. Twenty-five sets of false teeth <u>lay</u> at the bottom of
(8)
the pool. Amusement park workers also <u>has found</u> glass eyes,
(9)
hearing aids, and toupees beneath coaster tracks. Who knows what
workers <u>discovered</u> under future rides.
(10)

---

1. A. will have happened
   B. were happening
   C. had happened
   D. Correct as is

2. A. will ride
   B. rode
   C. is riding
   D. Correct as is

3. A. had been
   B. will have been
   C. was being
   D. Correct as is

4. A. will be speaking
   B. has spoken
   C. spoke
   D. Correct as is

5. A. says
   B. will say
   C. had said
   D. Correct as is

6. A. lose
   B. have lost
   C. will be losing
   D. Correct as is

7. A. will drain
   B. drained
   C. drains
   D. Correct as is

8. A. laid
   B. has laid
   C. are laying
   D. Correct as is

9. A. have found
   B. will be finding
   C. must find
   D. Correct as is

10. A. are discovering
    B. were discovering
    C. will discover
    D. Correct as is

VERBS

LESSON 1 — What Is a Verb?

① Here's the Idea

▶ **A verb is a word used to express an action, a condition, or a state of being.** The two main types of verbs are **action verbs** and **linking verbs**. Both kinds can be accompanied by helping verbs.

Action Verbs

An **action verb** tells what its subject does. The action it expresses may be either **physical** or **mental**.

> **The roller coaster climbs up a hill.** (physical action)

> **Then the coaster plunges straight down.** (physical action)

> **Some people hate amusement parks.** (mental action)

> **Others enjoy them.** (mental action)

Linking Verbs

A **linking verb** links its subject to a word in the predicate. The most common linking verbs are forms of the verb *be.*

Linking Verbs	
Forms of *be*	be, is, am, are, was, were, been, being
Verbs that express condition	appear, become, feel, grow, look, remain, smell, sound, taste

LINKS

The Cyclone is a roller coaster.
LINKING VERB

Its name sounds dangerous.

CHAPTER 4

Some verbs can serve as either action or linking verbs.

LINKS

A passenger looks at the roller coaster. She looks eager.
    ACTION VERB   LINKING VERB

She feels ready. She feels the steel bar across her lap.
    LINKING VERB   ACTION VERB

Helping Verbs and Verb Phrases

Helping verbs help main verbs express precise shades of meaning. The combination of one or more helping verbs with a main verb is called a **verb phrase.**

VERB PHRASE
Many people will ride the Cyclone this weekend.
  HELPING   MAIN

They must want some thrills in their lives.

Some verbs can serve both as main verbs and as helping verbs. For example, *has* stands alone in the first sentence below but is a helping verb in the second sentence.

Rich Rodriguez has no fear of roller coasters.
    MAIN VERB

He has set a world roller coaster record.
    HELPING VERB

Common Helping Verbs	
Forms of *be*	be, am, is, are, was, were, been, being
Forms of *do*	do, does, did
Forms of *have*	have, has, had
Others	could, should, would may, might, must can, shall, will

VERBS

❷ Why It Matters in Writing

You often can express strong feelings by using action verbs instead of linking verbs. Notice the difference that the change to an action verb makes in the sentence below.

The Cyclone ~~is scary to~~ *petrifies* me.

❸ Practice and Apply

A. CONCEPT CHECK: What Is a Verb?

Write the verb or verb phrase in each of the following sentences.

The King of Coaster Jockeys
1. Rich Rodriguez has ridden a roller coaster longer than anyone else in the world.
2. He set the record on the Big Dipper in Blackpool, England.
3. His record is 1,013.5 hours over 47 days.
4. Guidelines allow a rider two hours a day off a coaster.
5. Rodriguez slept on the roller coaster.
6. By the end, Rodriguez had traveled 11,362 miles.
7. The wind rubbed his face raw.
8. The Big Dipper is a complete-circuit roller coaster.
9. It travels about 65 miles per hour.
10. But Rodriguez calls the Cyclone his favorite.

➡ **For a SELF-CHECK and more practice, see the EXERCISE BANK, p. 326.**

CHALLENGE

Label each verb above as *Action* or *Linking*.

B. WRITING: Using Action Verbs

Write an action verb for each numeral in the paragraph below.

The Chiller
    Imagine a trip on the Chiller, a roller coaster in New Jersey. The coaster **(1)** from 0 to 70 miles per hour in four seconds. Its launch **(2)** you. Ahead **(3)** a tunnel and then a sharp rise. Halfway through the ride, the train **(4)** and hurtles you backwards. The ride **(5)** only 45 seconds.

Action Verbs and Objects

❶ Here's the Idea

Action verbs are often accompanied by words that complete their meaning. These complements are **direct objects** and **indirect objects**.

Direct Objects

▶ **A direct object is a noun or pronoun that names the receiver of a verb's action.** The **direct object** answers the question *what* or *whom*.

GAINED WHAT?

Evel Knievel gained **much** fame.
  ACTION VERB   DIRECT OBJECT

He performed **dangerous stunts on a motorcycle.**

Indirect Objects

▶ **An indirect object tells *to what* or *whom* or *for what* or *whom* an action is done.** Verbs that often take indirect objects include *bring, give, hand, lend, make, send, show, teach, tell,* and *write.*

Knievel gave a thrill. (Gave a thrill to whom?)

TO WHOM?

Knievel gave **his** fans **a thrill.**
  INDIRECT OBJECT   DIRECT OBJECT

Knievel taught **his** son **some stunts.**

If the word *to* or *for* appears in the sentence, the word that follows is **not** an indirect object. It is the object of a preposition.

Show the stunt to us.
                    OBJECT OF PREPOSITION

Show us the stunt.
      INDIRECT OBJECT

Transitive and Intransitive Verbs

An action verb that has a direct object is called a **transitive verb**. An action verb that does not have a direct object is called an **intransitive verb**.

Knievel cleared nineteen cars in one stunt.

TRANSITIVE VERB ⬆   ⬆ DIRECT OBJECT

His motorcycle sailed through the air.

⬆ INTRANSITIVE VERB (NO OBJECT)

Sometimes an intransitive verb is followed by a word that looks like a direct object but is really an adverb. An adverb tells where, when, how, or to what extent, but a direct object answers the question *what* or *whom*.

CRASHED WHAT?

Knievel crashed his motorcycle.

TRANSITIVE VERB ⬆   ⬆ DIRECT OBJECT

CRASHED WHEN?

He crashed frequently.

INTRANSITIVE ⬆   ⬆ ADVERB
VERB

❷ Why It Matters in Writing

Use direct objects that are specific nouns to make your writing clearer and more interesting to readers. Notice how the model below uses specific nouns as direct objects.

PROFESSIONAL MODEL

> Knievel became as tough as Butte [Montana]. He held **school records** for push-ups and sit-ups. He played **pro hockey**. . . . He raced **stock cars, sprint cars,** and **motorcycles**. . . .
>
> —Jerry Garrett, "Midnight in the Garden of Good and Evel"

➌ Practice and Apply

A. CONCEPT CHECK: Action Verbs and Objects

Write the 15 complements in these sentences, identifying each as a direct object or an indirect object.

Jumping a Canyon

1. In 1974, Evel Knievel staged the most famous feat of his career.
2. He chose the Snake River Canyon in Idaho.
3. He bought himself a steam-powered vehicle.
4. Knievel's promoter publicized the danger of the jump.
5. Fans wished Knievel good luck.
6. TV cameras showed viewers the quarter-mile-wide chasm.
7. The launch gave spectators a fright.
8. A parachute opened its canopy early.
9. The vehicle hit the floor of the canyon.
10. The failure gave the famous daredevil no desire for another try at the canyon.

➜ **For a SELF-CHECK and more practice, see the EXERCISE BANK, p. 326.**

B. WRITING: Using Specific Nouns

The photograph below shows Evel Knievel's son Robbie jumping his motorcycle over the Grand Canyon. Write a short description of him in action based on what you see in the photo. Use some of the nouns in this list as direct objects.
air, Grand Canyon, ground, helmet, motorcycle, record, reputation, rocks, scaffold, stunt

Linking Verbs and Predicate Words

LESSON 3

❶ **Here's the Idea**

The word that a linking verb connects its subject to is called a **subject complement.** The subject complement identifies or describes the subject. Some common linking verbs are *is, feel, seem,* and *look.*

IDENTIFIES

Paul Revere's mount was **a saddle horse.**
SUBJECT   VERB   SUBJECT COMPLEMENT

DESCRIBES

The mare seemed **very fast.**
SUBJECT   VERB   SUBJECT COMPLEMENT

Predicate Nouns and Predicate Adjectives

A subject complement can be a **predicate noun** or a **predicate adjective.**

▶ **A predicate noun is a noun that follows a linking verb and identifies, renames, or defines the subject.**

IDENTIFIES

Brown Beauty was **the mare's name.**
SUBJECT   VERB   PREDICATE NOUN

Mr. Larkin was **the horse's owner.**

▶ **A predicate adjective is an adjective that follows a linking verb and modifies the subject.**

MODIFIES

Saddle horses are **powerful.**
SUBJECT   VERB PREDICATE ADJECTIVE

They look **distinctive.**

CHAPTER 4

❷ Why It Matters in Writing

You can use predicate adjectives to evaluate a subject or show judgment. Notice author William Saroyan's use of a predicate adjective to evaluate a horse.

LITERARY MODEL

"I do not know what to think," he said. "The horse is **stronger** than ever. Better-tempered, too. I thank God."

—William Saroyan, "The Summer of the Beautiful White Horse"

❸ Practice and Apply

CONCEPT CHECK: Linking Verbs and Predicate Words

Identify each linking verb, predicate noun, and predicate adjective in the sentences below.

A Narrow Escape

1. On the night of Paul Revere's ride, the weather was mild.
2. His mount's canter was graceful.
3. Revere himself felt calm.
4. Suddenly, Revere's horse became nervous.
5. The two horsemen on the road ahead were enemy soldiers.
6. The result was a brief chase off the original route.
7. A clay pit became a trap for one soldier's horse.
8. Brown Beauty was faster than the other soldier's horse.
9. Revere's detour seemed a nuisance.
10. But his new route was safer.

➜ For a **SELF-CHECK** and more practice, see the **EXERCISE BANK**, p. 327.

VERBS

Principal Parts of Verbs

❶ Here's the Idea

▶ **Every verb has four basic forms called its principal parts: the present, the present participle, the past, and the past participle.** These principal parts are used to make all of the forms and tenses of the verb. Here are some examples.

PRESENT
Balloonists sail on wind currents.

PRESENT PARTICIPLE
They often are riding jet streams.

PAST
Bertrand Piccard and Brian Jones circled the earth in a balloon in 1999.

PAST PARTICIPLE
Many balloonists have tried the feat.

The Four Principal Parts of a Verb			
Present	**Present Participle**	**Past**	**Past Participle**
sail	(is) sailing	sailed	(has) sailed
lift	(is) lifting	lifted	(has) lifted

Notice that helping verbs are used with the present participle and the past participle.

Regular Verbs

There are two kinds of verbs: regular and irregular.

▶ **A regular verb is a verb whose past and past participle are formed by adding -ed or -d to the present.** It forms the present participle by adding -ing to the present.

Present	Present Participle	Past	Past Participle
succeed	(is) succeed + **ing**	succeed + **ed**	(has) succeed + **ed**

You will learn about irregular verbs in the next lesson.

CHAPTER 4

❷ Why It Matters in Writing

The principal parts of verbs help you show changes in time in your writing. In the model below, notice how the writer uses the past and the present to show two different times.

PROFESSIONAL MODEL

Piccard and Jones finished their around-the-world trip in 20 days. Their feat stands as a world record.

PAST

PRESENT

—Martha Schmitt

VERBS

❸ Practice and Apply

CONCEPT CHECK: Principal Parts of Verbs

Identify each underlined principal part as the present, the present participle, the past, or the past participle.

An Around-the-World Balloon Flight

Piccard and Jones **(1)** traveled in a combination hot-air and helium balloon called *Breitling Orbiter 3*. In terms of comfort, the balloon greatly **(2)** outclasses earlier aircraft. Inside a pressurized, heated cabin, engineers have **(3)** equipped the balloon with a bunk bed, toilet, and kitchen. When one pilot is **(4)** sleeping, the other **(5)** sits at the control panel. Then the pilots **(6)** switch places. Other equipment on the flight **(7)** included a fax machine and satellite telephones. Solar-charged batteries **(8)** provided power for the onboard equipment. Other pilots have **(9)** used similar balloons in around-the-world attempts. Engineers are continually **(10)** improving the design of high-altitude balloons.

➜ For a SELF-CHECK and more practice, see the EXERCISE BANK, p. 327.

Irregular Verbs

LESSON 5

① Here's the Idea

▶ **Irregular verbs are verbs whose past and past participle forms are not made by adding -ed or -d to the present.**

The following chart shows you how to form the past and past participle forms of many irregular verbs.

Common Irregular Verbs			
	Present	**Past**	**Past Participle**
Group 1 The forms of the present, the past, and the past participle are all the same.	**burst** cost cut hurt let put set shut	**burst** cost cut hurt let put set shut	(has) **burst** (has) cost (has) cut (has) hurt (has) let (has) put (has) set (has) shut
Group 2 The forms of the past and the past participle are the same.	**bring** build catch feel keep lay leave lend make pay say sell shine sit sting swing teach think win wind	**brought** built caught felt kept laid left lent made paid said sold shone sat stung swung taught thought won wound	(has) **brought** (has) built (has) caught (has) felt (has) kept (has) laid (has) left (has) lent (has) made (has) paid (has) said (has) sold (has) shone (has) sat (has) stung (has) swung (has) taught (has) thought (has) won (has) wound

CHAPTER 4

Common Irregular Verbs *(continued)*

	Present	Past	Past Participle
Group 3 The past participle is formed by adding *-n* or *-en* to the past.	**bite** break choose freeze lie speak steal tear wear	**bit** broke chose froze lay spoke stole tore wore	(has) **bitten** (has) broken (has) chosen (has) frozen (has) lain (has) spoken (has) stolen (has) torn (has) worn
Group 4 The past participle is formed from the present, often by adding *-n* or *-en*.	**blow** do draw drive eat fall give go grow know rise run see shake take throw write	**blew** did drew drove ate fell gave went grew knew rose ran saw shook took threw wrote	(has) **blown** (has) done (has) drawn (has) driven (has) eaten (has) fallen (has) given (has) gone (has) grown (has) known (has) risen (has) run (has) seen (has) shaken (has) taken (has) thrown (has) written
Group 5 The last vowel changes from *i* in the present to *a* in the past, to *u* in the past participle.	**begin** drink ring shrink sing sink spring swim	**began** drank rang shrank sang sank sprang swam	(has) **begun** (has) drunk (has) rung (has) shrunk (has) sung (has) sunk (has) sprung (has) swum

The Irregular Verb *Be*

	Present	Past	Past Participle
The past and past participle do not follow any pattern.	**am, are, is**	**was, were**	(has) **been**

VERBS

❷ Why It Matters in Writing

Skilled writers use irregular verb forms correctly. You probably already know the principal parts of many irregular verbs. To avoid mistakes, memorize any that you do not know. Notice the student writer's correct use of irregular verbs in the model below.

> **STUDENT MODEL**
>
> My brother Mike **took** part in "Ride the Rockies," Colorado's famous bike ride through the Rocky Mountain range. In one day he **rode** 67 miles. "Half of that **was** uphill!" **said** my brother when I congratulated him after the event.

❸ Practice and Apply

CONCEPT CHECK: Irregular Verbs

In the sentences below, choose the correct forms of the verbs in parentheses.

On the Rebound

1. American bicyclist Lance Armstrong (win, won) the 2,287-mile Tour de France in 1999.
2. Several years earlier, doctors (give, gave) him less than a 40 percent chance of surviving cancer.
3. Armstrong (chose, chosen) an aggressive treatment plan.
4. Now Armstrong has (beat, beaten) the disease.
5. After the cancer, he (began, begun) his career all over.
6. The experience has (gave, given) him a different outlook.
7. It also has (leave, left) him with a leaner body.
8. Armstrong's lighter weight (pay, paid) off when he had to cycle through the mountains.
9. So (did, done) his training, in which he cycled the toughest portions of the course.
10. Armstrong's amazing victory has (teach, taught) other cancer patients to maintain hope.

➜ For a SELF-CHECK and more practice, see the EXERCISE BANK, p. 328.

Simple Tenses

❶ Here's the Idea

▶ **A tense is a verb form that shows the time of an action or condition.** Verbs have three **simple tenses:** the present, the past, and the future.

Understanding Simple Tenses

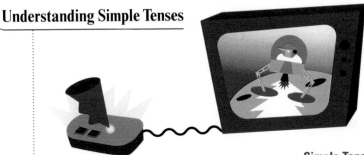

Simple Tenses

The **hatch of the lunar module opens.**
— The **present tense** shows that an action or condition occurs now.

The **module reached Tranquillity Base 30 minutes ago.**
— The **past tense** shows that an action or condition was completed in the past.

Soon the occupants **will walk** on the moon.
— The **future tense** shows that an action or condition will occur in the future.

A **progressive form** of a verb expresses an action or condition in progress. The progressive forms of the three simple tenses are used to show that actions or conditions were, are, or will be in progress.

Progressive Forms

You **are operating** a virtual-reality model of the Apollo 11 mission.
— Present Progressive

You **were blasting** off before.
— Past Progressive

You **will be sharing** the game with a friend.
— Future Progressive

Forming Simple Tenses

The **present tense** of a verb is the present principal part. The **past tense** is the past principal part. To form the **future tense,** add *will* to the present principal part.

Forming Simple Tenses	Singular	Plural
Present (present principal part)	I moonwalk you moonwalk he, she, it moonwalks	we moonwalk you moonwalk they moonwalk
Past (past principal part)	I moonwalked you moonwalked he, she, it moonwalked	we moonwalked you moonwalked they moonwalked
Future (*will* + present part)	I will moonwalk you will moonwalk he, she, it will moonwalk	we will moonwalk you will moonwalk they will moonwalk

To make the progressive form of one of these tenses, add the present, past, or future form of *be* to the present participle.

Present Progressive: **I am moonwalking.**

Past Progressive: **I was moonwalking.**

Future Progressive: **I will be moonwalking.**

❷ Why It Matters in Writing

The simple tenses help you express basic time frames. Notice how the model uses the past and present tenses to shift between the writer's childhood and her adulthood.

> **LITERARY MODEL**
>
> I held on to the knowledge tightly afterward, and I still hold it to this day. I learned what flying was for my father and for the other early aviators. . . .
>
> —Reeve Lindbergh, "Flying"

PAST

PRESENT

❸ Practice and Apply

A. CONCEPT CHECK: Simple Tenses

Identify each underlined verb as present, past, future, present progressive, past progressive, or future progressive.

The *Eagle* Has Landed
1. What <u>was</u> the first moon landing like?
2. A virtual-reality game <u>recreates</u> the experience.
3. Inside the lunar module *Eagle,* you <u>head</u> for a plain called the Sea of Tranquillity.
4. A computer <u>sounds</u> several alarms.
5. Mission Control <u>will override</u> the alarms.
6. You <u>are running</u> out of fuel in the search for a good landing spot.
7. You <u>will have</u> only thirty seconds left.
8. But you <u>will land</u> without a bump.
9. Before the real take-off, Neil Armstrong <u>doubted</u> the mission's likelihood of success.
10. He <u>set</u> the odds at 50-50.

Rewrite sentences 2, 3, 4, 5, and 8, changing the verbs to progressive forms.

➜ For a SELF-CHECK and more practice, see the EXERCISE BANK, p. 328.

B. WRITING: Using Simple Tenses

Use time frame clues to write each verb in parentheses in the correct simple tense: present, past, or future.

Shuttle Commander Collins

NASA (select) Eileen Collins as the first female space-shuttle pilot in 1990. She (pilot) her first mission in February 1995. In 1997, she (return) to space, piloting *Atlantis* to the *Mir* space station. Today, Collins's husband, Pat Youngs, (take) care of their daughter during her space missions. He (handle) that job during Collins's future flights for NASA.

❶ Here's the Idea

Understanding Perfect Tenses

The **present perfect tense** places an action or condition in a stretch of time leading up to the present.

> **Many people have rafted through the Grand Canyon.** | People rafted through the canyon at unspecified times before the present.

The **past perfect tense** places a past action or condition before another past action or condition.

> **After the guide had straightened the raft, we entered the rapids.** | The straightening occurred before the entering.

The **future perfect tense** places a future action or condition before another future action or condition.

> **We will have cleared many rapids before the trip ends.** | The clearing will occur before the ending.

Rafters will have passed this point soon.

Forming Perfect Tenses

To form the present perfect, past perfect, or future perfect tense, add the present, past, or future form of *have* to the past participle.

Forming Perfect Tenses

	Singular	**Plural**
Present Perfect (*has* or *have* + past participle)	I have rafted you have rafted he, she, it has rafted	we have rafted you have rafted they have rafted
Past Perfect (*had* + past participle)	I had rafted you had rafted he, she, it had rafted	we had rafted you had rafted they had rafted
Future Perfect (*will* + *have* + past participle)	I will have rafted you will have rafted he, she, it will have rafted	we will have rafted you will have rafted they will have rafted

In a perfect form, the tense of the helping verb *have* shows the verb's tense.

VERBS

❷ Why It Matters in Writing

When writing a narrative, you can use the perfect tenses to make the timing of events clear. Notice how the use of the past perfect tense and the future perfect tense makes the time relationships clear in the model.

STUDENT MODEL

Just before the trip began, our guide had warned us about Lava Falls, the largest rapid in the Grand Canyon. He now says that by the time the trip ends, at least one raft will have flipped in its churning currents.

PAST PERFECT

FUTURE PERFECT

❸ Practice and Apply

A. CONCEPT CHECK: Perfect Tenses

Identify the verb in each sentence, and indicate whether its tense is present perfect, past perfect, or future perfect.

A Grand Ride

1. The guide had compared a trip through the Grand Canyon to a roller coaster.
2. Soon I will have experienced the journey myself.
3. Within eight days, we will have ridden more than 70 rapids.
4. I have taken other rafting trips.
5. But the Grand Canyon trip will have been the longest and wildest.
6. At Hermit Rapid, huge waves had swept over our boat.
7. The roar of the waves had muffled our voices.
8. Someone has called Lava Falls the world's fastest navigable white-water rapid.
9. I never have rafted through anything like it.
10. By the end of Lava Falls, the river had dropped 37 feet.

→ **For a SELF-CHECK and more practice, see the EXERCISE BANK, p. 329.**

B. WRITING: Using Perfect Tenses

Add verbs to this narrative in the tense indicated in parentheses. Choose verbs from this list:

climb, travel, see, return, take

The Best Trip

The ride through the Grand Canyon was the best trip I ever (present perfect). Before it was over, we (past perfect) nearly 280 miles in just eight days. We (past perfect) up the rocks along waterfalls and jumped into the pools below. We (past perfect) mule deer and bighorn sheep as well as fossils of sea creatures millions of years old. I hope that by the time I graduate from college I (future perfect) to the Grand Canyon.

Using Verb Tenses

❶ Here's the Idea

A good writer uses different verb tenses to indicate that events occur at different times. If you do not need to indicate a change of time, do not switch from one tense to another.

Writing About the Present

▶ **The present tenses convey actions and conditions that occur in the present.** When you write about the present, you can use the present tense, the present perfect tense, and the present progressive form.

People ride many animals besides horses. **Tourists in India sightsee on the backs of elephants.**	The **present tense** places the actions in the present.
Indians have trained elephants for thousands of years. **They have used elephants for transportation and work.**	The **present perfect tense** places the actions in a period of time leading up to the present.
Elephant handlers are continuing an old tradition. **They are passing the tradition on to their children.**	The **present progressive form** shows the actions in progress now.

Writing About the Past

▶ **The past tenses convey actions and conditions that came to an end in the past.** When you write about the past, you can use past verb forms to indicate the order in which events occurred. Using these forms correctly will make it easier for readers to follow the events.

In 218 B.C., Hannibal's army **crossed** the Alps with elephants.

His army **included** thirty-eight elephants.

> The **past tense** shows actions that began and were completed in the past.

Other generals **had used** elephants in war before Hannibal did.

Almost a century after Persians **had ridden** elephants in battle, Hannibal led elephants against Rome.

> The **past perfect tense** places the actions before other past actions.

Hannibal's elephants **were scaring** the Roman army's horses, as well as its soldiers.

Hannibal **was winning** battle after battle.

> The **past progressive forms** show that the actions were in progress in the past.

Elephants **were frightening** Hannibal's opponents.

Writing About the Future

▶ **The future tenses convey actions and conditions that are yet to come.** By using the different future verb forms, you can show how future events are related in time.

Maybe you will ride an elephant one day.

You will mount the largest land animal on earth.

> The **future tense** shows that the actions have not yet occurred.

By the time you are an adult, perhaps elephants will have survived threats to their existence.

With luck, people will have protected enough elephants to keep the species from becoming extinct.

> The **future perfect** tense places the actions before other future actions.

Elephant herds will be prospering with protection.

Their numbers will be growing.

> The **future progressive** forms show that the actions will be continuing in the future.

❷ Why It Matters in Writing

The present tense is useful when you are describing or explaining something. Notice how the writer consistently uses the present tense in the model below.

> **PROFESSIONAL MODEL**
>
> A mahout ... is one who **trains** and **drives** an elephant. The mahout **sits** on the elephant's neck, just behind the head, and **guides** the animal through a series of spoken and physical commands.
>
> —Malcolm C. Jensen, "Elephants of War"

❸ Practice and Apply

A. CONCEPT CHECK: Using Verb Tenses

In the sentences below, choose the correct tense or form for each verb in parentheses.

Park Rangers on Elephants

1. In the Kanha National Park in India, mahouts (patrol, will patrol) the park every day.
2. In India, mahouts (have ridden, had ridden) elephants for centuries.
3. On their daily patrols, the mahouts at Kanha (protect, will protect) the park's Bengal tigers from poachers.
4. Bengal tigers (are becoming, became) increasingly rare.
5. A mahout and his elephant (remained, will remain) together for life.
6. Yesterday, a mahout (takes, took) several tourists into the jungle.
7. They (were hoping, will be hoping) for a glimpse of the tigers.
8. During the ride, the mahout (was pointing, have pointed) out tigers in the bamboo and elephant grass.
9. By the end of the ride, the tourists (had learned, were learning) a great deal about tigers.
10. Every day for the next month, the mahout (will have taken, will be taking) tourists on elephant rides.

→ For a SELF-CHECK and more practice, see the EXERCISE BANK, p. 329.

B. EDITING: Correcting Verb Tenses

Rewrite this paragraph, correcting inconsistencies in the use of verb tenses. There are five errors.

The Elephants at Kanha

At Kanha, each elephant has a caretaker. What do the caretakers do? In the late afternoon, the caretakers have given the elephants their baths and fed them. Then they set the elephants free in the jungle. In the middle of the night, the caretakers woke up and will round up the elephants. They dust off the animals and will be saddling them for the mahouts.

🗎 **Working Portfolio:** Find your **Write Away** from page 90 or a sample of your most recent work. Identify any errors in the use of verb tenses and correct them.

Troublesome Verb Pairs

❶ Here's the Idea

Some verbs seem similar but are actually different words with different meanings. Troublesome verb pairs include *lie* and *lay*, *sit* and *set*, *rise* and *raise*, and *let* and *leave*.

Lie and *Lay*

Lie means "to rest in a flat position." It does not take an object. *Lay* means "to put or place." It does take an object.

The worker lies near the tree.

He lays a bucket near the tree.

Lie and *Lay*		
Present	**Past**	**Past Participle**
lie Al **lies** down.	lay Al **lay** down.	lain Al has **lain** down.
lay Al **lays** the sponge down.	laid Al **laid** the sponge down.	laid Al has **laid** the sponge down.

Lie and lay are confusing because the present principal part of *lay* has the same spelling as the past principal part of *lie*.

Sit and *Set*

Sit means "to be seated." It does not take an object.

Set means "to put or place." It does take an object.

The worker sits by the window.

He sets the squeegee near the sill.

Sit and *Set*		
Present	**Past**	**Past Participle**
sit He **sits** on the ledge.	sat He **sat** on the ledge.	sat He has **sat** here often.
set Amy **sets** down the screen.	set Amy **set** down the screen.	set Amy has **set** down the screen.

VERBS

Rise and Raise

Rise means "to move upward" or "to get out of bed." It does not take an object. *Raise* means "to lift" or "to care for or bring up." It does take an object.

Lee rises before dawn every morning.

Lee raises the window.

Rise and *Raise*		
Present	**Past**	**Past Participle**
rise The hot air **rises**.	rose The hot air **rose**.	risen The hot air has **risen**.
raise Irene **raises** the screen.	raised Irene **raised** the screen.	raised Irene has **raised** the screen.

Let and Leave

Let means "to allow" or "to permit." *Leave* means "to depart" or "to allow something to remain where it is." Both *let* and *leave* may take an object.

Frank let his son operate the rig.

Marta leaves the windows closed.

Let and *Leave*		
Present	**Past**	**Past Participle**
let Anna **lets** me help.	let Anna **let** me help.	let Anna has **let** me help.
leave Tom **leaves** for work at noon.	left Tom **left** for work at noon yesterday.	left Tom has **left** for work.

❷ Practice and Apply

A. CONCEPT CHECK: Troublesome Verb Pairs

Choose the correct verb in parentheses for each of the following sentences.

Riding to the Top

1. (Let, Leave) me tell you about the job of washing the windows of a skyscraper.
2. On some buildings, the window washer (sits, sets) in a chair attached by ropes to the top of the building.
3. To move the chair up and down the building, a worker (rises, raises) and lowers the ropes.
4. From this high perch, a window washer can watch the sun (rise, raise).
5. On some skyscrapers, sliding scaffolds (rise, raise) the workers up and down.
6. One window washer began work at 5:00 A.M. and (let, left) work before the afternoon sun got too hot.
7. Another (lay, laid) asleep during the day and worked at night.
8. Would you like to (lie, lay) on a scaffold along the Sears Tower and watch the stars?
9. Window washers have to watch where they (sit, set) their tools.
10. They cannot just (lie, lay) them anywhere.

➡ **For a SELF-CHECK and more practice, see the EXERCISE BANK, p. 330.**

B. PROOFREADING: Correcting Errors in Verb Usage

List the five verbs that are used incorrectly in the following paragraph. Then change them to the correct verb forms.

At the Top

Imagine what it's like to set in a window-washing rig 70 stories up in the air. The cement sidewalk lays far below. As you look down, goose bumps raise on your skin. Don't sit your squeegee on that bird's nest on the window ledge! Let the nest alone, or you may be attacked by an angry bird.

Grammar in Social Studies

Using Verbs Effectively

In social studies you study major events in history. You use verbs—especially action verbs—to relate what happened. Creating an annotated map is a good way to describe a series of unfolding events. The map itself shows important locations. The annotations allow you to describe important events that took place at those locations. Below is an annotated map of part of the Oregon Trail, a pathway that settlers followed to get to the West in the mid-1800s.

Moving West Along the Oregon Trail

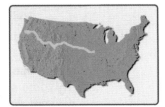

5 Three Island Crossing. Here settlers **can risk** a direct river crossing, or they **can travel** the long route around the river bend.

4 South Pass. South Pass **marks** the halfway point.

2 Ash Hollow. Most travelers **rest** here. They **taste** fresh water and **gaze** at the first trees in 100 miles.

3 Ft. Laramie. This fort **is** the gateway to the Rocky Mountains. Some people **decide** to go back.

1 Shawnee Mission. Oxen or mules **pull** wagons along the overland trail. Many settlers **walk** alongside them, barefoot. They **begin** a 2,000-mile journey.

Practice and Apply

A. USING VERBS TO RELATE EVENTS

Use your own ideas and the information on the map to write an imaginary journal entry by a settler on the Oregon Trail. Choose one of the landmarks on the map. Write what the settler might do, think, feel, or say upon arriving at that location. Your journal entry may answer questions like these:

• What might the settler do when he or she first arrives?

• What might the settler see?

• What might the settler wish?

B. WRITING: Making A Map

Draw a map of the route you follow to go to school or to go to another local spot. Label at least three landmarks along the route, and write a one-sentence annotation to indicate what you do at each one. You might include landmarks such as these:

• buildings

• natural features, such as rivers, hills, and lakes

• constructed features, such as bridges, overpasses, and railroad tracks

VERBS

home

I **meet** a friend at 7:35.

I **start** my trip at 7:30.

We always **check** the clock on the bank

Mixed Review

A. Correcting Errors in Verb Usage Find and correct the 15 incorrect verbs in the following sentences. Watch out for irregular verbs and members of troublesome verb pairs.

An Unusual Soap-Box Derby

1. Each year, the Sand Hill Challenge, a soap-box derby race in California, promoted driver safety among teenagers.
2. For several years, business firms sponsor the race teams, and technology companies build the race cars.
3. In the past, some cars will be having high-tech designs.
4. For a race in 1997, designers build a three-wheeled car.
5. Driver Amy Han laid down in the car and will steer it.
6. In the Whimsy Division, car designers typically will be worrying more about style than speed.
7. One year, a group will have made a car from bread.
8. In the past, both adult and high school teams participate in the races, but they will be having separate divisions.
9. Besides the driver, a typical team will be including two people who have pushed the car for the first 40 yards down a hill.
10. A "catcher" at the bottom of the hill slowed down and stopped the car.

B. Using Verb Tenses Imagine yourself in a soap-box derby race in a car of your own design. Write five sentences answering the following questions about the race. Be sure to use verb tenses correctly.

1. What thoughts or feelings did you have before the race?
2. What is your prediction about the outcome of the race?
3. How does the race start?
4. How does your car perform during the race?
5. What is the outcome of the race?

Choose the best way to rewrite each underlined word or group of words.

Nannette Baker admits to a fear of heights. Nevertheless, she takes up the sport of parachuting a number of years ago. When she (1) skydives, Baker lets her fears behind. In a typical dive, she free-falls (2) (3) for about 60 seconds and then opens her parachute. As she free-falls, she sometimes will be attaining a speed of 200 miles per hour. (4) In 1995, while she was skydiving with 102 other women, Baker (5) helped set a record for most women in a free-fall formation. But she will have jumped in even larger formations. For Baker, this sport (6) was the greatest thrill of all. According to Baker, it feels like she (7) floated, not falls, through the air. Although Baker is one of the few (8) African-American women in this sport, she gains company. In the (9) future, others probably will be drawn to the thrill of this sport. (10)

1. A. is taking
   B. took
   C. will take
   D. Correct as is

2. A. leaves
   B. has left
   C. had let
   D. Correct as is

3. A. has free-fallen
   B. had free-fallen
   C. was free-falling
   D. Correct as is

4. A. is attaining
   B. was attaining
   C. attains
   D. Correct as is

5. A. skydives
   B. will skydive
   C. is skydiving
   D. Correct as is

6. A. has jumped
   B. was jumping
   C. is jumping
   D. Correct as is

7. A. is
   B. will be
   C. had been
   D. Correct as is

8. A. will float
   B. had floated
   C. floats
   D. Correct as is

9. A. may gain
   B. was gaining
   C. gained
   D. Correct as is

10. A. were drawn
    B. are drawn
    C. had drawn
    D. Correct as is

Student Help Desk

Verbs at a Glance

A verb expresses action, condition, or state of being.
The two main kinds of verbs are **action verbs** and **linking verbs.**

People **ride** many kinds of vehicles.   A glider **is** a quiet craft.
     ACTION VERB   LINKING VERB

Principal Parts of Regular Verbs

Present	Present Participle	Past	Past Participle
present	present + *-ing*	present + -ed or -d	present + -ed or -d
coast	(is) coasting	coasted	(has) coasted
bicycle	(is) bicycling	bicycled	(has) bicycled
gallop	(is) galloping	galloped	(has) galloped
land	(is) landing	landed	(has) landed
race	(is) racing	raced	(has) raced
raft	(is) rafting	rafted	(has) rafted
roll	(is) rolling	rolled	(has) rolled
steer	(is) steering	steered	(has) steered
trot	(is) trotting	trotted	(has) trotted
walk	(is) walking	walked	(has) walked
cry	(is) crying	cried	(has) cried

Time to Sail

Keeping Tenses Straight

Tense	What It Conveys	Example
Present	Action or condition occurring in the present	I **sail** the boat.
Past	Action or condition occurring in the past	I **sailed** the boat.
Future	Action or condition occurring in the future	I **will sail** the boat.
Present perfect	Action or condition occurring in the period leading up to the present	I **have sailed** the boat.
Past perfect	Past action or condition preceding another past action or condition	I **had sailed** the boat before my sister did.
Future perfect	Action or condition preceding another future action or condition	I **will have sailed** the boat nine times by the weekend.

VERBS

The Bottom Line

Checklist for Verb Usage

Have I . . .

____ used action verbs to express actions?

____ used linking verbs with predicate nouns and predicate adjectives?

____ used direct objects and indirect objects to answer the questions *whom, what,* and *to whom* or *to what*?

____ used the correct principal parts of irregular verbs?

____ used tenses correctly to express the times of actions and conditions?

____ used *sit* and *set, lie* and *lay, rise* and *raise,* and *let* and *leave* correctly?

Adjectives and Adverbs

goblet—ceremonial
golden
ornate
concave
bejeweled

Theme: One of a Kind

Following the Clues

Can you find the particular goblet that this treasure hunter has
been seeking? Use the words listed on the treasure map to
learn what makes this goblet different from the others.

What makes something one of a kind? To explain why
something is unique, you would need to describe it by
answering questions like *what kind, which one,* and *to what
extent.* Words that do this are called **adjectives** and **adverbs.**

Write Away: One of a Kind

Pick another object in the treasure box. Write a description of
the object without naming it. Be sure your description is so
complete that someone could find the object you have in mind.
Save the paragraph in your 📁 **Working Portfolio.**

For each numbered item, choose the letter of the term that identifies it.

> In 1926 Benny Benson was in <u>seventh</u> grade. Benny's ethnic
> (1)
> background was a combination of <u>Aleutian, Russian,</u> and Swedish
> (2)
> ancestry. The teenager decided to enter a contest to create a design
> for the territory of Alaska. The contest asked people to make a
> design that would fit <u>artistically</u> on a flag. Benny Benson was <u>shy</u>.
> (3)   (4)
> He loved nature and looking at the stars. All these things came
> <u>together</u>, and he began <u>very</u> quickly to sketch his design. He wrote,
> (5)   (6)
> "The blue field is for the Alaska sky and the forget-me-not, an
> Alaska flower." Benny <u>also</u> explained that the big star showed
> (7)
> Alaska's future as the <u>most northern</u> state. Both houses of the
> (8)
> Alaska legislature voted <u>unanimously</u> to accept this design for the
> (9)
> flag. No one stood <u>more proudly</u> than Benny Benson the day his
> (10)
> flag was first raised outside his school.

1. A. adjective
   B. predicate adjective
   C. adverb
   D. intensifier

2. A. proper adjectives
   B. demonstrative pronouns
   C. predicate adjectives
   D. comparative adjectives

3. A. adverb telling when
   B. adverb telling where
   C. adverb telling how
   D. adverb telling to what extent

4. A. demonstrative pronoun
   B. comparative adjective
   C. predicate adjective
   D. proper adjective

5. A. adverb modifying *things*
   B. adverb modifying *All*
   C. adjective modifying *things*
   D. adverb modifying *came*

6. A. adverb modifying adjective
   B. adverb modifying adverb
   C. adverb modifying verb
   D. adjective modifying pronoun

7. A. adverb modifying verb
   B. adverb modifying adverb
   C. adverb modifying adjective
   D. adjective modifying noun

8. A. superlative adjective
   B. superlative adverb
   C. comparative adjective
   D. comparative adverb

9. A. adjective
   B. adverb modifying verb
   C. adverb modifying adjective
   D. adverb modifying adverb

10. A. comparative adjective
    B. comparative adverb
    C. superlative adjective
    D. superlative adverb

LESSON 1

What Is an Adjective?

❶ Here's the Idea

▶ **An adjective is a word that modifies, or describes, a noun or a pronoun.**

MODIFIES   MODIFIES

Extraordinary weather can cause strange events.
ADJECTIVE   NOUN   ADJECTIVE   NOUN

Adjectives help you see, feel, taste, hear, and smell all the experiences you read about. Notice how adjectives make the second sentence in this pair more descriptive.

> **During a storm, a boat capsized in the waves.**

> **During a violent storm, a large boat capsized in the enormous waves.**

Adjectives answer the questions *what kind, which one, how many,* and *how much.*

Adjectives			
What kind?	a **sudden** blizzard	a **brisk** wind	a **destructive** flood
Which one or ones?	the **first** warning	the **Mexican** earthquake	the **last** weather report
How many or how much?	**several** tornadoes	a **few** drifts	**more** ice

What kind? a **deadly** storm

Which one? the **worst** storm of the decade

How many? **three** men

CHAPTER 5

Articles

The most commonly used adjectives are the **articles** *a, an,* and *the. A* and *an* are forms of the **indefinite article.** The indefinite article is used before a noun that names an unspecified person, place, thing, or idea.

A weather radar can predict an unusual storm.
↑INDEFINITE ARTICLE   ↑INDEFINITE ARTICLE

Use *a* before a word beginning with a consonant sound ("a ball"); use *an* before a word beginning with a vowel sound ("an egg").

The is the **definite article.** It points to a particular person, place, thing, or idea.

The six-o'clock news predicted the tornado.
↑DEFINITE ARTICLE   ↑DEFINITE ARTICLE

Proper Adjectives

Many adjectives are formed from common nouns.

Nouns and Adjectives	
Common Noun	**Common Adjective**
cloud	cloudy
nation	national
statue	statuesque
friend	friendly

A **proper adjective** is formed from a proper noun. Proper adjectives are always capitalized.

Proper Nouns and Proper Adjectives	
Proper Noun	**Proper Adjective**
Honduras	Honduran
Olympus	Olympian
North America	North American
(Queen) Elizabeth	Elizabethan

ADJ. & ADV.

❷ Why It Matters in Writing

Fiction writers use adjectives to supply important details that help set a scene and provide background for a story.

> **LITERARY MODEL**
>
> It was a **dark autumn** night. The **old** banker was pacing from corner to corner of his study, recalling to his mind the party he gave in the autumn **fifteen** years ago. There were many **clever** people at the party and much **interesting** conversation. They talked among **other** things of **capital** punishment.
>
> —Anton Chekhov, "The Bet"

❸ Practice and Apply

CONCEPT CHECK: What Is an Adjective?

Write each adjective in these sentences, along with the noun or pronoun it modifies. Do not include articles.

How Strong Was It?
1. Scientists are amazed by the terrific power of a tornado.
2. The circular winds in strong tornadoes cause more damage than winds in other storms of a similar size.
3. Large hailstones often accompany a typical tornado.
4. One hailstone weighed two pounds, or about one kilogram.
5. It fell in the small Kansan town of Coffeyville.
6. A Chinese newspaper reported a rain of monstrous hailstones that killed a hundred people.
7. Tornadoes can drive large pieces of timber into thick walls.
8. A tornado hit the Midwestern town of Coralville.
9. The winds carried a heavy mechanical part a long way through the air.
10. Another tornado in 1875 carried a metal coop four miles.

➜ For a **SELF-CHECK** and more practice, see the **EXERCISE BANK, p. 331.**

Write and label the proper adjectives in your answers above. For each proper adjective, write the proper noun from which it is formed.

LESSON 2 Predicate Adjectives

❶ Here's the Idea

▶ **A predicate adjective is an adjective that follows a linking verb and describes the verb's subject.** The linking verb connects the predicate adjective with the subject.

DESCRIBES

Some people are extraordinary.
SUBJECT   LINKING VERB

DESCRIBE

They are very energetic or calm.

Predicate adjectives can follow linking verbs other than forms of *be*. Forms of *taste, smell, feel, look, become,* and *seem* are often used as linking verbs.

DESCRIBES

You usually feel lucky to know such a person.
LINKING VERB   PREDICATE ADJECTIVE

❷ Why It Matters in Writing

Writers often use predicate adjectives to supply key details about characters. Notice how predicate adjectives capture in just a few words the personality and appearance of this writer's teacher.

> **PROFESSIONAL MODEL**
>
> Miss Bindle . . . was **tiny, scrawny,** and **fierce,** with an eighty-year-old face and twenty-year-old red hair. . . .
> Miss Bindle was extremely **short,** only about half the size of some of the larger boys. When Miss Bindle grabbed them by the hair and took off for the office, they had to trail along behind her in a bent-over posture. . . .
>
> —Patrick F. McManus, "The Clown"

❸ Practice and Apply

A. CONCEPT CHECK: Predicate Adjectives

Write each predicate adjective in these sentences, along with the noun or pronoun it modifies. There may be more than one predicate adjective in a sentence.

Barreling Along!

1. Anna Edson Taylor was brave.
2. She grew certain that she could achieve fame by trying a dangerous feat.
3. Taylor had been a teacher, but she was now financially independent.
4. She felt eager to go over Niagara Falls in a barrel.
5. Her barrel was wooden and contained a rubber hose so that she could breathe.
6. According to the press, Taylor was "intelligent and venturesome."
7. When the barrel reached the edge of the falls, it appeared motionless for a moment.
8. After the plunge, the wait for the appearance of the barrel seemed endless.
9. Meanwhile, the daredevil herself was unconscious.
10. As the only woman survivor of a plunge over Niagara Falls, Anna Taylor remains unique.

→ For a SELF-CHECK and more practice, see the EXERCISE BANK, p. 331.

CHALLENGE Rewrite five of the sentences above by substituting a new predicate adjective.

B. WRITING: Creating a Character Description

Describe a person who you think is one of a kind. Use predicate adjectives and linking verbs in your description.

LESSON 3 Other Words Used as Adjectives

Here's the Idea

In addition to their usual uses, many pronouns and nouns can be used as adjectives. They can modify nouns to make their meanings more specific.

Pronouns as Adjectives

Demonstrative Pronouns *This, that, these,* and *those* are demonstrative pronouns that can be used as adjectives.

LOOP

MODIFIES
This fingerprint is a loop.

MODIFIES
That fingerprint is a whorl.

PLAIN WHORL

Possessive Pronouns *My, our, your, her, his, its,* and *their* are possessive pronouns that are used as adjectives.

DOUBLE LOOP

MODIFIES   MODIFIES
My thumbprint is a double loop, but your thumbprint is a tented arch.

Indefinite Pronouns Indefinite pronouns such as *all, each, both, few, most,* and *some* can be used as adjectives.

MODIFIES
All fingerprints fit one of seven patterns.

MODIFIES
But each fingerprint is unique.

TENTED ARCH

ACCIDENTAL

PLAIN ARCH

CENTRAL POCKET LOOP

ADJ. & ADV.

Nouns as Adjectives

Like pronouns, nouns can be used as adjectives. In the expression "crime story," for example, the word *crime* (normally a noun) is used to modify *story*. Notice the examples of nouns used as adjectives in the sentences below.

MODIFIES

The fingerprint evidence convicted the murderer.

MODIFIES

She was convicted on murder charges.

❷ Why It Matters in Writing

By using nouns as adjectives, writers can convey a lot of descriptive information in a single word. Notice how much information is contained in the nouns used as adjectives in the passage below.

LITERARY MODEL

The country is India. A large **dinner** party is being given in an **up-country** station by a colonial official and his wife. The guests are **army** officers and **government** attachés and their wives, and an American naturalist.

—Mona Gardner, "The Dinner Party"

Dinner at Haddo House (1884), Alfred Edward Emslie. National Portrait Gallery, London.

❸ Practice and Apply

A. CONCEPT CHECK: Other Words Used as Adjectives

Write each noun or pronoun that is used as an adjective in these sentences, along with the word it modifies.

Don't Touch!
1. Why do your fingerprints leave their marks on objects?
2. The fingers have skin ridges on their surface.
3. These ridges are coated with both sweat and body oil.
4. When a criminal touches a surface with his fingers, these ridges leave an impression.
5. These impressions are often not visible to the human eye.
6. But detectives in a crime investigation use special chemicals to reveal those fingerprints.
7. Police can also reveal these clues by using laser light.
8. The first criminal convicted on fingerprint evidence was Alfred Stratton.
9. He left his fingerprint on a cash box at the crime scene.
10. Many criminals do not make this mistake anymore, because they wear latex gloves.

→ **For a SELF-CHECK and more practice, see the EXERCISE BANK, p. 332.**

Write five sentences using nouns as adjectives and five sentences using pronouns as adjectives.

B. REVISING: Using Nouns as Adjectives

Make this e-mail message more detailed by adding a noun from the list below to modify each of the nouns in boldface type.

city   super-sleuth   ridge   foot-sole   leather   body

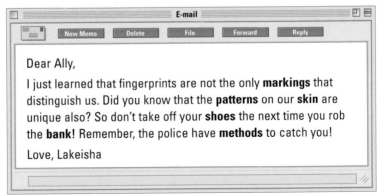

Dear Ally,

I just learned that fingerprints are not the only **markings** that distinguish us. Did you know that the **patterns** on our **skin** are unique also? So don't take off your **shoes** the next time you rob the **bank**! Remember, the police have **methods** to catch you!

Love, Lakeisha

LESSON 4

CHAPTER 5

❶ Here's the Idea

▶ **An adverb is a word that modifies a verb, an adjective, or another adverb.**

MODIFIES

Teenagers often make a unique impression.
ADVERB   VERB

MODIFIES

They wear very creative clothing.
ADVERB   ADJECTIVE

MODIFIES

They nearly always have their own way of talking.
ADVERBS

Adverbs answer the questions *how, when, where,* or *to what extent.*

Adverbs			
How?	successfully	quietly	terribly
When?	soon	later	now
Where?	inside	close	together
To what extent?	nearly	completely	quite

Adverbs can appear in several different positions.

Shari completed the exam quickly. (after verb)

Shari quickly completed the exam. (before verb)

Quickly, Shari completed the exam. (beginning of sentence)

Intensifiers are adverbs that modify adjectives or other adverbs. They are usually placed directly before the word they modify. Intensifiers usually answer the question *to what extent.*

MODIFIES

How does Shari work so quickly?

Intensifiers				
almost	extremely	quite	so	usually
especially	nearly	really	too	very

Forming Adverbs

Many adverbs are formed by adding the suffix -ly to adjectives. Sometimes a base word's spelling changes when -ly is added.

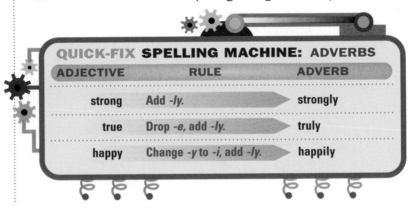

QUICK-FIX **SPELLING MACHINE:** ADVERBS

ADJECTIVE	RULE	ADVERB
strong	Add -ly.	strongly
true	Drop -e, add -ly.	truly
happy	Change -y to -i, add -ly.	happily

❷ Why It Matters in Writing

Adverbs can add information that makes verbs clearer and more specific. What would be lost if the adverbs in the model below were removed?

PROFESSIONAL MODEL

Yehudi Menuhin played the violin spectacularly. He began to study quite early, at the age of four. When he performed onstage, he always received thunderous applause. He first appeared in *Who's Who* at the age of 15 and was written about frequently in the world's press throughout his long career.

—C. Podojil

ANSWERS HOW

ANSWERS WHEN

ANSWERS WHERE

ANSWERS TO WHAT EXTENT

❸ Practice and Apply

A. CONCEPT CHECK: What Is an Adverb?

Write each adverb and the word it modifies. Identify the modified word as a verb, an adjective, or an adverb. There may be more than one adverb in a sentence.

The Green Scene

1. Alison and James Henry climb trees professionally.
2. To some people, this seems quite extraordinary.
3. This is because Alison and James are unusually young for such a job.
4. They became professionals when they were only 17 and 16.
5. They are certified arborists, and they care for trees expertly.
6. They may ascend trees daily if their services are needed.
7. The two teenagers climb high in order to cut branches that might suddenly fall on a house or wire.
8. They work very carefully when they are up in the tops of trees.
9. They were once called in the middle of the night to remove a tree that had fallen dangerously close to a house.
10. So far, Alison and James are the only teenagers to have this particularly impressive professional title.

➜ For a SELF-CHECK and more practice, see the EXERCISE BANK, p. 332.

B. WRITING: Adding Adverbs

Add adverbs to modify the numbered words in the paragraph below. Choose adverbs that will make the words clear and specific.

Julie **(1)** walked to the library. She had **(2)** thought she would **(3)** win the math contest. She was **(4)** good at math. But the new student from across town also **(5)** completed her math assignments. She would be a **(6)** tough competitor for Julie. I'll just have to **(7)** work, Julie thought as she **(8)** entered the library.

In your 📂 **Working Portfolio,** find the description you wrote for the **Write Away** on page 124. Use verbs and adverbs to expand your description.

Making Comparisons

❶ Here's the Idea

Special forms of modifiers are used to make comparisons.

▶ **Use the comparative form of an adjective or adverb when you compare a person or thing with one other person or thing.**

Earth is larger than Venus.

Earth orbits the sun more slowly than Venus.

▶ **Use the superlative form of an adjective or adverb when you compare someone or something with more than one other person or thing.**

Which of the four inner planets is the hottest?

Which of the five outer planets rotates most quickly?

Regular Forms of Comparisons

For most one-syllable modifiers, add -er to form the comparative and -est to form the superlative.

One-Syllable Modifiers	Base Form	Comparative	Superlative
Adjective	light	lighter	lightest
	slow	slower	slowest
Adverb	close	closer	closest
	soon	sooner	soonest

You can also add -er and -est to some two-syllable adjectives. With other two-syllable adjectives, and with all two-syllable adverbs, use the words *more* and *most.*

Two-Syllable Modifiers	Base Form	Comparative	Superlative
Adjectives	windy	windier	windiest
	massive	more massive	most massive
Adverbs	brightly	more brightly	most brightly
	quickly	more quickly	most quickly

With adjectives and adverbs having three or more syllables, use *more* and *most*.

Modifiers with More than Two Syllables			
	Base Form	**Comparative**	**Superlative**
Adjectives	successful mysterious	**more** successful **more** mysterious	**most** successful **most** mysterious
Adverbs	awkwardly eloquently	**more** awkwardly **more** eloquently	**most** awkwardly **most** eloquently

Use only one sign of comparison at a time. Don't use *more* and *-er* together or *most* and *-est* together.

INCORRECT: **Earth is the most greenest planet.**

CORRECT: **Earth is the greenest planet.**

Irregular Forms of Comparisons

The comparatives and superlatives of some adjectives and adverbs are formed in irregular ways.

Irregular Modifiers			
	Base Form	**Comparative**	**Superlative**
Adjectives	good bad	better worse	best worst
Adverbs	much little well	more less better	most least best

❷ Why It Matters in Writing

When you write about science or technology, you can often explain your subject more clearly by comparing it to another.

PROFESSIONAL MODEL

Venus is **hotter** than Earth—about 800 degrees **hotter.** The atmosphere on Venus is **more unfriendly** too. It rains sulfuric acid, and the pressure is 90 times **greater** than that on Earth. —T. Bagwell

❸ Practice and Apply

A. CONCEPT CHECK: Making Comparisons

Choose the correct comparative or superlative form to complete each sentence.

Nine of a Kind

1. Which do you think is the (fascinatingest/ most fascinating) planet in the solar system?
2. Earth is (wettest/wetter) than Mars.
3. Venus orbits the sun (quicker/more quickly) than it rotates on its axis.
4. This means that a day on Venus is (longer/longest) than its year.
5. Mars has a volcano that is (taller/more taller) than any one on Earth.
6. It also has a canyon that is (longer/longest) than the Grand Canyon.
7. Jupiter is the (most massive/more massive) planet in the system.
8. If Jupiter were many times (larger/more large) than it is, it might have ignited to become a star.
9. Neptune is the planet on which winds blow the (most rapidly/more rapidly).
10. If Neptune had a solid surface, you'd never be able to stand upright on this (windiest/windier) of planets.

➜ **For a SELF-CHECK and more practice, see the EXERCISE BANK, p. 333.**

B. WRITING: Creating Comparisons

Write five sentences in which you compare and contrast the planets shown, using comparative and superlative forms. Use the information given.

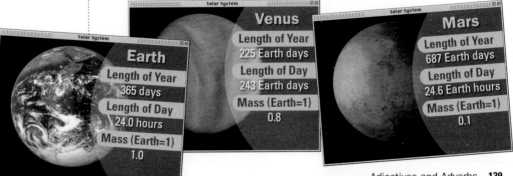

Earth
Length of Year
365 days
Length of Day
24.0 hours
Mass (Earth=1)
1.0

Venus
Length of Year
225 Earth days
Length of Day
243 Earth days
Mass (Earth=1)
0.8

Mars
Length of Year
687 Earth days
Length of Day
24.6 Earth hours
Mass (Earth=1)
0.1

Adjective or Adverb?

❶ Here's the Idea

Some pairs of adjectives and adverbs are often a source of confusion and mistakes in speaking and writing.

Good or Well *Good* is always an adjective; it modifies a noun or pronoun. *Well* is usually an adverb, modifying a verb, an adverb, or an adjective. *Well* is an adjective when it refers to health.

MODIFIES

Poetry is a good way to express your individuality.
ADJECTIVE ↗ ↖ NOUN

MODIFIES

Good poems can communicate ideas well.
VERB ↗ ADVERB ↗

MODIFIES

You can write poems even when you don't feel well.
PRONOUN ↗ ADJECTIVE ↗

Real or Really *Real* is always an adjective; it modifies a noun or pronoun. *Really* is always an adverb; it modifies a verb, an adverb, or an adjective.

MODIFIES

Reciting poetry is a real talent.
ADJECTIVE ↗ ↖ NOUN

MODIFIES

If you really work at it, you can become good at it.
ADVERB ↗ ↖ VERB

Bad or Badly *Bad* is always an adjective; it modifies a noun or pronoun. *Badly* is always an adverb; it modifies a verb, an adverb, or an adjective.

MODIFIES   MODIFIES

That wasn't a bad poem, but you read it badly.
ADJECTIVE ↗ ↖ NOUN   ↖ VERB   ↖ ADVERB

MODIFIES

Oh, I feel bad about that.
PRONOUN ↗ ↖ ADJECTIVE

❷ Why It Matters in Writing

The pairs of words you have just studied are often misused in everyday speech. When you find yourself using one of these words in writing, stop and make sure you have the correct one.

STUDENT MODEL

My sister wants to be in the *Guinness Book of Records*.
She wants this ~~real bad~~ *really badly*. She swims ~~good,~~ *well* so she thinks she

will try to tread water longer than anyone else. I will feel
~~badly~~ *bad* for her if she fails but ~~well~~ *good* if she succeeds.

❸ Practice and Apply

ADJ. & ADV.

CONCEPT CHECK: Adjective or Adverb?

For each sentence, choose the correct modifier from those given in parentheses. Identify each word you choose as an adjective or an adverb.

Setting Real Records

1. If you are (good/well) at something, you can try to get into the *Guinness Book of Records.*
2. You may climb (bad/badly) or be a (real/really) poor runner.
3. But maybe you grow vegetables or flowers that are large and make a (real/really) statement.
4. Or maybe you blow big bubble-gum bubbles (good/well).
5. It helps if you attempt a (real/really) feat in public.
6. At least you must have (good/well) documentation by a person with (real/really) excellent community standing.
7. If it's just you and the huge bubble, that's (bad/badly).
8. The Guinness people will react (bad/badly) to your claim.
9. Those same folks also suggest that you take (good/well) safety precautions when you try to set a record.
10. After all, you don't want to get your award while lying in a hospital bed, feeling (bad/badly).

➡ For a **SELF-CHECK** and more practice, see the **EXERCISE BANK, p. 334.**

Avoiding Double Negatives

❶ Here's the Idea

A **negative word** is a word that implies that something does not exist or happen. Some common negative words are listed below.

Common Negative Words				
barely	never	none	nothing	can't
hardly	no	no one	nowhere	don't
neither	nobody	not	scarcely	hasn't

If two negative words are used where only one is needed, the result is a **double negative.** Avoid double negatives in your speaking and writing.

NONSTANDARD:
> You **don't** have **no** business climbing Mt. Rushmore.

STANDARD:
> You **don't** have **any** business climbing Mt. Rushmore.

> You have **no** business climbing Mt. Rushmore.

❷ Why It Matters in Writing

Many of the situations where success counts most—school, work, and interviews—require language that is free of double negatives. The following model is an example of what NOT to say in an interview.

> **PROFESSIONAL MODEL**
>
> For example, suppose you are being interviewed for a job as an airline pilot, and your prospective employer asks you if you have any experience, and you answer: "Well, I ain't never actually flied no actual airplanes or nothing, but I got several pilot-style hats and several friends who I like to talk about airplanes with."
>
> —Dave Barry, "What Is and Ain't Grammatical"

❸ Practice and Apply

A. CONCEPT CHECK: Avoiding Double Negatives

Write the word in parentheses that correctly completes each sentence.

> **Big Foot or Big Fake?**
> 1. You (can/can't) scarcely imagine how many people believe in one-of-a-kind monsters.
> 2. You (can't/can) barely read a newspaper or a magazine without seeing a reference to one.
> 3. The "abominable snowman" (is/isn't) nothing like the kind you build.
> 4. No one has (never/ever) been able to prove it exists.
> 5. Researchers investigating the Loch Ness Monster (haven't/have) had nothing to show for their efforts.
> 6. People trying to prove the existence of Bigfoot haven't come up with (nothing/anything) either.
> 7. Evidence of such creatures (is/isn't) nowhere to be found.
> 8. Nobody has ever taken a photograph of one (either/neither).
> 9. No one (has/hasn't) ever gotten one on videotape.
> 10. Some people believe in such creatures, but I don't think there are (none/any).

➜ For a SELF-CHECK and more practice, see the EXERCISE BANK, p. 334.

B. PROOFREADING: Eliminating Double Negatives

In the draft below, find and correct five double negatives. There is more than one way to correct each double negative.

> **STUDENT MODEL**
>
> You won't find no animal more unusual than the duck-billed platypus. Since it lays eggs, you wouldn't hardly guess that it's a mammal. It has a bill like a duck, but it can't fly neither. You shouldn't never judge things by appearances. Duck-billed platypuses are odd looking, but there isn't an animal better designed for its environment nowhere.

Grammar in Literature

Using Adjectives and Adverbs to Describe

When you write a character description, using adjectives and adverbs allows you to make a person come alive. Adjectives and adverbs help writers clearly express what they see, think, and feel. As you read the following passage from a science-fiction story, notice how writer Daniel Keyes uses adjectives and adverbs to describe an adult student's impressions of his special-education teacher. The student, Charlie, has had brain surgery that has made him more intelligent, and he feels as if he is seeing his teacher clearly for the first time.

Flowers for Algernon
by Daniel Keyes

April 28 I don't understand why I never noticed how beautiful Miss Kinnian really is. She has brown eyes and feathery brown hair that comes to the top of her neck. She's only thirty-four! I think from the beginning I had the feeling that she was an unreachable genius—and very, very old. Now, every time I see her she grows younger and more lovely.

We had dinner and a long talk. When she said that I was coming along so fast that soon I'd be leaving her behind, I laughed.

Max Seabaugh/MAX

"It's true, Charlie. You're already a better reader than I am. You can read a whole page at a glance while I can take in only a few lines at a time. And you remember every single thing you read. I'm lucky if I can recall the main thoughts and the general meaning."

"I don't feel intelligent. There are so many things I don't understand."

> **ADJECTIVES**
> describe Miss Kinnian's appearance.

> **ADVERBS**
> add to the description of changes in Charlie by telling how and when actions occur.

> **ADJECTIVES**
> compare the skills of Miss Kinnian and Charlie.

CHAPTER 5

Practice and Apply

ACROSS the CURRICULUM
LITERATURE

A. USING ADJECTIVES AND ADVERBS

The following passage is a possible journal entry describing the dinner from Miss Kinnian's point of view. Follow the directions below to make the entry clearer. Add adjectives and adverbs to the numbered sentences.

April 28 Today, Charlie was not in class. **(1)** His absence worried me, so I decided to call him. I asked him to meet me at City Restaurant. **(2)** We had a dinner and a talk. **(3)** The surgery has changed him. **(4)** Just weeks ago, he could not carry on a conversation. **(5)** Now, he expresses himself. He can read a book in just minutes. I believe that he will be smarter than his doctors.

1. Add an adverb that emphasizes that Miss Kinnian was worried.
2. Add adjectives to describe what kind of dinner and what kind of talk you think they had.
3. Add an adverb to emphasize that Charlie has changed.
4. Use your imagination and add adjectives to describe how many weeks ago and what kind of conversation he used to make.
5. Add an adverb to describe how Charlie expresses his ideas now, and when he may become smarter than his doctors.

ADJ. & ADV.

B. WRITING: Description

Charlie uses a variety of adjectives and adverbs to describe his favorite teacher. Write a paragraph in which you use adjectives and adverbs to describe someone whom you admire. Save your paragraph in your ▭ **Working Portfolio.**

A. Using Adjectives Write each adjective in the sentences below and give the word it modifies. Do not include articles. Then add as many of the following descriptions as apply (may be none).

predicate adjective
proper adjective
demonstrative pronoun
indefinite pronoun

noun used as adjective
comparative form of adjective
superlative form of adjective
possessive pronoun

1. The animal world is full of unique characteristics.
2. Most insects are small, and many mammals are large.
3. But a kind of mammal is actually a smaller creature than a bumblebee.
4. This creature—the Kitti's hog-nosed bat—is the tiniest mammal.
5. Actually, the honeybee makes the food with the most impressive additive.
6. That's right, honey tastes fresher after time on the shelf than some foods because of its natural preservatives.
7. Despite the purple dinosaur you see on television, the African blesbok is unique.
8. His coat is purple, and he is the only land animal to have that color.
9. When you think of sharks, you probably see them in their wide oceans and their salty seas.
10. But the bull shark also likes fresh water, such as Mississippi River water.

B. Using Adverbs Write each adverb in the paragraph below, tell what word it modifies, and tell whether the word it modifies is a verb, an adverb, or an adjective.

LITERARY MODEL

When I had waited a long time, very patiently, without hearing him lie down, I resolved to open a little—a very, very little crevice in the lantern. So I opened it—you cannot imagine how stealthily, stealthily—until, at length, a single dim ray, like the thread of the spider, shot from out the crevice and fell full upon the vulture eye.

—Edgar Allan Poe, "The Tell-Tale Heart"

For each numbered item, choose the letter of the term that identifies it.

Satchel Paige, who played in both the Negro Leagues and the major leagues, was one of the greatest players in <u>American</u> baseball.
(1)
He is the only person who played <u>professionally</u> into his sixties.
(2)
He is also the <u>oldest</u> player ever to play in the All-Star Game. As if
(3)
that were not enough, Paige pitched <u>more</u> games than anyone in the
(4)
history of baseball—about 2,500!

Satchel Paige pitched <u>more distinctively</u> than other pitchers.
(5)
Batters gritted <u>their</u> teeth when they were up against "Satch." His
(6)
"bee ball" was <u>extremely</u> fast, and batters swore they could hear it
(7)
buzz. His "pea ball" appeared <u>small</u> as it zipped over the plate. Some
(8)
people remember Paige <u>best</u> for his words of wisdom. He said, "If your
(9)
stomach disputes you, lie <u>down</u> and pacify it with cool thoughts."
(10)

ADJ. & ADV.

1. A. pronoun used as adjective
   B. comparative adjective
   C. proper adjective
   D. predicate adjective

2. A. adverb modifying *person*
   B. adverb modifying *is*
   C. adverb modifying *played*
   D. intensifier

3. A. comparative adjective
   B. superlative adjective
   C. comparative adverb
   D. superlative adverb

4. A. adjective modifying *pitched*
   B. adjective modifying *games*
   C. adjective modifying *anyone*
   D. adjective modifying *Paige*

5. A. superlative adjective
   B. comparative adverb
   C. comparative adjective
   D. superlative adverb

6. A. demonstrative pronoun
   B. noun used as adjective
   C. possessive pronoun
   D. proper adjective

7. A. adverb telling to what extent
   B. adverb telling how
   C. adverb telling where
   D. adverb telling when

8. A. predicate adjective
   B. comparative adjective
   C. superlative adjective
   D. pronoun used as adjective

9. A. comparative adverb
   B. superlative adjective
   C. superlative adverb
   D. comparative adjective

10. A. adverb telling when
    B. adverb telling where
    C. adverb telling how
    D. adverb telling to what extent

Student Help Desk

Adjectives and Adverbs at a Glance

Adjectives modify nouns and pronouns.

The Jamaican runner finished first. She was fast!

Adverbs modify verbs, adverbs, and adjectives.

The usually quiet student spoke very emphatically.

Modifiers in Comparisons

Bigger and Better

	Comparative	Superlative
fast	faster	fastest
speedy	speedier	speediest
unusual	more unusual	most unusual
original	more original	most original
quickly	more quickly	most quickly
good	better	best
bad	worse	worst

Avoiding Double Forms

Double Trouble

Double Negative	Fix
we can't never	we can never we can't
we don't hardly	we hardly we don't
Double Comparison	**Fix**
more better	better
most luckiest	luckiest

Modifier Problems

Good and Well

I have a **good** reason.
    ↑ ADJECTIVE

Do you feel **good** about that?
    ↑ PREDICATE
    ADJECTIVE

I can sing **well**.
    ADVERB ↑

You don't look **well**.
  PREDICATE ADJECTIVE ↑

Real and Really

She's a **real** gem.
    ↑ ADJECTIVE

She's **really** friendly.
    ADVERB ↑

Bad and Badly

That's not a **bad** idea.
    ↑ ADJECTIVE

She feels **bad** about it.
    ↑ PREDICATE
    ADJECTIVE

He drives **badly**.
    ADVERB ↑

ADJ. & ADV.

The Bottom Line

Checklist for Adjectives and Adverbs

Have I . . .

____ used adjectives to add detail to my nouns?

____ capitalized proper adjectives?

____ used adverbs to describe actions clearly?

____ used the correct comparative or superlative form?

____ avoided using adjectives as adverbs?

____ avoided double negatives?

Prepositions, Conjunctions, Interjections

Theme: Robots

Brains the Size of Planets

Robots may seem to move and even speak independently, but the real brains behind robots are the human beings who program them. Humans use very precise codes to direct and sequence the robots' movements. Like computer codes, our language includes small but critical signals that communicate such things as direction, location, order, and even relationships. Prepositions, conjunctions, and interjections provide those signals in our language.

Write Away: My Personal Robot
What would you want a robot to do for you? Write a paragraph about your personal robot. Describe what it does. Does it hang up your clothes, serve your food, entertain your friends, or pitch balls? Save the paragraph in your 🖿 **Working Portfolio.**

Diagnostic Test: What Do You Know?

Choose the letter of the term that correctly identifies each underlined item.

> How great would it be if you had a robot? It isn't such a wild idea. People <u>around the world</u> have robots. One teenager designed a robot that responded to musical <u>tones</u>. There were different tones <u>for different commands</u>. It had claws that opened and closed. The robot <u>not only</u> picked up objects <u>but also</u> moved them from place to place. Another teenager designed a robot with sonar. This robot bumped <u>into</u> objects <u>and</u> learned where the objects were located. <u>Wow!</u> Unfortunately, sometimes the bumper switches would stick. The robot dashed <u>across the room</u> wildly. It looked frantically for a way <u>out</u>. These robots may seem primitive, <u>but</u> they are really complex systems that operate independently.
>
> (1) around the world
> (2) tones
> (3) for different commands
> (4) not only ... but also
> (5) into
> (6) and
> (7) Wow!
> (8) across the room
> (9) out
> (10) but

1. A. coordinating conjunction
   B. correlative conjunction
   C. prepositional phrase
   D. preposition

2. A. coordinating conjunction
   B. correlative conjunction
   C. object of a preposition
   D. preposition

3. A. correlative conjunction
   B. coordinating conjunction
   C. adjective phrase
   D. adverb phrase

4. A. coordinating conjunction
   B. correlative conjunction
   C. prepositional phrase
   D. interjection

5. A. coordinating conjunction
   B. preposition
   C. interjection
   D. adverb

6. A. coordinating conjunction
   B. correlative conjunction
   C. preposition
   D. adjective

7. A. correlative conjunction
   B. preposition
   C. subordinating conjunction
   D. interjection

8. A. coordinating conjunction
   B. correlative conjunction
   C. adverb phrase
   D. adjective phrase

9. A. correlative conjunction
   B. preposition
   C. adverb
   D. adjective

10. A. coordinating conjunction
    B. correlative conjunction
    C. preposition
    D. adjective

What Is a Preposition?

❶ Here's the Idea

▶ **A preposition is a word that shows a relationship between a noun or pronoun and some other word in the sentence.**

Robots in outer space perform useful functions.

⬆ PREPOSITION

Here, the preposition *in* shows the relationship between *robots* and *space*. In the sentences below, notice how each preposition expresses a different relationship between the robot and the spacecraft.

The robot is above the spacecraft.

The robot is below the spacecraft.

The robot is beside the spacecraft.

The robot is inside the spacecraft.

Common Prepositions				
about	at	despite	like	to
above	before	down	near	toward
across	behind	during	of	under
after	below	except	off	until
against	beneath	for	on	up
along	beside	from	out	with
among	between	in	over	within
around	beyond	inside	past	without
as	by	into	through	

CHAPTER 6

Some prepositions, called **compound prepositions,** are made up of more than one word. These include *according to, instead of,* and *apart from.*

Prepositional Phrases

▶ **A prepositional phrase consists of a preposition, its object, and any modifiers of the object.** The object of the preposition is the noun or pronoun following the preposition.

PREPOSITIONAL PHRASE
Robots conduct missions for the space program.
PREPOSITION   OBJECT

Among their many tasks is photographing the planets.
PREPOSITION   MODIFIER   OBJECT

Compound Objects in Prepositional Phrases

A preposition may have a compound object made up of two or more nouns or pronouns joined by *and* or *or,* as shown below.

PREPOSITIONAL PHRASE
Robots conduct a series of tests and experiments.
PREPOSITION   COMPOUND OBJECT

Experiments can be performed by robots or people.
COMPOUND OBJECT

Preposition or Adverb?

Sometimes the same word can be used as a preposition or as an adverb. If the word has no object, then it is an adverb.

PREPOSITIONAL PHRASE
The spacecraft has no gravity within its walls.
PREPOSITION   OBJECT

The spacecraft has no gravity within.
ADVERB

For more on adverbs, see pp. 134–135.

❷ Why It Matters in Writing

When writing for science, you can use prepositions to describe where objects are located in relation to other objects. Notice how the prepositions in the model show the robot's location in relation to Mars.

> **PROFESSIONAL MODEL**
>
> The *Sojourner* microrover rolled **onto** the planet Mars. Controllers guided it **over** the rough terrain.
>
> —R. Golub

❸ Practice and Apply

CONCEPT CHECK: What Is a Preposition?

Write the preposition in each sentence, along with its object or objects.

A Viking in Space
1. The *Viking 1* lander used a robot arm in outer space.
2. Scientists encoded computer programs with instructions and rules.
3. The instructions inside the computer's memory directed the robot.
4. They designed the lander according to the functions it would perform.
5. It communicated data between Mars and Earth.
6. The lander's mechanical arm reached beyond the spacecraft.
7. The lander photographed the surface of Mars.
8. The robot arm reached below the surface.
9. For later tests and analysis, the robot arm collected soil and rocks.
10. Unfortunately, a faulty command from Earth caused the lander to malfunction.

➜ For a SELF-CHECK and more practice, see the EXERCISE BANK, p. 335.

📁 **Working Portfolio:** Find your **Write Away** from page 150 or a sample of your most recent work. Add at least one prepositional phrase that helps explain the location of your robot or other topic.

Using Prepositional Phrases

LESSON 2

❶ Here's the Idea

A prepositional phrase is always related to another word in a sentence. It modifies the word in the same way an adjective or adverb would.

Adjective Phrases

▶ **An adjective prepositional phrase modifies a noun or a pronoun.** Like an adjective, a prepositional phrase can tell which one, how many, or what kind.

WHAT KIND?

Robots perform several jobs **in the automobile industry.**
NOUN ↗ ADJECTIVE PHRASE

WHICH ONE?

The sprayer **on an assembly line** is an industrial robot.

Adverb Phrases

▶ **An adverb prepositional phrase modifies a verb, an adjective, or an adverb.** An adverb prepositional phrase can tell where, when, how, why, or to what extent.

WHERE?

Industrial robots operate **from fixed positions.**
VERB ↗ ADVERB PHRASE

HOW?

These robots are reprogrammable **for various tasks.**
ADJECTIVE ↗

Several prepositional phrases can work together. Often, each phrase after the first modifies the object in the phrase before it.

Some industrial robots load frozen slabs **of meat**
in meat lockers **with subzero temperatures.**

PREPOSITIONS

Placement of Prepositional Phrases

When you write, try to place each prepositional phrase as close as possible to the word it modifies. Otherwise, you may confuse—or unintentionally amuse—your readers.

Unclear

In a chorus line, we watched 15 robots.

(Who or what was in a chorus line?)

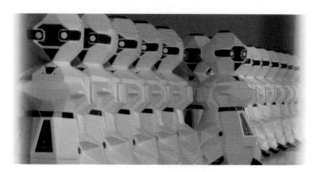

Clear

We watched 15 robots in a chorus line.

(Now the readers know who or what was in a chorus line.)

❷ Why It Matters in Writing

When you write technical information that shows how to do something or how something works, prepositional phrases can help make your explanations clear. Use them to tell *where, how, which one,* and *what kind.* Notice that the prepositional phrases in the model tell *where, how,* and *which one.*

> **PROFESSIONAL MODEL**
>
> The wheels, located on the bottom of the robot's body, are set in a triangular pattern. The two back wheels are the "drive" wheels, and they propel the robot either forward, backward, or sideways. Each drive wheel can be driven independently of the other, allowing the robot to turn right or left.
>
> —Margaret Baldwin and Gary Pack, *Robots and Robotics*

TELLS WHERE

TELLS WHICH ONE

TELLS HOW

❸ Practice and Apply

A. CONCEPT CHECK: Using Prepositional Phrases

Write the prepositional phrase in each sentence, along with the word it modifies. Then write whether the phrase is an adjective phrase or an adverb phrase.

On the Job

1. Automobile manufacturers around the world have installed robots.
2. In factories, robots work quickly and efficiently.
3. Many factory robots are arms on moving rails.
4. Mechanical arms move systematically down an assembly line.
5. Robots work chiefly under hazardous conditions.
6. With great precision, robots spray-paint cars.
7. They are immune to dangerous paint fumes.
8. Mold-maker robots inject red-hot metal into molds.
9. Robots handle materials that would cause damage to human flesh.
10. Arc welding is another job among the many risky jobs that robots perform.

➜ **For a SELF-CHECK and more practice, see the EXERCISE BANK, p. 335.**

B. WRITING: Explaining with Prepositional Phrases

Write the prepositional phrase that best completes each sentence in the paragraph.

a. below the surface   **d.** of the sea exploration team
b. on shore   **e.** with cameras
c. between the coral reef and some large rocks

As a member ___(1)___, the robot plunged into the deep icy water. It sank quickly ___(2)___. Equipped ___(3)___, it scanned the ocean floor. The broken oil pipeline ___(4)___ was identified. Scientists ___(5)___ received the data.

A diving robot works under the water.

PREPOSITIONS

Conjunctions

❶ Here's the Idea

▶ **A conjunction is a word used to join words or groups of words.** Different kinds of conjunctions are used in different ways.

Coordinating Conjunctions

▶ **A coordinating conjunction connects words used in the same way.** The words joined by a conjunction can be subjects, objects, predicates, or any other kind of sentence parts.

SUBJECTS
Motors and software control a robot named Cog.
COORDINATING CONJUNCTION

Common Coordinating Conjunctions						
and	but	for	or	nor	so	yet

Use *and* to connect similar ideas. Use *but* or *yet* to contrast ideas.

Cog can make eye contact and track motion.
(*And* connects two of Cog's abilities.)

Cog is a computer-driven machine, but it acts like a human being.
(*But* contrasts what Cog is with how it acts.)

Use *or* or *nor* to introduce a choice.

Kismet, another robot, can smile or look sad.
(*Or* introduces another choice for a facial expression.)

CHAPTER 6

Correlative Conjunctions

▶ **Correlative conjunctions are pairs of words that connect words used in the same way.** Like coordinating conjunctions, correlative conjunctions can join subjects, objects, predicates, and other sentence parts.

OBJECTS

Cog moves not only its head but also its arms.
CORRELATIVE CONJUNCTION

SUBJECTS

Both Cog and Kismet are robots with intelligence.
CORRELATIVE
CONJUNCTION

Common Correlative Conjunctions		
both . . . and	either . . . or	not only . . . but also
neither . . . nor	whether . . . or	

You will learn about conjunctions of another type—subordinating conjunctions—in Chapter 8.

❷ Why It Matters in Writing

When writing descriptions, you can use conjunctions to help the reader know how details relate to each other. Notice how the conjunctions in the model help you picture the arrangement of features on the monster.

LITERARY MODEL

It had a flat head **and** the overhanging brows of a Neanderthal man. Its face was crisscrossed with crude stitching, **and** two electrodes stuck out of its neck.

—Daniel Cohen, "Man-Made Monsters," from
A Natural History of Unnatural Things

❸ Practice and Apply

A. CONCEPT CHECK: Conjunctions

Write the conjunction in each sentence, along with the words or groups of words that it joins.

Cog and Kismet

1. Cog and Kismet are two robots developed at MIT, the Massachusetts Institute of Technology.
2. The robot Cog has an upper body, but it doesn't have any legs.
3. Cog's achievements are few, yet they are impressive.
4. Cog not only stares at strangers but also follows them with its gaze as they cross a room.
5. Cog can play drums and even played them in a rock video.
6. It can move a toy or pick up a stuffed animal.
7. Kismet needs constant stimulation, yet it is easily amused.
8. Its features are cartoon-like, and its big blue eyes open wide.
9. Kismet can respond to its handlers' actions with a smile or a look of interest.
10. Neither Cog nor Kismet is programmed with emotions.

➜ For a SELF-CHECK and more practice, see the EXERCISE BANK, p. 336.

Identify each conjunction in items 1–10 above as a coordinating conjunction or a correlative conjunction.

B. REVISING: Changing Conjunctions

Using the right conjunctions helps you say what you mean. Rewrite the conjunctions so that the following paragraph makes sense.

Robot Danger?

(1) We may have a basic fear of robots, **nor** we depend on them. (2) Robots can work faster **but** are stronger than people. (3) They never grow tired **for** get bored. (4) All robots are cold **but** unfeeling. (5) They can injure a human being **nor** just keep working. Is our fear justified?

Interjections

❶ Here's the Idea

▶ **An interjection is a word or phrase used to express emotion.**

Hey, how do you like my automatic scanner?

It's fast! **Wow!**

> An interjection can stand alone or be set off by a comma.

❷ Why It Matters in Writing

The 5th Wave by Rich Tennant

"Shoot, that's nothing! Watch me spin him!"

> *Shoot* is an interjection.

Writers often use interjections to express strong emotions, such as anger, joy, concern, surprise, terror, and disgust. What emotion is the crew member on the left in the cartoon expressing?

❸ Practice and Apply

📁 **Working Portfolio:** Find your **Write Away** from page 150 or a sample of your most recent work. Add to your writing three interjections that express emotions. Use the interjections in the Student Help Desk on page 167 for ideas.

Grammar in Science

Using Prepositions to Write About Science

When you take notes on a science book or a documentary film, the proper use of prepositions can help you keep things straight in your mind. Prepositions are especially important when you are describing how a machine works. In the notebook below, a student has used notes and a diagram to describe the movement of *Dante II*, a robot used to explore the inside of volcanoes.

Dante II

The frames are connected **by a track** Each frame can slide **along the track** **toward the ends of the other frame.** Most **of the time**, **at least** one frame has all four **of its legs** **on the ground.**

Dante consists **of two frames**; there are four legs attached **to each frame.**

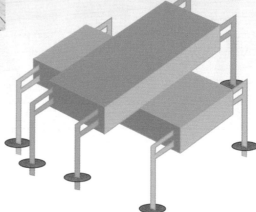

How Dante Walks
It begins **with all eight legs** **on the ground.** Then one frame lifts its four legs **from the ground** and slides forward **on the track** When it can slide no further, it stops, planting its legs **on the ground** again. **At that point**, the second frame lifts its legs and repeats the process.

Practice and Apply

ACROSS the CURRICULUM
SCIENCE

WRITING: Using Prepositions

For a project on robots, your class has designed robots for a variety of tasks. Your robot, shown below, is meant to answer the door. Using the information provided in the labels, write a short description of how the robot functions. Use prepositional phrases to describe the relationship between moving parts as well as the movements themselves. Useful prepositions might include the words *on, into, toward, from,* or *at.* Underline the prepositional phrases in your summary. Save your work in your 🗂 **Working Portfolio.**

PREP. CONJ. INTER.

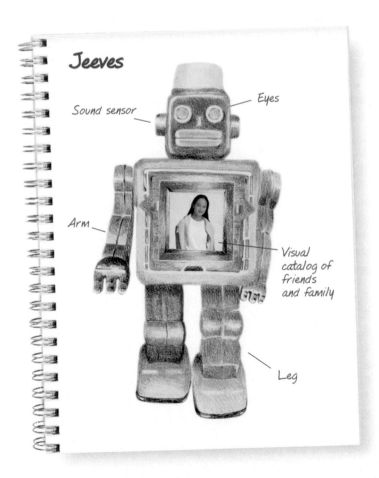

Jeeves

Sound sensor

Eyes

Arm

Visual catalog of friends and family

Leg

A. Prepositions, Conjunctions, Interjections Choose the correct word in parentheses to complete each sentence. Then identify the word as a preposition, a conjunction, or an interjection.

The Future Is Now!

1. Someday scientists will develop robots that think. (Wow!, After!)
2. Many theorists believe that machine intelligence is possible, (yet, or) scientists are far from copying the human brain.
3. (Whether, Both) robots help their operators (or, to) perform new jobs, they hold the future.
4. The invention of (both, neither) smarter tools (and, nor) more exotic devices will happen.
5. (With, Between) advanced robot technology, labor-saving devices will be even more common.
6. We barely notice, (and, but) robots have already taken over many tedious tasks.
7. Factories hum (to, after) a steady robot rhythm.
8. Mine shafts are dug (by, from) tireless automated moles.
9. Our banking is done (below, at) automated terminals.
10. (During, Among) surgery, robots drill bones and assist doctors.

B. Prepositional Phrases Read the passage and answer the questions below it.

Can You Give Me a Hand?

(1) A jointed-arm robot can perform a number of complex actions. (2) The arm's various sections move the same way as a human arm. (3) With seven joints, the arm can change positions. (4) Its attached hand can grasp anything within reach. (5) The robot-arm can be trained by a human. (6) A person can stand beside the robot-arm, hold the arm, and repeat a motion. (7) After a few repetitions, the robot performs the job independently.

1. What is the prepositional phrase in sentence 1?
2. What is the prepositional phrase in sentence 2?
3. What word does the prepositional phrase modify in sentence 2?
4. What word does the prepositional phrase modify in sentence 3?
5. What is the preposition in sentence 4?
6. What is the object of the preposition in sentence 5?
7. What is the prepositional phrase in sentence 6?
8. What word or words does the prepositional phrase modify in sentence 6?
9. What is the prepositional phrase in sentence 7?
10. What word does the prepositional phrase modify in sentence 7?

Choose the letter of the term that correctly identifies each underlined item.

Have you heard the story <u>about ancient Egyptian robots</u>? Some
(1)
ancient Egyptians believed that statues could speak <u>and</u> that the
(2)
statues could also answer their questions. <u>According to early
(3)
accounts,</u> Egyptian statues <u>both</u> spoke <u>and</u> even moved their
(4)   (4)
arms. Archaeologists have discovered some of these <u>statues</u>, which
(5)
are hollow. A man would put his head <u>into the statue's head</u> and
(6)
talk <u>through</u> the mouth. <u>Alas!</u> What a ruse! Some people believed
(7)   (8)
that the statue spoke, but it was really a man <u>inside</u>. The man
(9)
made the arms move up and down <u>with strings</u> attached to the
(10)
statue's arms.

1. A. adverb phrase
   B. adjective phrase
   C. conjunction
   D. object of a preposition

2. A. conjunction
   B. interjection
   C. preposition
   D. adverb phrase

3. A. prepositional phrase
   B. preposition
   C. conjunction
   D. adverb

4. A. coordinating conjunction
   B. correlative conjunction
   C. compound preposition
   D. interjection

5. A. coordinating conjunction
   B. correlative conjunction
   C. object of a preposition
   D. adverb

6. A. coordinating conjunction
   B. correlative conjunction
   C. adverb phrase
   D. adjective phrase

7. A. object of a preposition
   B. preposition
   C. coordinating conjunction
   D. correlative conjunction

8. A. correlative conjunction
   B. coordinating conjunction
   C. adverb phrase
   D. interjection

9. A. correlative conjunction
   B. preposition
   C. adverb
   D. interjection

10. A. coordinating conjunction
    B. correlative conjunction
    C. adverb phrase
    D. adjective phrase

Student Help Desk

Prepositions, Conjunctions, Interjections at a Glance

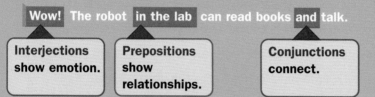

Wow! The robot **in the lab** can read books **and** talk.

| Interjections show emotion. | Prepositions show relationships. | Conjunctions connect. |

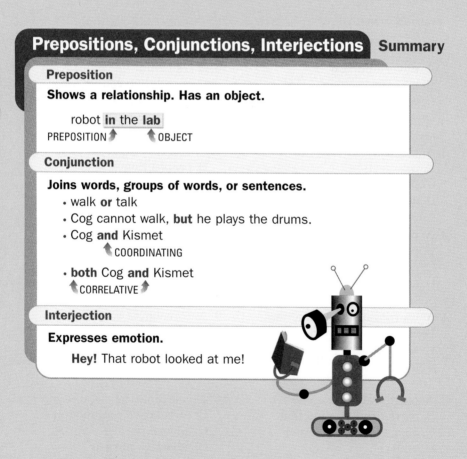

Prepositions, Conjunctions, Interjections Summary

Preposition

Shows a relationship. Has an object.

robot **in the lab**

PREPOSITION ⬆   ⬆ OBJECT

Conjunction

Joins words, groups of words, or sentences.

- walk **or** talk
- Cog cannot walk, **but** he plays the drums.
- Cog **and** Kismet
  ⬆ COORDINATING
- **both** Cog **and** Kismet
  ⬆ CORRELATIVE ⬆

Interjection

Expresses emotion.

Hey! That robot looked at me!

Prepositional Phrases

What Do They Do?

Adjective Phrases

Modify a noun or a pronoun.

Tell *which one*	The robot known as ROBODOC
Tell *what kind*	is a type of industrial robot.

Adverb Phrases

Modify a verb, an adjective, or another adverb.

Tell *when*	Surgeons use it during surgery
Tell *where*	at the hospital
Tell *why*	for precise work
Tell *how* or *to what extent*	with a drill.

Interjections!

Just a Few Ideas . . .

To express concern	oh-oh, oh no, oops
To express terror	eek, help, yipes
To express disgust	yuck, ick, gross
To express joy	awesome, hooray, yea
To express surprise	wow, what, whoops
To draw attention to	hey

The Bottom Line

Checklist for Prepositions and Conjunctions

Have I . . .

____ used prepositions to show relationships between things?

____ placed prepositional phrases close to the words they modify?

____ used coordinating conjunctions to connect words and groups of words?

____ used both parts of correlative conjunctions?

____ used interjections to express strong emotions?

Verbals and Verbal Phrases

> Hurrying down the dark street, Jeff knew that someone—or something— was right behind him. To turn and look seemed like a bad idea. He kept walking, but suddenly . . .

Theme: Scary Stories

It Was a Dark and Stormy Night . . .

What happens next? Chances are, your favorite character will be running headlong into . . . verbals! A verbal is a verb form that acts as another part of speech. Can you spot two verbals in the passage above? You already know that strong verbs can make your writing livelier. Verbals, too, can add further interest and excitement to anything you write.

Write Away: A Tale of Terror
Copy the story starter above and write a paragraph that describes what happens next. Or, if you prefer, freewrite a paragraph about a scary event of your own choosing, either real or imagined. Save your thriller in your
📁 **Working Portfolio**.

For each numbered item, choose the letter of the answer that correctly identifies it.

<u>Driving</u> home late one night, a man was startled to see a girl
(1)
<u>dressed in white</u> appear in front of his car. The driver stopped;
(2)
<u>screeching</u> echoed in the night air. He stopped just in front of the
(3)
girl, whose <u>torn</u> coat hung from her shoulder. The man got out
(4)
<u>to offer help</u>. The girl said that she had been in an accident and
(5)
asked the man <u>to drive her home</u>. Her only wish was <u>to get home</u>.
(6)   (7)
After <u>giving directions to her house</u>, the girl did no further talking.
(8)
When they arrived, the man turned—and saw that the girl had
vanished! The girl's mother told him that her daughter had been
killed in a car accident two months earlier!

---

1. A. gerund
   B. present participle
   C. past participle
   D. infinitive

2. A. past participial phrase
   B. gerund phrase
   C. infinitive phrase
   D. present participle

3. A. infinitive
   B. past participle
   C. gerund
   D. present participle

4. A. past participle
   B. present participle
   C. gerund
   D. infinitive

5. A. gerund phrase
   B. gerund
   C. infinitive phrase
   D. participial phrase

6. A. infinitive phrase used as subject
   B. infinitive phrase used as adjective
   C. infinitive phrase used as direct object
   D. infinitive phrase used as adverb

7. A. gerund used as subject
   B. infinitive phrase used as subject
   C. gerund used as direct object
   D. infinitive phrase used as predicate noun

8. A. gerund phrase used as object of a preposition
   B. gerund phrase used as direct object
   C. gerund phrase used as subject
   D. gerund phrase used as predicate noun

Gerunds and Gerund Phrases

① Here's the Idea

A **verbal** is a word that is formed from a verb and that acts as a noun, an adjective, or an adverb. There are three kinds of verbals: gerunds, infinitives, and participles.

▶ **A gerund is a verbal that ends in *ing* and acts as a noun.** Like nouns, gerunds may be subjects, predicate nouns, direct objects, indirect objects, and objects of prepositions.

Inventing can be dangerous.

▶ **A gerund phrase consists of a gerund plus its modifiers and complements.** Like a gerund, a gerund phrase functions as a noun.

GERUND PHRASE

Writing *Frankenstein* must have given Mary Shelley goose bumps!

Using Gerund Phrases	
Subject	**Calling the monster Frankenstein** is a mistake.
Predicate noun	Frankenstein's error was **creating the monster.**
Direct object	I like **watching horror movies.**
Object of a preposition	The monster was responsible for **killing three people.**

② Why It Matters in Writing

A gerund can create a "special effect" in a sentence by adding a sense of motion or action. Notice how the gerund in the model communicates what the speaker is hearing.

LITERARY MODEL

My head ached, and I fancied a **ringing** in my ears: but still they sat and still chatted. The **ringing** became more distinct. . . .

—Edgar Allan Poe, "The Tell-Tale Heart"

❸ Practice and Apply

A. CONCEPT CHECK: Gerunds and Gerund Phrases

Write the gerund or gerund phrase for each sentence.

Dream Story
1. Mary Shelley is famous for creating the Gothic novel *Frankenstein.*
2. Completing *Frankenstein* at 19 was an incredible accomplishment.
3. One night, after listening to ghost stories, Mary and three others agreed to write their own horror stories.
4. Mary Shelley heard her husband and a friend discuss the possibility of reviving a corpse.
5. Another idea was assembling a human being from various body parts.
6. Falling asleep was difficult for Mary that night.
7. She dreamed of a man who was responsible for creating a ghastly creature.
8. After seeing this mental image, Mary was terrified.
9. Opening her eyes reminded her that the vision was not real.
10. Imagining this ghastly creature inspired *Frankenstein.*

➜ **For a SELF-CHECK and more practice, see the EXERCISE BANK, p. 336.**

Tell how each gerund or gerund phrase functions in the sentences above.

B. REVISING: Using Gerunds for Concise Writing

In the following paragraph, replace the words in parentheses with gerunds or gerund phrases. You may need to add, change, or remove words.

Dr. Jekyll, the main character in *Dr. Jekyll and Mr. Hyde,* tries to transfer all of his own evil to another character. The young scientist concocts a potion to isolate his wicked impulses. However, after (he drinks) the liquid, he becomes a man controlled by those impulses. His dream (to improve) himself has failed. He has become Mr. Hyde, a villainous version of himself. (To break) all rules of society seems to be Hyde's goal. Jekyll's mistake is (that he fails) to foresee that his bad side might be stronger than his good side.

Participles and Participial Phrases

❶ Here's the Idea

▶ **A participle is a verb form that acts as an adjective.** It modifies a noun or a pronoun.

MODIFIES   MODIFIES

The **exhausted** campers found a **crumbling** schoolhouse.

Present and Past Participles

There are two kinds of participles: present participles and past participles. The **present participle** always ends in *ing*.

MODIFIES

Creaking eerily, the door swung open.

The **past participle** of a regular verb ends in *ed*. Past participles of irregular verbs, such as *fall,* are formed in a variety of ways.

MODIFIES

The **deserted** building was old and decrepit. (regular verb)

MODIFIES

Fallen bricks blocked the entry. (irregular verb)

Gerunds, present participles, and main verbs in progressive forms all end in *ing.* Here's how you can tell them apart.

Using Words That End in *ing*		
	Example	**Clue**
Participle	What's that **scampering** sound?	Could be replaced by an adjective
Gerund	It's the **scampering** of rodents.	Could be replaced by a noun
Verb	Mice are **scampering** beneath the floorboards.	Always preceded by a helping verb

Need help in remembering past participles of irregular verbs? See page 102.

Participial Phrases

▶ **A participial phrase consists of a participle plus its modifiers and complements.** The entire phrase modifies a noun or pronoun.

MODIFIES

They spied a shape lurking in the dark shadows.

MODIFIES

Frightened by the sight, they stopped cold.

❷ Why It Matters in Writing

If your descriptive writing seems dull, you can use participial phrases to enliven it. Notice how the participial phrases in the model present strong visual images.

LITERARY MODEL

He was thin, nondescript, with a cap **pulled down over his eyes.** . . . I was just slowing down for one of the tunnels—when I saw him— **standing under an arc light by the side of the road.** I could see him quite distinctly. The bag, the cap, even the spots of fresh rain **spattered over his shoulders.**

—Lucille Fletcher, *The Hitchhiker*

❸ Practice and Apply

A. CONCEPT CHECK: Participles and Participial Phrases

Write the participles and participial phrases in these sentences, along with the words they modify.

"The Legend of Sleepy Hollow"
1. Washington Irving's "The Legend of Sleepy Hollow" is still a frightening story.
2. A schoolmaster named Ichabod Crane falls in love with the bewitching Katrina Van Tassel.
3. Handsome Brom Bones, annoyed by Ichabod's flirtations, turns against him.
4. Knowing of the schoolmaster's superstitious nature, Brom tells Ichabod of his encounter with the Headless Horseman of Sleepy Hollow.
5. The horseman is the ghost of a beheaded soldier who appears at night.
6. After that chilling story, Ichabod sets out for home through the woods.
7. Suddenly, he is confronted by a hideous figure riding on a horse!
8. The horseman hurtles something resembling a head at Ichabod!
9. Scared out of his wits, Ichabod Crane flees from Sleepy Hollow forever.
10. Did Brom, disguised as the ghost, scare Ichabod away?

➜ For a SELF-CHECK and more practice, see the EXERCISE BANK, p. 337.

B. REVISING: Using Participial Phrases

For each blank, choose the correct participial phrase.

a. learning about the house's history
b. known for sentencing many people to death
c. neglected for many years
d. staring at him

"An Account of Some Strange Disturbances in Aungier Street" is a ghost story by Sheridan Le Fanu. A house **(1)** _____ suddenly has new occupants. One night, one of them sees a huge, dark monster **(2)** _____, and he tries to learn the cause of the appearance. **(3)** _____, he finally begins to understand the odd events. Many years earlier, the house had belonged to an old judge **(4)** _____. Now the judge's ghost haunts the house.

Infinitives and Infinitive Phrases

❶ Here's the Idea

▶ **An infinitive is a verb form that usually begins with the word *to* and acts as a noun, an adjective, or an adverb.**

INFINITIVE

Mars is a place some people want to visit.

▶ **An infinitive phrase is an infinitive plus its modifiers and complements.** The entire phrase functions as a noun, an adjective, or an adverb.

INFINITIVE PHRASE

To believe in life on Mars was common in the 1930s.
(ACTS AS NOUN)

INFINITIVE PHRASE

Martians might use flying saucers to invade Earth.
(ACTS AS ADVERB)

INFINITIVE PHRASE

I took time to read an old science fiction book.
(ACTS AS ADJECTIVE)

Using Infinitive Phrases	
Noun	To colonize Mars is a real possibility. (SUBJECT)
	My dream is to live on Mars. (PREDICATE NOUN)
	Would you like to go there? (DIRECT OBJECT)
Adverb	Science fiction writers wrote about little green Martians to scare readers.
Adjective	Even some scientists believed Mars to be inhabited.

On some evenings, the planet Mars seems to be red.

Is the phrase an infinitive phrase or a prepositional phrase? If a verb follows *to,* the phrase is an infinitive phrase. If a noun or pronoun follows *to,* the phrase is a prepositional phrase.

PREPOSITIONAL PHRASE

Of all the planets, Mars is most similar to Earth.

↑NOUN

INFINITIVE PHRASE

It was easy to imagine creatures on Mars.

VERB ↑

Would you like to travel to Mars?

VERB ↑   ↑ NOUN

I prefer to go to libraries for information.

❷ Why It Matters in Writing

Infinitive phrases are useful for communicating goals, wishes, and plans. Notice how the infinitive phrases in the model let readers know what the old man wishes.

> **LITERARY MODEL**
>
> "I'd like **to go to India myself**," said the old man, "just **to look round a bit**, you know."
>
> "Better where you are," said the sergeant-major, shaking his head. . . .
>
> "I should like **to see those old temples and fakirs and jugglers**," said the old man.
>
> —W. W. Jacobs, "The Monkey's Paw"

❸ Practice and Apply

A. CONCEPT CHECK: Infinitives and Infinitive Phrases

Identify the infinitives and infinitive phrases in the following sentences.

The War of the Worlds

1. It's possible to scare an entire nation with an imaginary story.
2. One day in 1938, Orson Welles began to broadcast a radio play about a Martian invasion.
3. It was not Welles's intention to cause a nationwide panic, but that's what he did.
4. Welles had designed the play to sound like an actual broadcast with flash news bulletins.
5. People tuning in were shocked to hear that giants from Mars had landed in New Jersey!
6. A later bulletin reported that the invaders had started to destroy entire cities!
7. Ready to wade across the Hudson River, the Martians were headed to New York!
8. Many hysterical listeners tried to escape their homes.
9. Some rushed outside with wet handkerchiefs over their faces to protect them from the Martians' lethal gas.
10. The media's ability to influence the public is astonishing.

→ For a SELF-CHECK and more exercises, see the EXERCISE BANK, p. 337.

B. WRITING: Using Infinitives and Infinitive Phrases

Use each of these infinitive phrases in a sentence of your own. Tell whether the infinitive phrase is used as a noun, an adjective, or an adverb.

1. to read mysteries
2. to be choosy
3. to surprise my friends
4. to entertain myself on the weekend
5. to find out the ending

C. REVISING: Using Verbal Phrases

Return to your **Write Away** assignment. Add three verbal phrases—gerund, participial, or infinitive—to make your writing more interesting and fluent. Then underline each verbal phrase you used.

Grammar in Literature

Using Verbals in Descriptive Writing

When you describe an eerie scene, you can use verbals to create energetic images. Because they are formed from verbs, verbals often lend a feeling of action to descriptions. Notice how Aiken's use of gerunds and participles shows the vivid actions of the struggling swan, as well as the quiet energy of Mr. Peters and the woods themselves.

from

The Third Wish

by JOAN AIKEN

As Mr. Peters entered a straight, empty stretch of road he seemed to hear a faint crying, and a struggling and thrashing, as if somebody was in trouble far away in the trees. He left his car and climbed the mossy bank beside the road. Beyond the bank was an open slope of beech trees leading down to thorn bushes through which he saw the gleam of water. He stood a moment waiting to try and discover where the noise was coming from, and presently heard a rustling and some strange cries in a voice which was almost human—and yet there was something too hoarse about it at one time and too clear and sweet at another. Mr. Peters ran down the hill and as he neared the bushes he saw something white among them which was trying to extricate itself; coming closer he found that it was a swan that had become entangled in the thorns growing on the bank of the canal.

> **GERUNDS**
> as direct objects of *hear* and *heard,* lend energy and vividness to the images.

> **PARTICIPIAL PHRASES**
> The first phrase modifies *trees;* although the trees are standing still, the phrase shows them in the act of leading.
> The second phrase modifies *He;* it shows that Mr. Peters waits and listens while he stands.

Practice and Apply

VERBALS

WRITING: Using Verbals

Follow the directions to write your own description of a person secretly watching or hearing a struggle. You can suggest what happens next to Mr. Peters, or you can create a passage about another character.

1. List four gerunds naming activities that are a part of the struggle being observed. You can describe a struggle that is bold and noisy, or one that is quiet and tense.
2. List four participles you might use as adjectives to describe both the character and his or her surroundings.
3. Use your responses to 1 and 2 to write a short scene about someone seeing or hearing a struggle. (You may decide not to use all of your participles or gerunds.)
4. Evaluate your work. How would your writing be different if you hadn't used participles or gerunds? Put your writing and your evaluation in your **Working Portfolio.**

1. Gerunds
   1. weeping
   2. whispering
   3.
   4.

2. Participles
   1. trapped
   2. darkening
   3.
   4.

Wallpaper design for *Swan, Rush and Iris*, Walter Crane (1845–1915). Victoria & Albert Museum, London, UK/Bridgeman Art Library, London/New York.

Mixed Review

A. Gerunds, Participles, and Infinitives In each of the following sentences, identify the word or words in italics as a gerund, a participle, or an infinitive.

1. *Writing* bestsellers has been Stephen King's specialty for a long time.
2. He seems to be able *to write* at least one book every year.
3. The *amazing* fact is that more than a hundred million copies of his books are in print.
4. King's popularity shows that people enjoy *scaring* themselves.
5. Every new King book results in a huge rush by customers *to buy* every copy.
6. Several successful movies are *adapted* versions of his books and stories.
7. King has played small parts in many of those films, because he enjoys *acting*.
8. His books are constructed to keep suspense *building* from beginning to end.
9. It is safe *to predict* that King's work will be popular for a long time.
10. By *achieving* such remarkable success, King has shown that he would deserve a place in the Scary Writers' Hall of Fame if one existed.

B. Writing with Verbal Phrases Write five sentences using the phrases below. Follow the directions in parentheses. You may choose to add more details to the phrases.

Example: to write five fresh sentences (Use as an infinitive phrase that acts as a direct object.)

Answer: I will soon begin to write five fresh sentences.

1. to walk home late one night (Use as an infinitive phrase that is the direct object in the sentence.)
2. shocked (Use as a participle.)
3. running away (Use as a gerund phrase that is the subject.)
4. speaking loudly (Use as a participial phrase.)
5. to advise you (Use as an infinitive phrase that acts as a noun.)

For each numbered item, choose the letter of the answer that correctly identifies it.

Not believing in ghosts, a reporter agreed to stay overnight in a
    (1)   (2)
"haunted" house where events considered weird had occurred.
                            (3)
Finding natural causes of the events was her goal. The reporter
            (4)
decided to take her niece along on the adventure. That night,
                   (5)
sitting in the front hall of the dark house, the woman and girl
               (6)
heard an upstairs door open and close. Then, echoing footsteps
                                  (7)
came down the stairs. After opening the lid of the piano in the
                                  (8)
next room, *something* began to play music! When the music
stopped, the footsteps seemed to go back upstairs.

---

1. A. gerund phrase
   B. infinitive phrase
   C. present participial phrase
   D. past participial phrase

2. A. gerund
   B. past participle
   C. present participle
   D. infinitive

3. A. gerund
   B. present participle
   C. infinitive
   D. past participle

4. A. gerund phrase used as direct object
   B. gerund phrase used as object of a preposition
   C. gerund phrase used as predicate noun
   D. gerund phrase used as subject

5. A. infinitive phrase used as subject
   B. infinitive phrase used as direct object
   C. infinitive phrase used as adverb
   D. infinitive phrase used as adjective

6. A. past participial phrase
   B. past participle
   C. present participial phrase
   D. present participle

7. A. past participial phrase
   B. past participle
   C. present participial phrase
   D. present participle

8. A. gerund phrase used as direct object
   B. gerund phrase used as object of a preposition
   C. gerund phrase used as predicate noun
   D. gerund phrase used as subject

VERBALS

Student Help Desk

Verbals and Verbal Phrases at a Glance

Verbal	Job	Example
Gerund	Noun	**Seeing** a horror show can jangle your nerves.
Participle	Adjective	The **terrifying** plot will make you gasp.
Infinitive	Noun	**To scare** you out of your wits is the director's aim.
	Adjective	The dark and lonely scenes are the ones **to watch.**
	Adverb	When a door slams shut, you're sure **to jump.**

Gerund, Participle, or Verb? Rolling, Rolling, Rolling

	Example	Clue
Gerund	**Running** was Jason's best sport.	Could be replaced by a noun
Participle	His daily **running** schedule was rigorous.	Could be replaced by an adjective
Verb	Friday night, Jason was **running** out of the horror movie!	Always preceded by a helping verb

To Cut to the Chase

Infinitives vs. Prepositional Phrases

	Example	Clue
Infinitive	He started **to run home.** VERB	A verb follows *to.*
Prepositional phrase	Instead, he returned **to work.** NOUN	A noun or pronoun follows *to.*

Understanding Infinitives To Weave a Plot

Noun

SUBJECT
To save the victims required a genius.

DIRECT OBJECT
An eccentric scientist tried **to find** a solution.

PREDICATE NOUN
His brilliant idea was **to catch** the spiders in their own webs.

Adjective

Victims' struggles in the mammoth sticky webs were a horrible sight **to see.**

Adverb

In the horror show, giant spiders were able **to trap** people in their webs.

The Bottom Line

Checklist for Verbals and Verbal Phrases

Have I . . .

____ used gerunds and gerund phrases to name actions and activities?

____ used participles and participial phrases to modify nouns and pronouns?

____ understood the different jobs of words that end in *ing*?

____ understood the difference between infinitives and prepositional phrases beginning with *to*?

____ used infinitives and infinitive phrases as nouns, adjectives, and adverbs?

____ used verbals and verbal phrases to add fluency and excitement to my writing?

Sentence Structure

Dark and slippery
Formed a chain to bring in gear
Started mapping from entrance
Sketched view of passage
Need to wear helmets with lights
Found stalagmites and stalactites
If lost

Theme: A Day in the Life . . .

One Step at a Time

How exactly will Brandon and Taylor describe their experience as underground cave explorers? The notes they made while helping their team map the cave are sketchy and brief. How could they turn these notes into sentences that give a better description of their experience? You, too, often have to translate sketchy thoughts into complete ideas. Knowing how sentences are structured can help you explore the best possible way to say what you want.

Write Away: Surprises Around the Corner
It's not necessary to travel underground in order to have an exciting or unusual day in your life. Sometimes the most ordinary day can turn out to be the most surprising. Write about a day in your life that turned out to be not so typical. Put your writing in your ▭ **Working Portfolio.**

Choose the letter of the term that correctly identifies each underlined section.

> While her friends relax on weekends, Davida works on her line
> (1)
> of fashion jeans and jackets. Right now she is making an evening
> (2)
> jacket. She is also working on a special order for a friend, and she
> is designing her first prom dress. Even though these projects take
> (3)   (4)
> a lot of time, each reflects a step toward Davida's dream. She
> (5)
> wants to be a fashion designer. This dream, which Davida has had
> (6)   (7)
> since childhood, keeps her focused. Davida's friends encourage her,
>
> but they wish she spent more time with them as well. Whenever
> (8)
> she can, Davida invites her friends to go along with her to junk
> (9)
> shops, and together they hunt for buttons and fabrics that can be
>
> used in Davida's designs. Davida searches the shops until she
> (10)
> finds just the right materials for her creations.

1. A. independent clause
   B. dependent clause
   C. compound sentence
   D. simple sentence

2. A. simple sentence
   B. dependent clause
   C. compound sentence
   D. complex sentence

3. A. part of a compound sentence
   B. sentence fragment
   C. part of a complex sentence
   D. simple sentence

4. A. coordinating conjunction
   B. subordinating conjunction
   C. noun clause
   D. relative pronoun

5. A. independent clause
   B. dependent clause
   C. compound sentence
   D. simple sentence

6. A. simple sentence
   B. compound sentence
   C. complex sentence
   D. compound-complex sentence

7. A. noun clause
   B. adjective clause
   C. adverb clause
   D. independent clause

8. A. coordinating conjunction
   B. subordinating conjunction
   C. relative pronoun
   D. clause

9. A. simple sentence
   B. compound sentence
   C. complex sentence
   D. compound-complex sentence

10. A. noun clause
    B. adjective clause
    C. adverb clause
    D. independent clause

What Is a Clause?

CHAPTER 8

❶ Here's the Idea

▶ **A clause is a group of words that contains a subject and a verb.** For example, the following sentence contains two clauses.

SUBJECT   VERB
Kate noted the day's events in her journal
before she went to bed.
SUBJECT   VERB

There are two kinds of clauses: independent and dependent.

Independent and Dependent Clauses

▶ **An independent clause expresses a complete thought and can stand alone as a sentence.**

Kate noted the day's events in her journal.
INDEPENDENT CLAUSE

▶ **A dependent clause does not express a complete thought and cannot stand alone as a sentence.**

Most dependent clauses are introduced by words like *although, before, because, so that, when, while,* and *that.*

before she went to bed
DEPENDENT CLAUSE

A dependent clause can be joined to an independent clause to add to the complete thought that the independent clause expresses.

Kate noted the day's events in her journal before she went to bed.

Some writers keep journals so that they can remember details about events.

HOT TIP

Dependent clauses are also known as subordinate clauses. These clauses cannot stand alone and are dependent on main clauses.

❷ Why It Matters in Writing

When you write, pay special attention to sentences that start with words such as *because, when, so that,* or other words that signal a dependent clause. Be sure you have not accidentally created a fragment. Notice how connecting the dependent clause to the preceding sentence in the model below makes a sentence that expresses a complete thought.

STUDENT MODEL

> Kate and her horse Scarlet are one of the
> best teams in the junior rodeo. Because
> they practice together every day.

INDEPENDENT CLAUSE

DEPENDENT CLAUSE

❸ Practice and Apply

A. CONCEPT CHECK: What Is a Clause?

Identify each underlined group of words as an independent clause or a dependent clause.

A Day in the Life of a Junior Rodeo Competitor
1. Thirteen-year-old Kate is devoted to her horse Scarlet.
2. They won their first competition together when Kate was only nine years old.
3. While her brothers sleep, Kate slips out to the stable.
4. After she feeds Scarlet, Kate brushes her coat and mane.
5. She does this so that Scarlet's coat stays shiny.
6. Because Scarlet needs exercise, Kate rides her daily.
7. Kate and Scarlet entered a barrel-racing competition, which was very competitive.
8. Entrants raced around barrels that were put in the ring.
9. Kate and Scarlet's performance brought cheers from the crowd because they put everything they had into the race.
10. Now Kate and Scarlet have more than a dozen ribbons, and Kate plans to keep competing in the rodeo.

➜ For a SELF-CHECK and more practice, see the EXERCISE BANK, p. 338.

B. EDITING: Fixing Fragments

Read the following first draft of a student's paragraph. Rewrite the paragraph to eliminate any sentence fragments.

STUDENT MODEL

My friend Derrick is a butterfly collector. He invited me to join him on Saturday. So that I could help him catch butterflies for his collection. We hunkered down in our back field and waited quietly. Because we didn't want to frighten away the butterflies. Derrick pointed toward the tall pink flowers nearby. We watched the flowers sway in the breeze. While a beautiful orange and black monarch hovered over them. Now I want to collect butterflies too.

C. WRITING: Creating a Caption

This photograph shows a junior rodeo contestant barrel-racing. On a separate sheet of paper, write a caption for the picture, describing what is happening. Use at least one independent clause and one dependent clause.

Simple and Compound Sentences

LESSON 2

❶ Here's the Idea

Simple Sentences

▶ **A simple sentence contains one independent clause and no dependent clauses.** Remember that even a simple sentence can include many details. Each of the following sentences has only a single independent clause.

> Malika sings.
> INDEPENDENT CLAUSE

> Ben competes at chess every day after school.

Compound Sentences

▶ **A compound sentence contains two or more independent clauses and no dependent clauses.** The clauses in a compound sentence must be closely related.

> Malika sings every day, and she practices with the choir.
> INDEPENDENT CLAUSE   INDEPENDENT CLAUSE

Independent clauses can be joined by a comma and a coordinating conjunction or by a semicolon.

> **The choir rehearsed late on Tuesday, and the director praised their hard work.**

> **The choir rehearsed late on Tuesday; the director praised their hard work.**

> **Coordinating Conjunctions**
> for   and   nor   or   but   so   yet

WATCH OUT

Don't mistake a simple sentence with a compound verb for a compound sentence. No punctuation should separate the parts of a compound verb.

Play Chess

> **Ben planned a chess tournament for interested students✗and promoted it.**

SENTENCES

Sentence Structure **189**

❷ Why It Matters in Writing

Too many short sentences can make your writing choppy. You can avoid this problem by using compound sentences. Notice how the writer of the model below combined related ideas to form compound sentences.

STUDENT MODEL

My grandfather enjoys listening to me sing. He has many favorite songs, *and* I sing them for him every night. He still has a pretty strong voice, *so* He sometimes joins in for a few verses.

> Related thoughts combined

❸ Practice and Apply

A. CONCEPT CHECK: Simple and Compound Sentences

Identify each sentence as simple or compound.

A Day in the Life of a Young Writer

1. Eighth-grader Max Marciano is working hard on his first mystery novel.
2. Max loves mysteries, and he has read every story about the detective Sherlock Holmes.
3. Max's older brother Tony and two friends are also fans of the famous detective.
4. Tony encourages Max with his novel.
5. Max writes a full page of text on most mornings, but sometimes he isn't inspired.
6. Max's friend Sophie made a suggestion.
7. She formed a small writing group, and now they meet once a week.
8. The writing group has motivated Max, and he now meets his writing goal each morning.

9. The main character in Max's story is named De Soto, and he is a master of disguise.
10. Max read his latest chapter to Sophie and Tony, and they loved it.

→ **For a SELF-CHECK and more practice, see the EXERCISE BANK, p. 338.**

B. REVISING: Combining Sentences

Combine each pair of sentences to form a compound sentence, using one of the coordinating conjunctions *and, but, for, or, nor, so,* and *yet.* Remember to use a comma before the coordinating conjunction.

Meeting Challenges Daily

1. Fourteen-year-old Marisha was born with both of her legs broken. No one noticed anything was wrong at first.
2. She has a rare bone disease. Her bones are brittle and soft.
3. Marisha has already had seven operations. She may need more in the future.
4. After an operation, physical therapy is a big part of Marisha's rehabilitation. She has four sessions of physical therapy a day.
5. A typical day in physical therapy always includes swimming. It also can include bike riding.
6. Sheri is Marisha's physical therapist. She is also Marisha's friend.
7. Together they work on exercises like sit-ups and leg lifts. They talk about Marisha's progress.
8. Sometimes Marisha feels a lot of pain. She doesn't like to show it.
9. Marisha works hard on her school work. She still has time for fun.
10. Marisha isn't sure of her future career. She thinks of becoming a pediatrician.

Working Portfolio: Revising Reread what you wrote for the **Write Away** paragraph on page 184. Check to see if any short sentences can be combined to form compound sentences.

Complex Sentences

❶ Here's the Idea

▶ **A complex sentence contains one independent clause and one or more dependent clauses.**

INDEPENDENT CLAUSE   DEPENDENT CLAUSE

Mr. Hernandez, who is a professional storyteller, performs at many different festivals.

When Mr. Hernandez performs, he enchants the audience.

Young people love the way he tells stories because he changes his voice and wears costumes.

Most dependent clauses are introduced by subordinating conjunctions. A **subordinating conjunction** relates the dependent clause to the independent clause. The following is a list of the most common subordinating conjunctions.

Commonly Used Subordinating Conjunctions			
after	as though	so that	whenever
although	because	than	where
as	before	though	wherever
as if	even though	unless	while
as long as	if	until	
as soon as	since	when	

❷ Why It Matters in Writing

You can use complex sentences to clarify relationships between ideas. Notice how the writer of the model on the next page used dependent clauses to convey details of character and plot.

"When the merchant arrived, he asked her if she could spin. "Spin?" answered the old woman, while the poor embarrassed girl stood by with bowed head. "Spin! The hanks [of linen fibers] disappear so fast you would think she was drinking them like water."

—"The Souls in Purgatory," retold by Guadalupe Baca-Vaughn

TELLS THE TIME OF THE EVENT

PROVIDES A DETAIL OF THE PLOT

TELLS HOW THE GIRL FEELS

❸ Practice and Apply

CONCEPT CHECK: Complex Sentences

Write these sentences on a sheet of paper. Underline each independent clause once and each dependent clause twice.

A Day in the Life of a Storyteller

1. Rick and José Hernandez enjoy hearing their father's stories because he performs them so cleverly.
2. When Mr. Hernandez performed on Saturday, he told the story "Aunty Misery."
3. Since the main character is a very old woman, Mr. Hernandez crumpled his face and walked with a stoop.
4. Aunty Misery, who lives alone, is teased by children.
5. When these children yell insults at the old woman, Mr. Hernandez makes his voice squeaky and high-pitched.
6. After she is kind to a stranger, she is given one wish.
7. Mr. Hernandez pulls a cape across his face so that the stranger looks mysterious.
8. Because her wish comes true, the children stick to a tree.
9. She ignores their cries until the children promise not to bother her.
10. The audience laughs when Mr. Hernandez portrays the naughty children stuck to the pear tree.

➡ **For a SELF-CHECK and more practice, see the EXERCISE BANK, p. 339.**

Kinds of Dependent Clauses

① Here's the Idea

Adjective Clauses

▶ **An adjective clause is a dependent clause used as an adjective.** An adjective clause modifies a noun or a pronoun. It tells what kind, which one, how many, or how much.

MODIFIES NOUN

Devon Kim is a climber who likes challenges.

ADJECTIVE CLAUSE

Adjective clauses are usually introduced by relative pronouns.

Relative Pronouns
who   whom   whose   that   which

His hardest climb, which took him three days, was Mount Whitney.

Notice that a clause that begins with *which* is set off with commas. Use commas when the clause isn't necessary to understand the meaning of a sentence.

Adverb Clauses

▶ **An adverb clause is a dependent clause used as an adverb.** It modifies a verb, an adjective, or an adverb. An adverb clause might tell where, when, how, why, to what extent, or under what conditions.

Adverb clauses are introduced by subordinating conjunctions such as *if, because, before, than, as, even though, than, so that, while, where, when, as if,* and *since.*

MODIFIES VERB

They checked their gear before they started the climb.

ADVERB CLAUSE

MODIFIES ADJECTIVE

They were cautious **because** ice made the trails slippery.

MODIFIES ADVERB

Devon worries about the weather more **than** Andy does.

When Devon started his climb, the weather was good.

ADVERB CLAUSE

An adverb clause should be followed by a comma when it comes before an independent clause. When an adverb clause comes after an independent clause, a comma may or may not be needed before it.

Because the weather was bad, Devon canceled the climb.

Devon canceled the climb **because** the weather was bad.

For more about adjectives and adverbs, see pages 126–136.

Noun Clauses

▶ **A noun clause is a dependent clause used as a noun.**
Like a noun, a noun clause can serve as a subject, a direct object, an indirect object, an object of a preposition, or a predicate noun.

NOUN CLAUSE SERVING AS SUBJECT

That the dedicated actor practiced her role every day surprised no one.

NOUN CLAUSE SERVING AS DIRECT OBJECT

The director determined who would design the set.

NOUN CLAUSE SERVING AS AN INDIRECT OBJECT

The set designer gave whoever helped **a bonus.**

NOUN CLAUSE SERVING AS A PREDICATE NOUN

A love of theater is what motivates her.

NOUN CLAUSE SERVING AS AN OBJECT OF A PREPOSITION

She takes great satisfaction in whatever they perform.

Noun clauses are often introduced by words such as those shown in the following chart.

Words That Introduce Noun Clauses

that, how, when, where, whether, why, what, whatever,

who, whom, whoever, whomever, which, whichever

If you can substitute the word *something* or *someone* for a clause in a sentence, it is a noun clause.

The director determined who would design the set.

The director determined something.

❷ Why It Matters in Writing

You can use dependent clauses to add detail and to provide explanations. Notice how the writer of the model below used adverb clauses to add information about the characters.

LITERARY MODEL

Because Annie was home for a semester break from college, we had decided to make a special Saturday visit. Now Annie was in bed, groaning theatrically—she's a drama major—but I told my mother I'd go, anyway. I hadn't seen my grandmother since she'd been admitted to Lawnrest.

—Robert Cormier, "The Moustache"

Adverb clause tells why they decided to visit.

Adverb clause tells when the narrator last saw his grandmother.

❸ Practice and Apply

A. CONCEPT CHECK: Kinds of Dependent Clauses

Write these sentences on a sheet of paper. Underline each dependent clause, and identify it as an adjective clause, an adverb clause, or a noun clause.

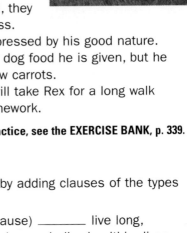

A Dog's Life
1. Rex is a yellow Labrador retriever who loves to chase squirrels.
2. As soon as he sees a squirrel, he yelps with delight.
3. After he has an exciting squirrel chase, Rex usually needs to take a very long nap.
4. That Rex is a swift runner is obvious to everyone.
5. Rachel and Jake have photos that show Rex as a puppy at the animal shelter.
6. He looks as if he wanted a good home.
7. Although Rex behaves well, they take him to obedience class.
8. Whoever meets Rex is impressed by his good nature.
9. Rex eagerly eats whatever dog food he is given, but he really likes lasagna and raw carrots.
10. Tonight Rachel and Jake will take Rex for a long walk because they have no homework.

➡ For a SELF-CHECK and more practice, see the EXERCISE BANK, p. 339.

B. WRITING: Using Clauses

Complete the sentences below by adding clauses of the types indicated in parentheses.

(1) Many dogs (adjective clause) _____ live long, healthy lives. (2) Dogs can help people live healthier lives (adverb clause) _____ . (3) Love and kindness are (noun clause) _____ .

Compound-Complex Sentences

❶ Here's the Idea

▶ **A compound-complex sentence contains two or more independent clauses and one or more dependent clauses.**

DEPENDENT CLAUSE   INDEPENDENT CLAUSE

While she was fishing, Amy saw many deer, and she tried not to disturb them.

INDEPENDENT CLAUSE

Amy unhooked the salmon from the line, and she threw it back into the stream so that it could live.

❷ Why It Matters in Writing

A rich, detailed description is hard to create with only simple sentences. Notice how Marjorie Kinnan Rawlings used compound-complex sentences in a detailed description of a day in the life of a boy.

LITERARY MODEL

When I left my bed in the cool morning, the boy had come and gone, and a stack of kindling was neat against the cabin wall. He came again after school in the afternoon and worked until time to return to the orphanage. His name was Jerry; he was twelve years old, and he had been at the orphanage since he was four.

      —Marjorie Kinnan Rawlings,
       "A Mother in Mannville"

DEPENDENT CLAUSE

INDEPENDENT CLAUSE

CHAPTER 8

❸ Practice and Apply

A. MIXED REVIEW: Compound, Complex, or Compound-Complex

Identify each sentence as compound, complex, or compound-complex.

Daily Life in the Middle Ages

1. Most young people in the Middle Ages spent their time on farm work, and they never learned reading and writing.
2. Boys and girls harvested grain, and they picked fruit.
3. Young boys in prosperous families were sent to school, where they studied grammar, rhetoric, and arithmetic.
4. Girls from wealthy families also learned reading and arithmetic so that they could manage households.
5. All girls were taught spinning when they were quite young, and they also learned weaving.
6. Wealthy families apprenticed their sons so that they could learn banking, business, and law.
7. If a young boy lived in a city, he could work for an artisan, and he could receive on-the-job training.
8. City life centered on the marketplace, where country people came to buy and sell; the shops offered all sorts of wares and services.
9. While housewives were at the marketplace, they met at the public fountain, and young people played games.
10. Although it was crowded and cramped, daily life in a medieval city could be lively and exciting.

➜ **For a SELF-CHECK and more practice, see the EXERCISE BANK, p. 340.**

B. WRITING: Creating Compound-Complex Sentences

Combine the following sentences to create a compound-complex sentence. Use *but* and *so that* in your new sentence.

Most young people in the Middle Ages worked. Today young people go to school. They learn reading and writing.

SENTENCES

Grammar in Literature

Using Dependent Clauses to Enrich Writing

When you write descriptions of powerful memories, you will probably use complex sentences. All complex sentences are made up of independent and dependent clauses. In the passage below, notice how author Jewell Parker Rhodes weaves dependent clauses into her sentences as she shares her memories of what it was like to grow up in Pittsburgh, Pennsylvania, in the 1950s.

BLOCK PARTY

by Jewell Parker Rhodes

We lived in the dark green hills of Pittsburgh where the smoke from J.L. Steel dusted our clothes gray and blanketed the sky, causing sunsets to streak bright pink and orange. Streetcar wires crisscrossed overhead, making perches for the hungry crows who flew high when the lumbering cars came, spewing electric sparks. Sometimes we'd put pennies in the metal tracks and wait for them to be squashed flat as the streetcars rumbled over them, carrying passengers down the hills into the heart of the city that rested by the three rivers: Ohio, Monongahela, and Allegheny.

But what I remember most about growing up in Pittsburgh was living in a neighborhood where everyone acted like a relative—an aunt, an uncle, a brother, or a sister. Lots of women acted like my mother, bossing me, feeding me. Many would hold me on their laps and tell me stories about High John the Conqueror or John Henry. Some felt no shame about whipping out a comb and fixing my hair when they thought I looked too raggedy. And days when I was lucky, one of my neighborhood mothers would jump in the circle and join me in a waist-twisting, hip-rolling hula-hoop.

ACROSS the CURRICULUM

LITERATURE

Practice and Apply

WRITING: Using Dependent Clauses

The notebook below contains a list of dependent clauses. Rewrite the following passage, using dependent clauses from the list. Follow the directions in parentheses to add noun clauses, adverb clauses, and adjective clauses. If you'd like to, make up your own dependent clauses.

We loved to use our hula-hoops (*adverb clause*). Hula-hoops were circular tubes of plastic (*adjective clause*). The challenge was to keep the hoops spinning (*adverb clause*). We practiced (*adverb clause*) and (*adverb clause*). Sometimes our older brothers and sisters (*adjective clause*) joined in the fun. Once my aunt (*adjective clause*) tried it herself (*adverb clause*). (*Noun clause*) was the champion spinner. (*Adverb clause*), we looked like we were doing the Hawaiian hula dance.

wherever there was enough room to play

as long as you could

when we really got going

when we had parties outside

who never played

whoever kept the hoop spinning the longest

whenever we had time

that you spun around your waist

who thought they were too old for toys

when we challenged her

SENTENCES

Mixed Review

A. Simple, Compound, and Complex Sentences Read this excerpt about a young Chinese-American chess champion. Then answer the questions below it.

> **LITERARY MODEL**
>
> **(1)** A man who watched me play in the park suggested that my mother allow me to play in local chess tournaments. **(2)** My mother smiled graciously, an answer that meant nothing. **(3)** I desperately wanted to go, but I bit back my tongue. **(4)** I knew she would not let me play among strangers. **(5)** So as we walked home I said in a small voice that I didn't want to play in the local tournament. **(6)** They would have American rules. **(7)** If I lost, I would bring shame on my family.
>
> —Amy Tan, "Rules of the Game"

1. Is sentence 1 simple or complex?
2. What is the adjective clause in sentence 1?
3. What is the noun clause in sentence 1?
4. Is sentence 3 complex or compound?
5. What is the coordinating conjunction in sentence 3?
6. What is the noun clause in sentence 5?
7. What is the independent clause in sentence 6?
8. What kind of sentence is sentence 6?
9. What is the dependent clause in sentence 7?
10. What is the subordinating conjunction in sentence 7?

B. Combining Clauses Rewrite the following paragraph, combining clauses to eliminate sentence fragments and to connect related ideas.

Learning the Yo-Yo

Jennifer Baybrook is a champion yo-yo player. Who began performing. When she was six. She was the first female ever to win national and world titles. Another American champion is Ed Giulietti. Who started when he was 11 years old. After he had practiced for only two years. He knew more than 500 tricks.

Choose the letter of the term that correctly identifies each underlined section.

Rob steps backstage, and he senses the electric atmosphere
(1)
among the actors as they prepare for the opening night of *My Fair*
(2)
Lady. Rob has been cast in the role of Professor Henry Higgins.
The role, which has always been one of Rob's favorites, calls for
(3)
wit, charm, and a touch of snobbery. As soon as Rob sees Angela
and James, the actors who are playing Eliza and Colonel
(4)
Pickering, he wishes them luck. Rob, Angela, and James have only
five minutes before the curtain rises, and they try to relax. That
(5)
the actors are a little nervous is understandable. Rob straightens
(6)   (7)
his bow tie and hat, which are supposed to make him look like a
professor, and he clears his throat. Rob watches for his cue.
(8)   (9)
Whatever happens onstage, he is ready.
(10)

---

1. A. independent clause
   B. dependent clause
   C. compound sentence
   D. simple sentence

2. A. adjective clause
   B. adverb clause
   C. noun clause
   D. independent clause

3. A. simple sentence
   B. compound sentence
   C. complex sentence
   D. noun clause

4. A. adjective clause
   B. adverb clause
   C. noun clause
   D. independent clause

5. A. adjective clause
   B. adverb clause
   C. noun clause
   D. independent clause

6. A. adjective clause
   B. adverb clause
   C. noun clause
   D. independent clause

7. A. independent clause
   B. dependent clause
   C. noun clause
   D. simple sentence

8. A. coordinating conjunction
   B. subordinating conjunction
   C. relative pronoun
   D. clause

9. A. simple sentence
   B. compound sentence
   C. complex sentence
   D. compound-complex sentence

10. A. independent clause
    B. dependent clause
    C. noun clause
    D. simple sentence

Student Help Desk

Sentence Structure at a Glance

SIMPLE SENTENCE = | independent clause |
Jamal practices his saxophone every day.

COMPOUND SENTENCE = | independent clause | + | independent clause(s) |
| He plays in the marching band, | and | he also plays in a jazz quartet. |

COMPLEX SENTENCE = | independent clause | + dependent clause(s)
| Before the band practiced, | they tuned their instruments. |

COMPOUND–COMPLEX SENTENCE =
| independent clauses | + dependent clauses
| Jamal played a solo, | and | Christine joined in for a duet | while they were
waiting for band practice to begin.

Punctuating Compound and Complex Sentences

Everyday Choices

Use Commas	Example
to join independent clauses with coordinating conjunctions	Christine plays the clarinet, **and** she also plays the piano.
after adverb clauses that begin sentences	After the band finished the practice, they rested.
to set off adjective clauses that begin with *which*	Jamal appreciates his dad's knowledge of jazz, **which he played as a young man,** and Jamal has learned much from him.
Use Semicolons	
to join independent clauses without conjunctions	Christine learned her music from her uncle; he is a piano teacher.

Avoiding Clause Confusion   Job Options

Dependent Clause	Function	Example
Adjective clause	• modifies noun or pronoun • tells what kind, which one, how many, or how much	The **students who attended the game** enjoyed the half-time performance.
Adverb clause	• modifies verb, adjective, or adverb • tells where, when, how, why, to what extent, or under what conditions	**Because it was raining,** the band got soaked.
Noun clause	• acts as subject, direct object, indirect object, object of a preposition, or predicate noun	**That Jamal and Christine won music scholarships** surprised no one.

The Bottom Line

Checklist for Sentence Structure

Have I improved my writing by . . .

____ eliminating sentence fragments?

____ creating compound sentences to link closely related ideas?

____ using dependent clauses to show how ideas are related?

____ using dependent clauses to add details?

____ punctuating compound and complex sentences correctly?

Subject-Verb Agreement

Are You a Drummer?

Our band are looking for you!
Does you have good rhythm? Can you
play up-beat music? Give us a call! We
needs a responsible team player with a
good sense of humor. Show-offs needs
not apply.

We has these drums
for you to use!

Theme: Elements of Personality

Agreeable People

These band members need to get their act together! They need a drummer who'll fit their music style and whose personality will fit well with their own. They want someone who will come to rehearsals, someone who will share ideas—someone agreeable.

In addition to all this, they need to work on the agreement of their subjects and verbs. Can you find the errors in their poster? Subject-verb agreement is important for communication in writing. Mistakes in agreement may confuse, frustrate, or annoy your readers. This chapter will help you use subjects and verbs correctly.

Write Away: Celebrity Profile

Write a biographical sketch about a musician you admire, whether it's someone famous or someone you know. Focus on the elements of this musician's personality and how they contribute to his or her music. Then save your writing in your ⬛ **Working Portfolio.**

For each numbered item, choose the letter of the best revision.

> Who are you? <u>You doesn't seem</u> exactly like anyone else. Your
> (1)
> personality is the particular pattern of how you think, feel, and
> act. <u>Heredity and environment shapes</u> your personality from the
> (2)
> time you are born. <u>Both influence</u> whether you are shy, good-
> (3)
> natured, or aggressive. <u>Scientists studying human behavior</u>
> (4)
> <u>believes</u> you inherit certain traits. However, your <u>surroundings</u>
> (5)
> <u>also affect</u> the kind of person you are. <u>Your family play</u> an
> (6)
> important role in your personality development, for instance, as do
> your school, your community, and your cultural heritage. From
> this combination of influences <u>result your unique personality</u>. <u>No</u>
> (7)
> <u>one else are quite like you.</u>
> (8)

1. A. You doesn't seemed
   B. You don't seems
   C. You don't seem
   D. Correct as is

2. A. Heredity and environment
   is shaping
   B. Heredity and environment
   shape
   C. Heredity and environment
   has shaped
   D. Correct as is

3. A. Both influences
   B. Both has influenced
   C. Both is influencing
   D. Correct as is

4. A. Scientists studying human
   behavior are believing
   B. Scientists studying human
   behavior has believed
   C. Scientists studying human
   behavior believe
   D. Correct as is

5. A. surroundings also affects
   B. surroundings also does affect
   C. surroundings also has
   affected
   D. Correct as is

6. A. Your family plays
   B. Your family are playing
   C. Your family have been
   playing
   D. Correct as is

7. A. results your unique
   personality
   B. have resulted your unique
   personality
   C. are resulting your unique
   personality
   D. Correct as is

8. A. No one else was quite
   like you.
   B. No one else is quite like you.
   C. No one else are being quite
   like you.
   D. Correct as is

Agreement in Number

❶ Here's the Idea

▶ **A verb must agree with its subject in number.**

Number refers to whether a word is singular or plural. A word that refers to one person, place, thing, idea, action, or condition is singular. A word that refers to more than one is plural.

Singular and Plural Subjects

▶ **Singular subjects take singular verbs.**

```
       AGREE        SINGULAR VERB
Marla works cooperatively with her classmates.
  SINGULAR SUBJECT
```

She listens **carefully to their suggestions.**

▶ **Plural subjects take plural verbs.**

```
        AGREE        PLURAL VERB
The players work together well as a team.
   PLURAL SUBJECT
```

They listen **carefully to the coach.**

Most nouns that end in s or es are plural. For example, *players* is a plural noun. However, most verbs that end in s are singular. *Works* is a singular verb form.

Verb Phrases

▶ **In a verb phrase, it is the first helping verb that agrees with the subject.** A verb phrase is made up of a main verb and one or more helping verbs.

```
 AGREE
Lou has volunteered for the teen hotline.
        SINGULAR HELPING VERB
```

```
 AGREE
He is answering calls from troubled kids.
```

AGREE

Callers have asked **for help.**
        ↟ PLURAL VERB

AGREE

They have been seeking **advice from their peers.**

Contractions *Doesn't* and *Don't*

Two contractions we often use are *doesn't* and *don't*. Use *doesn't* with all singular subjects except *I* and *you*. Use *don't* with all plural subjects and with the pronouns *I* and *you*.

Tiffany doesn't attend **folk concerts.**
SINGULAR VERB: does + not = doesn't

You don't like **to shop.**
WITH PRONOUN *YOU:* do + not = don't

They don't enjoy **noisy, crowded malls.**
PLURAL VERB: do + not = don't

S-V AGREEMENT

❷ Why It Matters in Writing

When you revise your writing, you sometimes change a subject from singular to plural, or vice versa. When you revise, errors in subject-verb agreement can occur. Check your final draft carefully to make sure that the verb agrees with the new subject.

STUDENT MODEL

DRAFT	REVISION
Tomorrow's tryout is not just a popularity contest. The **cheerleaders** need upbeat students with school spirit and athletic ability.	Tomorrow's tryout is not just a popularity contest. The cheerleading **squad** needs upbeat students with school spirit and athletic ability.

❸ Practice and Apply

A. CONCEPT CHECK: Agreement in Number

For each sentence, write the verb that agrees with the subject.

Birds of a Feather

1. A popular saying (is, are) "Opposites attract."
2. On the contrary, we (doesn't, don't) often seek relationships with people who hold values and attitudes different from our own.
3. Personality clashes (spoils, spoil) relationships.
4. Differences (creates, create) tension.
5. Typically, a talkative person (prefers, prefer) the company of other sociable people.
6. A quiet individual sometimes (feels, feel) more comfortable with fellow introverts.
7. Teens usually (selects, select) friends who are most like them.
8. They sometimes (forms, form) tight-knit groups called cliques.
9. Still, friendships (has, have) developed among those with different personalities.
10. Open communication (helps, help) all kinds of friends to get along.

➡ **For a SELF-CHECK and more practice, see the EXERCISE BANK, p. 341.**

B. PROOFREADING: Checking Subject-Verb Agreement

The following paragraph has five errors in subject-verb agreement. Rewrite the paragraph, correcting the errors.

> Sometimes the best friends is the ones you least expect. More than once I has met someone I didn't grow to like for several years. When I met my friend Kelli two years ago, she were obnoxious and I couldn't stand her. Now we hangs out almost every day! She don't seem like the same person I once met.

C. REVISING: Using Correct Subject-Verb Agreement

Return to the **Write Away** you completed on page 206. If it is written in the past tense, revise it to be in the present tense. Then make sure that your subjects and verbs agree in number.

Compound Subjects

LESSON 2

❶ Here's the Idea

A **compound subject** is made up of two or more subjects joined by a conjunction such as *and, or,* or *nor.*

Subjects Joined by *And*

▶ **A compound subject whose parts are joined by *and* usually takes a plural verb.**

Career counselors and employers match people with the right jobs.

Sometimes a compound subject joined by *and* refers to a single thing or idea, so a singular verb is used.

Law and order appeals strongly to Veronica.

Subjects Joined by *Or* or *Nor*

▶ **When the parts of a compound subject are joined by *or* or *nor*, the verb should agree with the part closest to it.**

AGREE

Neither outdoor work nor office tasks suit Matt very well.

AGREE

Neither office tasks nor outdoor work suits Matt very well.

❷ Why It Matters in Writing

When revising their work, writers sometimes reverse the order of compound subjects. When you do this in your own writing, you may need to change the verb so that it agrees with the nearer part of the subject.

Babysitting or odd jobs are what I like.

Odd jobs or babysitting is what I like.

S–V AGREEMENT

❸ Practice and Apply

A. CONCEPT CHECK: Compound Subjects

Proofread each of the following sentences to find the mistakes in subject-verb agreement. Then rewrite the sentence correctly. If a sentence contains no error, write *Correct*.

Working Ways

1. Psychologists and guidance counselors have linked personality types to occupations.
2. For example, carpentry or engineering sometimes attract introverted people.
3. Paramedics and police officers seeks adventure and risk.
4. On the other hand, structure and order suits those with good organizational ability.
5. Bookkeepers or office managers typically has stable, practical personalities.
6. Problem-solving skills and strong verbal communication is useful for judges and businesspeople.
7. Generally, neither lawyers nor the head of a company like to be told what to do.
8. Logic or good spatial perception is needed for jobs in engineering and mechanics.
9. Trial and error are one way to find the right job.
10. Neither your teacher nor your parents want to see you in a job that doesn't suit you.

➜ For a SELF-CHECK and more practice, see the EXERCISE BANK, p. 341.

B. REVISING: Making Compound Subjects and Verbs Agree

Revise the following announcement by reversing the order of the compound subjects. Make sure that the verbs agree with the new order. There are four compound subjects.

Calling All Theatrical Types

Auditions for *Hello, Dolly!* will be held on Thursday at 3 P.M. The musical score or scripts are available from Mr. Testaverde, Room 202. Actors and the lighting director report to the auditorium. Sound-effects creators and musicians come to the music room. Neither props nor a costume is needed to audition.

Agreement Problems in Sentences

① Here's the Idea

Some sentences can be tricky, such as those with subjects in unusual positions, those containing predicate nouns, or those in which prepositional phrases separate subjects and verbs. Here are some tips for choosing the correct verb forms in these situations.

Subjects in Unusual Positions

A subject can follow a verb or part of a verb phrase in a question, a sentence beginning with *here* or *there*, or a sentence in which an adjective, an adverb, or a phrase is placed first.

Madeline Albright is a first-born.

Subjects in Unusual Positions	
Type of Sentence	**Examples**
Question	Does birth **order** shape personality?
Sentence beginning with *here* or *there*	Here are some famous **first-borns** with successful careers.
Sentence beginning with phrase	From years of study come our **ideas** about birth order.

The following tips can help you find the subject in one of these kinds of sentences.

Here's How Choosing the Correct Verb

(Is, Are) **last-borns more rebellious than middle children?**

1. Turn the sentence around, putting the subject before the verb.
   Last-borns (is, are) more rebellious than middle children.

   Is Robin Williams a last-born?

2. Determine whether the subject is singular or plural.
   Last-borns (plural)

3. Make sure the subject and verb agree.
   Last-borns are more rebellious than middle children.

Predicate Nouns

In a sentence containing a predicate noun, the verb should agree with the subject, not the predicate noun.

AGREE

One interesting topic is dreams and their meaning.

AGREE

Dreams are the voice of the subconscious.

Prepositional Phrases

The subject of a verb is never found in a prepositional phrase. Don't be fooled by words that come between a subject and a verb. Mentally block out those words. Then it will be easy to tell whether the subject is singular or plural.

AGREE

This book by two psychologists describes personality traits.

AGREE

Some theories of personality development are complex.

➋ Why It Matters in Writing

Writers often use prepositional phrases to paint visual pictures. When you use a prepositional phrase between a subject and a verb, make sure that the verb agrees with the subject, not the object of the preposition.

LITERARY MODEL

At one o'clock in the morning I walked down through the same section [of San Francisco]. Everything still stood intact. There was no fire. And yet there was a change. A **rain** of ashes was falling.

PREPOSITIONAL PHRASE

—Jack London, "The Story of an Eyewitness"

❸ Practice and Apply

A. CONCEPT CHECK: Agreement Problems in Sentences

Correct problems with subject-verb agreement in the sentences below. If a sentence contains no error, write *Correct*.

Pet Personality
1. Does pets have personalities?
2. Studies of animal behavior suggest differences in temperament.
3. There is many cats and dogs with distinctive traits.
4. For example, pit bulls is an aggressive breed of terrier.
5. On the other hand, a chihuahua is a very timid dog.
6. From careful observation comes new insights into pet behavior.
7. Heredity is one factor in determining what your pet is like.
8. There is some pets with serious behavioral problems.
9. Has you ever seen a cat chew wool?
10. On local radio stations play a popular call-in show for pet owners.

→ For a SELF-CHECK and more practice, see the EXERCISE BANK, p. 342.

B. PROOFREADING AND EDITING: Correcting Agreement Errors

Find the four errors in subject-verb agreement in this paragraph. Then change the verbs to agree with the subjects.

Twin Traits
Does you know any identical twins? Then you can probably observe their obvious physical similarities. Although people commonly believe that identical twins raised apart will develop different personalities, the opposite appears to be true. From studies at the University of Minnesota have been gathered information comparing the personality traits of twins separated after birth. There are evidence that separated twins still develop similar traits. Apparently, genes is an important factor in personality development.

Indefinite Pronouns as Subjects

❶ Here's the Idea

Some pronouns do not refer to a definite, or specific, person, place, thing, or idea. These pronouns are called **indefinite pronouns.**

▶ **When used as subjects, some indefinite pronouns are always singular, some are always plural, and others can be singular or plural, depending on how they're used.**

Indefinite Pronouns			
Singular	another anything everybody neither nothing someone	anybody each everyone nobody one something	anyone either everything no one somebody
Plural	both	few	many	several
Singular or Plural	all	any	most	none	some

Singular indefinite pronouns take singular verbs.

Everyone wonders how twins get along.

Anything about twins fascinates me.

Plural indefinite pronouns take plural verbs.

Many of my friends know a pair of twins.

Several are twins themselves.

Both of the twins are wearing red robes.
Each of the twins is wearing sunglasses.

Singular or Plural?

The indefinite pronouns *all, any, most, none,* and *some* can be either singular or plural. When you use one of these words as a subject, think about the noun it refers to. If the noun is singular, use a singular verb; if it is plural, use a plural verb.

REFERS TO

Most of this book deals with twin research.

REFERS TO

All of the studies have been conducted by scientists.

Sometimes an indefinite pronoun refers to a noun in a previous sentence.

Sometimes Myla and Melissa coincidentally buy the same outfit. Both are surprised to find out.
INDEFINITE PRONOUN ↗   ↖ PLURAL VERB

❷ Why It Matters in Writing

When you write about the results of a classroom survey, you may use a number of indefinite pronouns as subjects. Using correct subject-verb agreement makes it easier for readers to understand your writing.

STUDENT MODEL

Many of the students surveyed know at least one pair of identical twins. Some feel that they cannot tell the twins apart, and a few have close friends who are twins. Of those students, all find that it gets easier to tell twins apart once they know them better.

SUBJECT

VERB

❸ Practice and Apply

A. CONCEPT CHECK: Indefinite Pronouns as Subjects

Proofread each of the following sentences. Then rewrite the sentences in which the verb does not agree with its subject. If a sentence is correct, write *Correct*.

Like Peas in a Pod

1. Some of my relatives has twins in their families.
2. Several have volunteered for twin research projects.
3. No one have explained why identical twins behave so similarly.
4. Many of the researchers believes that these twins act alike because they have the same genes.
5. Some feels that the similarities are due to a common upbringing.
6. Among twins, many have strange stories to tell.
7. Ask Royce and Brett; none of their friends likes to play certain games with them.
8. Each of the boys know what the other is thinking, so they have a competitive advantage.
9. Do anyone know how to explain this? At summer camp, twin sisters start singing in their sleep.
10. Both sing the same song!

➜ For a SELF-CHECK and more practice, see the EXERCISE BANK, p. 342.

B: WRITING: Agreement with Indefinite Pronouns

Have you seen these twins? Marian and Vivian Brown live in San Francisco. Write a caption for this photograph using indefinite pronouns. Then proofread your caption, checking for correct subject-verb agreement.

Problem Subjects

① Here's the Idea

When collective nouns, nouns ending in s, titles, and numerical expressions are used as subjects, it can be difficult to tell whether they take singular or plural verbs.

Collective Nouns

Collective nouns name groups of people or things.

Common Collective Nouns
group   class   team   staff   jury   family   committee

▶ **Many collective nouns can take singular or plural verbs, depending on how they are used.** When a collective noun refers to people or things acting as a group, it takes a singular verb.

> **The choir** performs **each year in the talent show.**
> (THE CHOIR MEMBERS ARE ACTING TOGETHER.)

When a collective noun refers to people or things acting as individuals, it takes a plural verb.

> **The choir** come **from three different schools.**
> (THE CHOIR MEMBERS ARE ACTING AS INDIVIDUALS.)

Singular Nouns Ending in *s*

▶ **Some nouns that end in *s* or *ics* look plural but are actually singular.** When used as subjects, they take singular verbs.

Singular Nouns with Plural Forms			
measles	news	politics	mathematics
physics	economics	ceramics	molasses

AGREE
> **Politics** attracts **people with strong leadership qualities.**

> **The weekend news** features **local personalities.**

Titles

▶ **Titles of works of art, literature, and music are singular.**
Even a title consisting of a plural noun takes a singular verb.

   ***The Outsiders* is a popular young-adult novel.**

Measures and Amounts

▶ **Words and phrases that express weights, measures, numbers, and lengths of time are often treated as singular.** They take singular verbs when they refer to amounts rather than numbers of individual items.

Measures and Amounts		
Measures	three cups forty miles	**Three pounds is** the approximate weight of an adult human's brain.
Amounts	two hours eight dollars	**Five hours is** a long time to wait for lunch.

A fraction can take a singular or plural verb, depending on whether it refers to a single part or to a number of items.

   One-tenth of the brain's cells are lost during a lifetime.
   (THE FRACTION REFERS TO A NUMBER OF CELLS.)

   One-half of the cerebrum controls the body's left side.
   (THE FRACTION REFERS TO ONE PART OF THE CEREBRUM.)

❷ Why It Matters in Writing

When you write about science or the history of science, you often need to use collective nouns, singular nouns that end in s, titles, weights, measures, and numbers. Be sure that your verbs agree with these problem subjects.

> **PROFESSIONAL MODEL**
>
> **Genetics,** or the study of heredity, was developed by an Austrian monk named Gregor Mendel. The **1860s** was the decade when he discovered the principles of genetics by observing that garden peas inherited traits in a way that he could predict.
>
> —Kathryn Strickland

❸ Practice and Apply

A. CONCEPT CHECK: Problem Subjects

Correct problems with subject-verb agreement in the sentences below. If a sentence contains no error, write *Correct*.

The Notion of Emotion

1. Pediatrics are the branch of medicine dealing with infants and children.

2. Our class learns the four emotions that newborns experience: excitement, surprise, relaxation, and distress.

3. Six weeks are the age when infants first express joy.

4. Twelve months is when babies first experience sadness.

5. Linguistics indicate that babies begin to imitate speech sounds at the age of eight months.

6. Two-thirds of the daycare group are absent today.

7. Five minutes seem a long time until parents arrive.

8. The family reacts to a child's different responses.

9. The public often seek advice about raising a child.

10. *Dr. Spock's Baby and Child Care* is a classic book.

➜ **For a SELF-CHECK and more practice, see the EXERCISE BANK, p. 342.**

B. WRITING: Agreement with Problem Subjects

Choose the correct verb forms to complete the sentences that interpret the bar graph.

1. Four-fifths of the children in Evansville (attends, attend) daycare.

2. One-fifth of the children (stays, stay) at home.

3. Six hours a day (is, are) the length of time two-fifths of the children spend at daycare.

Child Care in Evansville

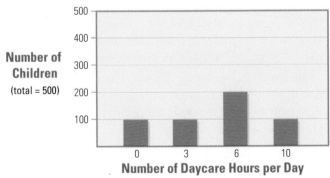

Number of Children (total = 500)

Number of Daycare Hours per Day

Grammar in Literature

Creative Writing and Subject-Verb Agreement

As you write, you may change from one tense to another. For example, you may choose to write descriptions or dialogues in the present tense. You may choose to write about past events in the past tense. When you choose to write in the present tense, you need to pay special attention to subject-verb agreement. As you read the passage from "A Mother in Mannville," notice the subjects and the verbs. Some verbs are in the present tense, others are past, but all of them agree with their subjects.

A MOTHER in MANNVILLE

by Marjorie Kinnan Rawlings

The orphanage is high in the Carolina mountains. Sometimes in winter the snowdrifts are so deep that the institution is cut off from the village below, from all the world. Fog hides the mountain peaks, the snow swirls down the valleys, and a wind blows so bitterly that the orphanage boys who take the milk twice daily to the baby cottage reach the door with fingers stiff in an agony of numbness.

"Or when we carry trays from the cook house for the ones that are sick," Jerry said, "we get our faces frostbit, because we can't put our hands over them. I have gloves," he added. "Some of the boys don't have any."

He liked the late spring, he said. The rhododendron was in bloom, a carpet of color, across the mountain-sides, soft as the May winds that stirred the hemlocks. He called it laurel.

SINGULAR SUBJECTS AND VERBS

PLURAL SUBJECTS AND VERBS

CHAPTER 9

Practice and Apply

A. DRAFTING: Using Different Tenses

The following passage from "A Mother in Mannville" is written in the past and past perfect tenses.

> He sat by the fire with me, with no other light, and told me of their two days together. The dog lay close to him and found a comfort there that I did not have for him. And it seemed to me that being with my dog, and caring for him, had brought the boy and me, too, together, so that he felt that he belonged to me as well as to the animal.

Imagine that as an author you are experimenting with the most effective tense to use for a scene like the one above. Write a version of the scene in the present tense. Notice that you need to pay attention to the subjects in order to choose the correct forms of the verbs. Check your subject-verb agreement.

B. WRITING: Description

Think of a place you know well. Write a few characteristics of that place and the people, animals, or things that you find there. Then name the actions that people, animals, or things might do. Write a description of this place in the present tense. Watch out for subject-verb agreement. Put your description in your
Working Portfolio.

Detail of *Pointer with Pheasant* (1700s), Anonymous. Benelli Collection, Florence. © Scala/Art Resource, New York.

A. Agreement in Number, Compound Subjects, and Indefinite Pronouns
Write the form of the verb that agrees with the subject of each sentence.

1. Everybody (has, have) a favorite character in a book or play.
2. Novelists and playwrights (creates, create) memorable portraits based on real or imaginary people.
3. A writer (uses, use) vivid description to bring characters to life.
4. Character traits such as honesty or shyness (is, are) developed through characterization.
5. For example, a character's own words or behavior (conveys, convey) his or her personality.
6. The words and actions of other characters also (reveals, reveal) character traits.
7. A main character usually (experiences, experience) the most development and growth.
8. Some of the most interesting characters (acts, act) courageously.
9. Many (changes, change) during the course of a novel or play.
10. A story with well-developed characters (entertains, entertain) readers.

B. Additional Agreement Problems Read the following newspaper help-wanted ad, identify the subject and verb in each sentence, and then correct the five errors in subject-verb agreement.

Do you like animals? Is you outgoing and well-spoken? Our demonstration team have a position for you.

The Pretty Pet Company seeks responsible, energetic individuals to demonstrate our exciting line of pet products. The company offer free training and flexible, part-time hours. Ten dollars are the hourly rate. Travel to pet stores throughout the tri-state area are required. For more information, please contact Mr. Finley, Ext. 315.

CHAPTER 9

Choose the letter of the best revision for each underlined section.

> The business world is highly competitive. Small businesses and
> (1)   (2)
> large corporations wants the right person for a job. Many gives
>   (3)
> personality tests to evaluate the attitudes, behavior, and skills of
> potential employees. Fifteen to thirty dollars are the average fee for
>   (4)
> a personality test. A test for high-level executives costs about $300.
>   (5)
> Since personality tests help match applicants with jobs, many
> companies use them to help in hiring. Some of these companies lose
>   (6)
> fewer employees and increase productivity. There is concerns,
>   (7)
> however, about the tests' accuracy and fairness. Critics questions
>   (8)
> whether these tests discriminate against qualified workers.

1. A. The business world are
   B. The business worlds are
   C. The business world was
   D. Correct as is

2. A. Small businesses and large
      corporations has wanted
   B. Small businesses and large
      corporations want
   C. Small businesses and large
      corporations is wanting
   D. Correct as is

3. A. Many is giving personality
      tests
   B. Many has given personality
      tests
   C. Many give personality tests
   D. Correct as is

4. A. Fifteen to thirty dollars is
      the average fee
   B. Fifteen to thirty dollars
      have been the average fee
   C. Fifteen to thirty dollars
      were the average fee
   D. Correct as is

5. A. A test for high-level
      executives cost
   B. A test for high-level
      executives are costing
   C. A test for high-level
      executives have cost
   D. Correct as is

6. A. Some of these company
      loses
   B. Some of these companies
      loses
   C. Some of these companies
      is losing
   D. Correct as is

7. A. There has been concerns
   B. There are concerns
   C. There was concerns
   D. Correct as is

8. A. Critics question
   B. Critics has questioned
   C. Critics is questioning
   D. Correct as is

Student Help Desk

Subject-Verb Agreement at a Glance

A singular subject takes a singular verb.

A plural subject takes a plural verb.

An **extrovert likes social activities.**

Introverts prefer being alone.

Subjects and Verbs

Tricky Cases

Subjects and Verbs	Tricky Cases
Verb phrase The first helping verb should agree with the subject.	**Jo** is playing darts. My **friends** are playing chess.
Prepositional phrase between subject and verb The subject of a verb is never in a prepositional phrase.	The **boys** down the street are shy.
Compound subject containing *and* Always use a plural verb.	**Soo** and **Meg** talk all the time.
Compound subject containing *or or nor* The verb should agree with the part of the subject closest to it.	Neither my **parents** nor my **sister** enjoys music.
Indefinite pronoun as subject Singular pronouns take singular verbs; plural pronouns take plural verbs. Some pronouns can be singular or plural.	**Everyone** thinks about the brain. **Few** understand it. **Most** of the research focuses on disorders. **Most** of the studies focus on disorders.
Collective noun Use a singular verb if it refers to a whole, a plural verb if it refers to individuals.	The **group** meets on Saturday. The **group** argue about the meeting time.
Singular noun ending in *s* Use a singular verb.	**Genetics** deals with inherited traits.
Title or amount Usually use a singular verb.	***Strange Personalities*** is my favorite book.

Other Agreement Problems

How to Deal with *Slippery* Subjects

Predicate noun Make sure the verb agrees with the subject.	**Teenagers** are the population with many identity questions. The **population** with many identity questions is teenagers.
Question Change the question to a statement to find the subject.	(Is, Are) personality tests a useful tool? Personality **tests** are a useful tool.
Sentence beginning with • *Here* or *There* • **phrase** Turn the sentence around to find the subject.	Here (is, are) a popular psychology course. A popular psychology **course** is here. On the shelf (is, are) stacked textbooks. **Textbooks** are stacked on the shelf.

The Bottom Line

Checklist for Subject-Verb Agreement

Have I . . .

____ used a singular verb with a singular subject?

____ used a plural verb with a plural subject?

____ made the helping verb in a verb phrase agree with the subject?

____ used a plural verb with compound subjects joined by *and?*

____ made the verb agree with the closest part of a compound subject joined by *or* or *nor?*

____ checked whether indefinite-pronoun subjects are singular or plural?

____ used singular verbs with subjects that are titles, measures, or amounts?

____ made verbs agree with subjects in unusual positions?

Capitalization

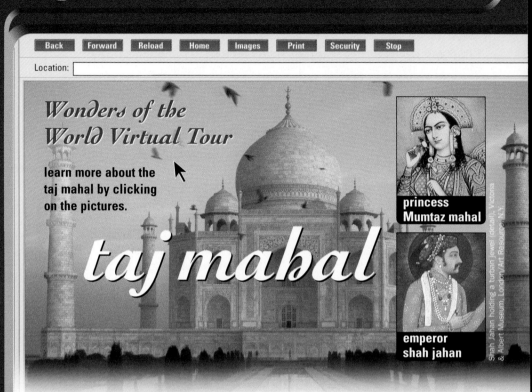

| Back | Forward | Reload | Home | Images | Print | Security | Stop |

Location:

Wonders of the World Virtual Tour

learn more about the taj mahal by clicking on the pictures.

taj mahal

princess Mumtaz mahal

emperor shah jahan

Shah Jahan holding a turban jewel (detail), Victoria & Albert Museum, London/Art Resource, N.Y.

Theme: Wonders of the World
Passport to the Wonders

If you were writing a report on man-made wonders, would you use the Web page shown on this page as a reliable source? Most people would probably not trust it because there are too many capitalization errors on the page. The rules of capitalization are just as important as spelling and grammar rules.

Write Away: Just Wonder

The Taj Mahal is considered one of the world's most beautiful and famous tombs. In a short paragraph, describe a place that you find amazing. It could be an interesting public building, a breathtaking natural area, or an unusual amusement park. Save your paragraph in your ▱ **Working Portfolio.**

Diagnostic Test: What Do You Know?

For each underlined passage, choose the letter of the correct revision.

> The Taj mahal, considered a man-made wonder, symbolizes the
> (1)   (2)
> country of india. It was built by Shah jahan, Mogul emperor of
>   (3)   (4)
> India, in memory of his wife Mumtaz Mahal. He had vowed to
>   (5)
> build her the most beautiful tomb ever imagined. He chose a site
> by the Jumna river in agra, India, and consulted with craftsmen
>   (6)   (7)
> from All over central Asia and european experts from France and
>   (8)   (9)
> Italy. With its slender towers and onion-shaped dome, an islamic
> symbol of both womanhood and paradise, the Taj Mahal has a
>   (10)
> fairytale quality. The white marble of the monument seems to take
> on different personalities at different times of the day. The inside
> of the tomb is decorated with carved marble screens inlaid with
> precious and semiprecious stones.

1. A. taj mahal
   B. taj Mahal
   C. Taj Mahal
   D. Correct as is

2. A. Symbolizes
   B. Country
   C. India
   D. Correct as is

3. A. Shah Jahan
   B. shah jahan
   C. shah Jahan
   D. Correct as is

4. A. Emperor of India
   B. Emperor of india
   C. emperor of india
   D. Correct as is

5. A. wife mumtaz mahal
   B. Wife Mumtaz mahal
   C. Wife Mumtaz Mahal
   D. Correct as is

6. A. The Jumna River
   B. the Jumna River
   C. the jumna river
   D. Correct as is

7. A. Agra, India, and Consulted
   B. Agra, India, and consulted
   C. Agra, India, And consulted
   D. Correct as is

8. A. all Over Central Asia
   B. all over central asia
   C. all over central Asia
   D. Correct as is

9. A. European Experts
   B. france and italy
   C. European experts
   D. Correct as is

10. A. Islamic Symbol
    B. Islamic symbol
    C. Womanhood and Paradise
    D. Correct as is

People and Cultures

LESSON 1

❶ Here's the Idea

Names and Initials

▶ **Capitalize people's names and initials.**

Cleopatra	**J.R.R.** Tolkien
Maria Theresa	Yasunari Kawabata

Personal Titles and Abbreviations

▶ **Capitalize titles and abbreviations of titles that are used before names and in direct address.**

Professor Anita Jones	Dr. Celia Brammer
Cardinal Richelieu	General Dwight D. Eisenhower

Mr. and Ms. Romer wrote a book entitled *The Seven Wonders of the World.*

Capitalize abbreviations of some titles when they follow names.

Ted Stein, **Jr.**	Sonia Rodriguez, **M.D.**
Mary Witt, **Ph.D.**	Meridyth Palmer, **D.D.S.**

▶ **Capitalize titles of heads of state, royalty, or nobility only when they are used before persons' names or in place of persons' names.**

Queen Marie Antoinette	Sir Thomas Browne

Chief Justice William H. Rehnquist

The temple of Artemis at Ephesus was built by King Croesus.

Do not capitalize titles when they are used without proper names.

The king will be remembered for his contributions to great architecture.

The Ruins at Ephesus

Family Relationships

▶ **Capitalize words indicating family relationships only when they are used as names or before names.**

Aunt Paula   Cousin Sue   Grandpa Klein

Dad and Mom would like to see the Great Pyramid in Egypt.

In general, do not capitalize a word indicating a family relationship when it follows the person's name or is used without a proper name.

Maria Tellez, my cousin, saw the Great Pyramid.

My aunt and uncle will see the Leaning Tower of Pisa.

The Pronoun *I*

▶ **Always capitalize the pronoun *I*.**

Grandpa and I read all about Stonehenge.

Religious Terms

▶ **Capitalize the names of religions, sacred days, sacred writings, and deities.**

Religions and Religious Terms	
Religions	Christianity, Hinduism, Judaism
Sacred days	Ramadan, Good Friday, Purim
Sacred writings	Bible, Koran, Torah
Deities	God, Yahweh, Allah

Do not capitalize the words *god* and *goddess* when they refer to gods of ancient mythology.

The statue of Zeus at Olympia honored the Greek god Zeus.

Nationalities, Languages, and Races

▶ **Capitalize the names of nationalities, languages, races, and most ethnic groups, as well as the adjectives formed from these names.**

Romans	Masai	Greek
Incan	African-American	Egyptian

❷ Practice and Apply

CONCEPT CHECK: People and Cultures

Write the words, abbreviations, and initials that should be capitalized in the paragraph below, and capitalize each correctly. If a sentence has no errors, write the word *Correct*.

Vanished Wonders

(1) In the book *Wonders of the World*, giovanni caselli gives a history of the Colossus of Rhodes. **(2)** The Colossus of Rhodes was a huge statue of helios, the Greek sun god. **(3)** After the people of Rhodes survived an invasion by the macedonians, they commissioned the greek sculptor chares to build the Colossus. **(4)** chares, a student of the famous sculptor Lysippus, worked on the bronze statue for about 12 years around 300 B.C. **(5)** The historian a. j. higgins believes the statue measured 120 feet in height. **(6)** The Colossus, i discovered, was nearly as tall as the Statue of Liberty. **(7)** The greeks weren't the only people to claim one of the ancient wonders; sometime between 283 B.C. and 246 B.C. the egyptians built the Pharos of Alexandria (also called the Lighthouse of Alexandria). **(8)** It was built during the reign of ptolemy II and designed by the greek architect sostratus. **(9)** The lighthouse may have been nearly 400 feet tall (larger than the Colossus and the Statue of Liberty), but an earthquake destroyed it after it had stood for almost 1,500 years.

Lighthouse of Alexandria

➡ For a SELF-CHECK and more practice, see the EXERCISE BANK, p. 343.

CHAPTER 10

First Words and Titles

LESSON 2

❶ Here's the Idea

Sentences and Poetry

▶ **Capitalize the first word of every sentence.**

The "seven wonders of the medieval world" date back to the Middle Ages.

▶ **In traditional poetry capitalize the first word of every line.**

> **LITERARY MODEL**
>
> The willow is like an etching,
> Fine-lined against the sky.
> The ginkgo is like a crude sketch,
> Hardly worthy to be signed.
>
> —Eve Merriam, "Simile: Willow and Ginkgo"

Modern poets sometimes choose not to begin each line of their poems with capital letters. If you make this choice in your own writing, make sure the meaning of your work is still clear.

Quotations

▶ **Capitalize the first word of a direct quotation if it begins a complete sentence.**

My teacher asked, "Has anyone read about the Colosseum?"

▶ **In a divided quotation, do not capitalize the first word of the second part unless it starts a new sentence.**

"I hear you're going to Italy," Theresa said. "Make sure you see the Leaning Tower of Pisa."

"Did you know," asked Theresa, "that the Leaning Tower has been tilting for 800 years?"

Outlines

▶ **Capitalize the first word of each entry in an outline and the letters that introduce major subsections.**

I. Famous buildings of the Middle Ages
  A. The Leaning Tower of Pisa
    1. Construction of bell tower
    2. Repairs to tower foundation
  B. The Tower of London
    1. Construction of royal fortress
    2. Additions to original site

Parts of a Letter

▶ **Capitalize the first word in the greeting and in the closing of a letter.**

Dear Ms. Song: Yours truly,

Leaning Tower of Pisa

Titles

▶ **Capitalize the first word, the last word, and all other important words in a title. Don't capitalize articles, coordinating conjunctions, or prepositions of fewer than five letters.**

Type of Media	Examples
Books	*The House of Dies Drear*, *A Wrinkle in Time*
Plays and musicals	*The Phantom of the Opera*, *The Miracle Worker*
Short stories	"The Tell-Tale Heart," "The Bet"
Poems	"Legacies," "Jazz Fantasia"
Magazines and newspapers	*YM*, *Next Generation*, *The New York Times*
Musical compositions	Beethoven's Fifth Symphony," "Jingle Bells"
Movies	*The Lion King*, *The Wizard of Oz*, *Home Alone*
Television shows	*The Practice*, *Dateline NBC*, *Total Request Live*
Works of art	*Starry Night*, *Venus de Milo*
Games	Warzone, TV Trivia, Brain Busters

❷ Practice and Apply

A. CONCEPT CHECK: First Words and Titles

Write the words that should be capitalized in each sentence.
Do not write words that are already capitalized.

> **The Secrets of Stonehenge**
> **1.** Kendra asked the tour guide, "what is Stonehenge?"
> **2.** The tour guide responded, "it is an ancient monument on
> a plain in England, composed of huge rough-cut stones
> set in a circle."
> **3.** "why are the stones there?" she continued. "what is their
> purpose?"
> **4.** the guide answered, "that's something that no one knows."
> **5.** "we do know that the ancient people who built
> Stonehenge were building something of great
> importance," she added. "It was probably used as a
> tribal gathering place."
> **6.** She continued, "there is also evidence that the stones
> were used as some sort of huge astronomical calendar."
> **7.** The meaning of Stonehenge was first discussed around
> 1139 in the book *history of the kings of Britain*.
> **8.** A modern book titled *stonehenge complete* covers every
> detail concerning the ancient monument.
> **9.** Writer Henry James once wrote about Stonehenge, "you
> may put a hundred questions to these rough-hewn giants as
> they bend in grim contemplation of their fallen
> companions."
> **10.** An outline for stone
> circles in England might
> begin like this:
> I. stone circles in England
>   A. stonehenge
>   B. Avebury
>
> ➡ For a SELF-CHECK and more
> practice, see the EXERCISE
> BANK, p. 344.

Stonehenge

B. WRITING: A Trip to the Stones

Write a letter to a travel agency, inquiring if its tours of England
go to any stone-circle sites, such as Stonehenge. Remember
to capitalize the first word in the greeting and in the closing of
your letter.

Places and Transportation

LESSON 3

❶ Here's the Idea

Geographical Names

▶ **In geographical names, capitalize each word except articles and prepositions.**

Geographical Names	
Divisions of the world	Southern Hemisphere, Continental Divide, Tropic of Cancer
Continents	Africa, North America, Australia
Bodies of water	Mediterranean Sea, Gulf of Mexico, Indian Ocean
Islands	Java, Bahamas, Easter Island
Mountains	Mount Everest, Sierra Nevada, Mount Olympus
Other landforms	Victoria Falls, Grand Canyon, Gobi Desert
Regions	Latin America, Southeast Asia, New England
Countries/nations	Greece, Italy, China, England
States	North Carolina, Maine, Colorado, Texas
Cities/towns	San Francisco, Miami, Fort Wayne, Austin
Roads and streets	Interstate 90, North Street, Prairie Road

Bodies of the Universe

▶ **Capitalize the names of planets and other specific objects in the universe.**

Big Dipper   Pluto   North Star

Do not capitalize *sun* and *moon*. Do not capitalize *earth* when it is preceded by *the* and when it does not refer to the planet Earth.

Ants and earwigs tunneled through the earth under the porch.

> **Venus is called Earth's twin.**

CHAPTER 10

Regions and Sections

▶ Capitalize the words *north, south, east,* and *west* when they name particular regions of the United States or the world or when they are parts of proper names.

The Golden Gate Bridge, the Empire State Building, and the Houston Astrodome are all modern wonders found in **N**orth America.

The Grand Canyon is one of the most popular tourist attractions in the **W**est.

 Do not capitalize these words when they indicate general directions or locations.

The Statue of Liberty is **s**outh of the Empire State Building in New York City.

Buildings, Bridges, and Other Landmarks

▶ Capitalize the names of specific buildings, bridges, monuments, and other landmarks.

Sears **T**ower   **G**reat **W**all of **C**hina

Big **B**en   **T**acoma **N**arrows **B**ridge

Many people consider the **S**ydney **O**pera **H**ouse in Sydney, Australia, to be a modern wonder.

Planes, Trains, and Other Vehicles

▶ Capitalize the names of specific airplanes, trains, ships, cars, and spacecraft.

Vehicle Names	
Airplanes	*Air Force One, Memphis Belle*
Trains	*Orient Express, City of New Orleans*
Ships	*Mayflower, Niña, Seawise Giant*
Cars	*Cavalier, Taurus, Grand Prix*
Spacecraft	*Sputnik, Challenger, Voyager 2*

❷ Practice and Apply

A. CONCEPT CHECK: Places and Transportation

Write the words that should be capitalized in the paragraph below and capitalize them correctly. Do not write words that are already capitalized.

The Wonders of France

(1) As the plane flew over the atlantic ocean, I read a book about the modern wonders that can be found in France. **(2)** Of course, I knew about the eiffel tower, which attracts more than 6 million visitors each year. **(3)** I also knew about versailles, which is 4 miles southwest of Paris. **(4)** Versailles is the home of the Grand palace of versailles, which was the creation of King Louis XIV, the Sun King. **(5)** However, back in Paris, the Sacré-coeur (Church of the Sacred heart) is also considered by many to be a modern wonder. **(6)** On the bank of the seine river, in downtown Paris, lies a controversial building. **(7)** Completed in 1977, the pompidou center is a famous example of high-tech architecture. **(8)** Finally, the fifth modern wonder is the pyramid-shaped entrance of the louvre Museum, which was constructed in the 1980s.

➡ **For a SELF-CHECK and more practice, see the EXERCISE BANK, p. 344.**

B. WRITING: Description

Write a short paragraph in which you use the facts below and the picture of the Hall of Mirrors to describe the Palace of Versailles.

Palace of Versailles
- about 1,300 rooms
- about 1,400 fountains
- 250 acres of gardens, lawns, and woods
- contains a royal chapel and a private theater
- took more than 40 years to complete

Organizations and Other Subjects

1 Here's the Idea

Organizations and Institutions

▶ **Capitalize all important words in the names of organizations, institutions, stores, and companies.**

> **M**uir **M**iddle **S**chool   **D**ave's **H**ardware
>
> **P**eace **C**orps   **N**ational **P**ark **S**ervice
>
> **N**iagara **F**alls **H**ospital   **S**ierra **C**lub

Do not capitalize words such as *hospital, school, company, church,* and *college* when they are not used as parts of names.

The renovations in our **c**hurch are now complete.

Organization and Business Abbreviations

▶ **Capitalize abbreviations of names of organizations, businesses, and institutions. Notice that these abbreviations are formed from the initial letters of the complete names and that the letters are usually not followed by periods.**

> **NFL** (National Football League)
>
> **MADD** (Mothers Against Drunk Driving)
>
> **NASA** (National Aeronautics and Space Administration)
>
> **USMC** (United States Marine Corps)

Historical Events, Periods, and Documents

▶ **Capitalize the names of historical events, periods, and documents.**

Historical Events, Periods, and Documents	
Events	Revolutionary War, Trail of Tears, Boston Massacre
Periods	Great Awakening, Roaring Twenties, Renaissance
Documents	National Environmental Policy Act, Treaty of Versailles

Thomas Jefferson wrote the **D**eclaration of **I**ndependence.

Time Abbreviations and Calendar Items

▶ **Capitalize the abbreviations B.C., A.D., A.M., and P.M.**

Niagara Falls, one of the natural wonders of the world, was probably formed around 10,000 **B.C.**

▶ **Capitalize the names of months, days, and holidays but not the names of seasons.**

April   **S**aturday   **A**rbor **D**ay

May   **T**uesday   spring

Mexico's Paricutín volcano appeared from a crack in the earth in a cornfield on **F**ebruary 20, 1943.

 When a season is used in the title of a festival or celebration (**G**rove **F**all **F**estival), capitalize all important words, including the season.

School Subjects and Class Names

▶ **Capitalize the names of school subjects only when they are names of languages, when they are followed by course numbers, or when they contain proper adjectives.**

algebra   **G**erman **L**iterature

Spanish   **B**iology **II**

▶ **Capitalize the words *freshman, sophomore, junior,* or *senior* only when they are used as parts of titles.**

The freshmen will attend **F**reshman **O**rientation **W**eek the last week in August.

Special Events, Awards, and Brand Names

▶ **Capitalize the names of special events and awards.**

Academy **A**wards   **P**ulitzer **P**rize

Nobel **P**rize   **W**orld **C**up

Ray and Abby are planning to watch the **S**uper **B**owl.

▶ **Capitalize the brand names of products but not common nouns that follow brand names.**

Fiji compasses   **S**taton tents

❷ Practice and Apply

A. CONCEPT CHECK: Organizations and Other Subjects

For each sentence, write the words that should be capitalized.

> **Saving National Forests and Parks**
> 1. Preservation of forests and parks has become an important issue for students at springhill middle school.
> 2. September is preservation awareness month.
> 3. Students who belong to the forest and park preservation society (fpps) hold annual fundraisers and give presentations about the organization.
> 4. Last year troy's auto shop donated $1,000.
> 5. On saturday, september 27, we will hold our first autumn day fest; we hope to raise $10,000.

→ **For a SELF-CHECK and more practice, see the EXERCISE BANK, p. 345.**

B. PROOFREADING: The Great Outdoors

Find and correct the errors in capitalization in the event calendar page below.

Grand Canyon National Park

July 2	Monday	9:00 a.m. hike at Bright Angel Point 7:00 P.M. sierra club presentation
July 3	Tuesday	7:00 P.M. flagstaff Middle School Independence day celebration
July 4	Wednesday	Independence day 9:00 p.m. fireworks
July 5	thursday	9:00 A.M. Audubon society hike at South Kaibab
July 6	Friday	7:00 p.m. National park service presentation at amphitheater
July 7	Saturday	1:00 p.m. national wildlife federation presentation at Desert View
July 8	Sunday	10:00 a.m. Izaak Walton league hike at Hermit's Rest

Grammar in Math

Using Correct Capitalization

When you write about the geometry of famous architecture, remember that correct capitalization helps clearly identify specific people, places, and things. Notice the capitalization highlighted in the following exercise.

Section 4 **Circles and Circumference**

The Circus Maximus

Setting the Stage

One of the wonders of the **R**oman **E**mpire was the **C**ircus **M**aximus. This enormous arena was the largest gathering place in ancient **R**ome, seating 250,000 screaming spectators. As many as 20 four-horse chariots raced around the low wall which ran down the middle of the arena.

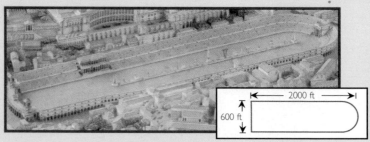

Think About It

1 Describe the shape of the track where the chariots raced.

2 How can you estimate the perimeter of the **C**ircus **M**aximus? How can you estimate the length of the curved part of the building?

3 The **A**strodome in **H**ouston, **T**exas, holds 60,000 people. About how many times as many people did the **C**ircus **M**aximus hold?

Practice and Apply

A. CAPITALIZING CORRECTLY

A **scale** is the ratio of a measurement on a model or a drawing to the corresponding measurement on the actual object. Study the diagram on page 242. Then use the scale 1 in. : 200 ft and your ruler and compass to make a scale drawing of the Circus Maximus. Label your drawing with the actual measurements, and write a brief caption based on the information on page 242.

B. WRITING: Using Capitalization in Math

With a small group of classmates, do some research and create a scale drawing or a scale model of one of the following structures:

• an architectural wonder in your community or state

• the Great Wall of China

• the Taj Mahal

• the Great Pyramid at Giza

Using correct capitalization, write a brief caption for your drawing or model. Include the location of the structure, its measurements, and other important information.

Save your drawings and captions in your 🗀 **Working Portfolio.**

CAPITALIZATION

The Great Wall of China

The Great Pyramid at Giza

The Taj Mahal

Mixed Review

A. Proofreading: Capitalization Identify and correct the 11 capitalization errors in the following paragraph.

STUDENT MODEL

The Channel Tunnel, which many people consider a modern wonder, was opened in may 1994. It links the towns of folkestone, England, and coquelles, France, via a tunnel that is 31 miles long—24 miles of which are 130 feet under the seabed of the english channel! Cars, buses, and trucks drive onto high-speed electric trains for the trip through the Channel Tunnel. Passengers also ride on high-speed electric trains. The company that operates the Channel Tunnel is called eurotunnel, so the Channel Tunnel is called the eurotunnel, too. Although the shore-to-shore part of the trip takes only 35 minutes, the trip east from london to Paris is three hours long. If you left London at 9:00 a.m., you would be in paris by lunchtime.

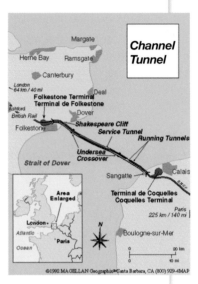

B. Capitalization of Book Titles Capitalize the following book titles correctly.

Wonders of the World Books
1. *the seven wonders of the ancient world*
2. *the stonehenge people*
3. *the world of the pharaohs*
4. *the empire state building*
5. *the great wall of china*

C. Revising: Capitalizing Important Words Look at the Web page on page 228. Using the capitalization rules in this chapter, identify and correct the ten capitalization errors. Each incorrect letter counts as one error.

For each underlined passage, choose the letter of the correct revision.

the first reference to making a list of notable places to visit was
(1)
written by herodotus in the fifth century b.c. About a century later,
(2)   (3)
when alexander the Great conquered most of the known world,
(4)
several greek writers, including antipater of Sidon, began
(5)   (6)
compiling lists of places that no traveler should miss. These lists
were eventually combined to make a list of the seven wonders of
the ancient world. Of these seven, all but the Great pyramid are
(7)
now gone. At some point during the middle Ages, another list
(8)
appeared, of the seven wonders of the medieval world, which
included some of the ancient marvels and some from the Middle
Ages, such as the Leaning Tower of pisa and the Great Wall of
(9)   (10)
China.

1. A. The first Reference
   B. The first reference
   C. The First Reference
   D. Correct as is

2. A. Was written by Herodotus
   B. was written by Herodotus
   C. was written By Herodotus
   D. Correct as is

3. A. Fifth Century B.C.
   B. fifth Century b.c.
   C. fifth century B.C.
   D. Correct as is

4. A. Alexander the great
   B. Alexander The Great
   C. Alexander the Great
   D. Correct as is

5. A. several Greek Writers
   B. several greek Writers
   C. several Greek writers
   D. Correct as is

6. A. Antipater of Sidon,
   B. Antipater of sidon,
   C. Antipater Of Sidon,
   D. Correct as is

7. A. The Great Pyramid
   B. the Great Pyramid
   C. the great Pyramid
   D. Correct as is

8. A. the Middle Ages
   B. the Middle ages
   C. The Middle ages
   D. Correct as is

9. A. Leaning tower of pisa
   B. leaning tower of pisa
   C. Leaning Tower of Pisa
   D. Correct as is

10. A. Great wall of China
    B. great wall of china
    C. great wall of China
    D. Correct as is

Student Help Desk

Capitalization at a Glance

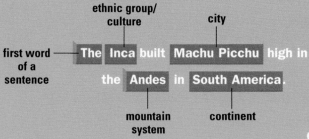

first word of a sentence — The [Inca] built [Machu Picchu] high in the [Andes] in [South America].

ethnic group/ culture — Inca

city — Machu Picchu

mountain system — Andes

continent — South America

Always Capitalize

Wonders of Capitalization

Proper nouns that name particular people, places, or things:

Mr. **S**chultz is taking the sixth grade class to the **G**rand **C**anyon.

Family words used with names or in place of names:

Asha listened as **U**ncle **A**sad told her about the Taj Mahal.

The first word of a sentence:

Did you read the book *Wonders of the World*?

The first word in every line of traditional poetry:

Whose woods these are I think I know.
His house is in the village, though;
He will not see me stopping here
To watch his woods fill up with snow.
　　　　—Robert Frost, "Stopping by Woods on a Snowy Evening"

The first word and all of the important words in a title:

The True Confessions of Charlotte Doyle

Proper nouns that name particular dates, holidays, events, or awards:

On **S**eptember 6, **L**abor **D**ay, our school is holding the annual **C**hampions **V**olleyball **T**ournament.

Never Capitalize

Ruins of Capitalization

Common nouns that name people, places, or things:
Our **c**oach is taking us on a tour of the **p**ark.

Family words used as common nouns:
My **a**unt bought a souvenir at a shop in the Empire State Building.

Word(s) after the first word of a closing in a letter:
Yours **t**ruly,   Sincerely **y**ours,

Articles, conjunctions, and short prepositions:
"How **t**o Paint **t**he Most Captivating Portrait **o**f **a** Bird"

Calendar items if they name a season:
Every **w**inter our school has a skiing contest on the slopes.

The Bottom Line

Checklist for Capitalization

Have I capitalized . . .

____ people's names and initials?

____ personal titles and religious terms?

____ names of ethnic groups, languages, cultures, and races?

____ names of bodies of the universe?

____ names of monuments, bridges, and other landmarks?

____ names of particular planes, trains, and other vehicles?

____ names of historical events, eras, and documents?

____ names of special events, awards, and product brands?

____ names of organizations, institutions, businesses, and their abbreviations?

____ names of school subjects when they contain a proper noun or proper adjective and class names when they are used as proper nouns?

Punctuation

What did you get Celia?

Theme: A History of Communication

Birthday Messages

Is the brother asking his sister what kind of present she bought Celia? Or is he asking Celia what kind of present she just opened?

If you heard the brother speaking, you could probably tell what he meant; however, to communicate clearly in writing, you need punctuation. A comma after the word *get* would tell you that the brother is talking to Celia.

Write Away: What's Your Point?

What kind of communication do you use? You might dash off a quick e-mail message for a friend's birthday, or you might write a birthday song or a poem. Write a birthday message to a friend or family member. Put your writing into your 📁 **Working Portfolio.**

Diagnostic Test: What Do You Know?

For each numbered item, choose the letter of the best revision.

Historians are not sure when the first books appeared, but evidence shows that they were written as early as 2700 B.C. in <u>Egypt?</u> These ancient <u>books, however</u> were made differently from
(1)   (2)
the books we use today. For <u>instance Egyptians</u> recorded facts
(3)
of their daily lives on scrolls made of <u>papyrus (a</u> material crafted
(4)
from papyrus stems). In Babylonia, people made marks on <u>soft clay</u>
(5)
<u>tablets</u> to document personal and cultural events. The <u>Babylonian's</u>
(6)
tablets relate information in the following <u>areas; business</u>, law,
(7)
government, and family life. Experts indicate <u>that "during</u> A.D. 300,
(8)
people made bound texts that resemble our own modern books. By the Middle Ages, some books, such as a copy of <u>"The Canterbury</u>
(9)
<u>Tales"</u> now in <u>London, England</u> included rich decorations.
(10)

1. A. Egypt!
   B. Egypt,
   C. Egypt.
   D. Correct as is

2. A. books however
   B. books, however,
   C. books however,
   D. Correct as is

3. A. instance, Egyptians
   B. instance, Egyptians,
   C. instance; Egyptians
   D. Correct as is

4. A. papyrus—a
   B. papyrus-a
   C. papyrus: a
   D. Correct as is

5. A. soft, clay, tablets
   B. soft, clay tablets
   C. soft, clay, tablets,
   D. Correct as is

6. A. Babylonians'
   B. Babylonians's
   C. Babylonians
   D. Correct as is

7. A. areas' business
   B. area's business
   C. areas: business
   D. Correct as is

8. A. that during
   B. "that during
   C. "that, during
   D. Correct as is

9. A. *"The Canterbury Tales"*
   B. *The Canterbury Tales*
   C. The Canterbury Tales
   D. Correct as is

10. A. London, England,
    B. London England
    C. London England,
    D. Correct as is

Periods and Other End Marks

❶ Here's the Idea

Periods, question marks, and exclamation points are known as **end marks** because they are used to indicate the end of a sentence. Periods have other uses as well.

Periods

▶ **Use a period at the end of a declarative sentence.** A declarative sentence makes a statement.

> The general wrote a message to the president **.**

▶ **Use a period at the end of almost every imperative sentence.** An imperative sentence gives a command. Some imperative sentences express excitement or emotion and therefore end with exclamation points.

> Take this message to the president **.**
> Wait **!** Use the faster horse **!**

▶ **Use a period at the end of an indirect question.**
An indirect question reports what a person asked without using the person's exact words.

> DIRECT   The aide asked, "Which route should I take, sir **?** "
>
> INDIRECT   The aide asked the general which route to take **.**

Question Marks

▶ **Use a question mark at the end of an interrogative sentence.** An interrogative sentence asks a question.

> Where are the maps **?**
> How soon can you pack and be ready to go **?**

Exclamation Points

▶ **Use an exclamation point to end an exclamatory sentence.** An exclamatory sentence expresses strong feeling.

The maps are missing**!** We're in trouble now**!**

▶ **Use an exclamation point after an interjection or any other exclamatory expression.**

What**!** Where could they be?

Quick**!** Search the woods for spies**!**

Other Uses of Periods

▶ **Use a period at the end of most abbreviations and initials.**

Common Abbreviations and Initials

Abbreviations

sec. second	**Dr.** Doctor	**Jr.** Junior	**tsp.** teaspoon
min. minute	**Oct.** October	**N.** North	**in.** inch
hr. hour	**Mon.** Monday	**Ave.** Avenue	**Co.** Company

Initials

P.O. post office	**A.M.** *ante meridiem* (before noon)
M.D. doctor of medicine	**U.S.A.** United States of America
B.A. bachelor of arts	**A.E.S.** Ann Elizabeth Stevens

Abbreviations Without Periods

CD compact disc	**TV** television
ER emergency room	**mph** miles per hour
MN Minnesota	**km** kilometer

▶ **Use a period after each number or letter in an outline or a list.**

Outline

Early Communication
I. Visual
   A. Sign language
   B. Writing
II. Oral
   A. Speech
   B. Song

List

Methods of Communication
1. Writing
2. Speaking
3. Sign language
4. Semaphores
5. Codes
6. Body language

❷ Practice and Apply

A. CONCEPT CHECK: Periods and Other End Marks

Write the words from the paragraph that should be followed by periods, question marks, or exclamation points. Include these punctuation marks in your answers.

Run till You Drop

Did you know that the modern marathon comes from ancient Greek history In 490 B.C., Greek military leaders ordered a young soldier, Pheidippides, to carry the news of their conquest of Persian armies The poor fellow He had to run from the city of Marathon to Athens, nearly 40 km (about twenty-six miles) Can you imagine running that distance When he finally arrived in Athens, Pheidippides shouted to the people, "Rejoice, we conquer" Unfortunately, he was unable to give more information because he immediately collapsed and died. How awful Aren't you glad that we have easier ways of sending messages

➔ For a SELF-CHECK and more practice, see the EXERCISE BANK, p. 346.

B. REVISING: A Message from a Machine

The computer below has written a message. Unfortunately, the message doesn't contain any end marks. Rewrite it, adding periods, question marks, and exclamation points where needed.

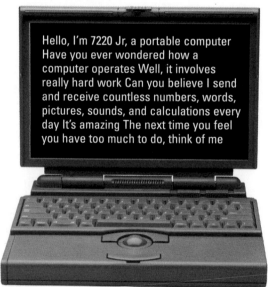

Hello, I'm 7220 Jr, a portable computer Have you ever wondered how a computer operates Well, it involves really hard work Can you believe I send and receive countless numbers, words, pictures, sounds, and calculations every day It's amazing The next time you feel you have too much to do, think of me

Commas in Sentences

❶ Here's the Idea

Commas are used to separate certain parts of sentences.

Commas in Compound Sentences

▶ **Use a comma before a conjunction that joins independent clauses in a compound sentence.**

Most people know Thomas Edison for his creation of the light bulb **,** **but** he also developed many communication devices.

Edison's inventions were completely new **,** **or** they were refined versions of older works.

Alexander Graham Bell devised the modern telephone **,** **and** Edison improved it by adding a stronger vocal transmitter.

 Sometimes a sentence has a compound verb but is not a compound sentence. Do not use a comma in this kind of sentence.

Edison also **constructed a model** and **tested the first phonograph.**

Commas with Items in a Series

▶ **Use a comma after every item in a series except the last one.** A series consists of three or more items.

Curiosity , ingenuity , and **determination** were qualities that helped shape Edison's career.

Edison's phonograph mainly consisted of **a metal disk , a steel needle ,** and **a rotating cylinder.**

In time, Edison's recording mechanism generated other inventions: **dictation machines , musical records ,** and **talking dolls.**

Thomas Edison in his famous laboratory.

PUNCTUATION

▶ **Use commas between two or more adjectives of equal rank that modify the same noun.**

Inventors are creative , practical people.

To decide whether to use a comma between two adjectives modifying the same noun, try the following tests.

> **Here's How** Adding Commas Between Adjectives
>
> **In his youth, Edison was a likable clever prankster.**
>
> 1. Place the word *and* between the adjectives.
>   **In his youth, Edison was a likable and clever prankster.**
> 2. If the sentence still makes sense, replace *and* with a comma.
>   **In his youth, Edison was a likable , clever prankster.**
> 3. Another test is to reverse the order of the adjectives.
>   **In his youth, Edison was a clever likable prankster.**
> 4. If the meaning of the sentence hasn't changed, use a comma.
>   **In his youth, Edison was a likable , clever prankster.**

Commas with Introductory Words and Phrases

▶ **Use a comma after an introductory word or phrase to separate it from the rest of the sentence.**

Slowly, Edison learned to use the telegraph.

Hampered by poor hearing, he invented the repeating telegraph.

Commas with Interrupters

▶ **Use commas to set off words or phrases that interrupt, or break, the flow of thought in a sentence.**

Edison, at last, could pick up whole telegraph messages.

Commas with Nouns of Direct Address

▶ **Use commas to set off nouns of direct address.** A noun of direct address names the person or group being spoken to.

Tell us, Kyla, how Edison helped the movie industry.

CHAPTER 11

254 Grammar, Usage, and Mechanics

Commas with Appositives

An **appositive** is a word or phrase that identifies or renames a noun or pronoun that comes right before it. Use commas when the appositive adds extra information; do not use commas when the appositive is needed to make the meaning clear.

Thomas Edison**, an American inventor,** is responsible for many patents. (The phrase *an American inventor* adds extra information.)

The American inventor **Thomas Edison** had patents for 1,093 inventions. (The phrase *Thomas Edison* tells which inventor and makes the sentence clear and complete.)

Commas to Avoid Confusion

▶ **Use a comma whenever the reader might otherwise be confused.**

UNCLEAR   Edison built a huge laboratory for inventing his life's work.

CLEAR   Edison built a huge laboratory for inventing , his life's work.

❷ Practice and Apply

CONCEPT CHECK: Commas in Sentences

Write the words and numbers from the paragraph that should be followed by commas.

Messages over the Air

Radio waves were discovered in 1888 and Guglielmo Marconi first used them to send messages in the 1890s. Although many claimed the credit, the first voice heard on the radio belonged to Reginald Fessendens. In 1906 Fessenden a physicist born in Canada spoke from Massachusetts to ships offshore. Generally speaking radio communication was most useful in rescues. The "wireless" was used for ship-to-ship and ship-to-shore messages. By 1930 radio was being used by airline pilots the police and military personnel. Commercial broadcasting began according to experts when a Pittsburgh station aired the 1920 presidential election results.

➔ **For a SELF-CHECK and more practice, see the EXERCISE BANK, p. 346.**

Commas: Dates, Addresses, and Letters

LESSON 3

❶ Here's the Idea

See these rules used in the letter below.

Commas in Dates, Addresses, and Letters	
Commas in dates	In dates, use a comma between the day and the year. (Use a comma after the year if the sentence continues.)
Commas in addresses	Use a comma between the city or town and the state or country. (Use a comma after the state or country if the sentence continues.)
Commas in letters	Use a comma after the greeting of a casual letter and after the closing of a casual or business letter.

```
1                    1810 Peach Tree Ln.
2                    Charleston, SC  29423
3                    June 28, 2000

4   Dear Samira,
5      I heard the most incredible story today.
6   Holley Anderson, who lived in Preston,
7   Connecticut, put a message into a bottle.
8   She then threw it into the Atlantic Ocean,
9   off the coast of Maine. She was eleven at
10  the time. Five years later, she got a letter
11  from a boy who lived in Järna, Sweden,
12  and who had found the bottle. It had
13  traveled nearly 5,000 miles!

14     I'm going to try to send a bottle
15  message tomorrow. Maybe I'll hear about
16  it by June 29, 2005, five years from now.
17  Wouldn't that be cool? Let me know if
18  you decide to send your own bottle
19  message.

20                   Your pal,
21                   Cindy
```

Line 2: comma between city and state

Line 3: comma between day and year

Line 4: comma after greeting

Lines 6–7: commas after town and state

Line 11: commas after city and country

Line 16: commas after day and year

Line 20: comma after closing

WATCH OUT

Do not use a comma between the state and the ZIP code.

❷ Practice and Apply

A. CONCEPT CHECK: Commas: Dates, Addresses, and Letters

Write the words and numbers from the letter that should be followed by commas.

688 Waveland Ave.
Providence RI 02904
May 22 2000

Dear Thad
    Ricardo and I were playing last week on the beach. While digging in the sand, Ricardo found a large, worn shell. At first, we didn't think it was anything special, but then I looked closer. On its side were some carved words and an old anchor. Ricardo and I immediately showed it to my mom. It reminded her of valuable examples of scrimshaw she had seen in Mystic Connecticut at a naval museum.
    I'm hoping to find more shells when my family visits San Juan Puerto Rico to see relatives. I should be back by June 10 2000 my fourteenth birthday.
                                                    Your friend

                                                    Rosa

➡ For a SELF-CHECK and more practice, see the EXERCISE BANK, p. 346.

B. WRITING: Dear Friend

Choose one of the notes written in this cartoon and rewrite it as a complete letter. Be sure to include all the elements of a letter.

Zits by Jerry Scott & Jim Borgman

©1999 Zits Partnership. Distributed by King Features Syndicate.

Punctuating Quotations

❶ Here's the Idea

To punctuate quotations, you need to know where to put quotation marks, commas, and end marks.

Direct Quotations

A direct quotation is a report of a speaker's exact words.

▶ **Use quotation marks at the beginning and end of a direct quotation.**

"In the mid-1800s, Ada, countess of Lovelace, created the first computer program," explained Carla.

▶ **Use commas to set off explanatory words used with direct quotations (whether they occur at the beginning, in the middle, or at the end of the sentence).**

Mark said, "She also wrote about an early computer."

"She also," said Mark, "wrote about an early computer."

"She also wrote about an early computer," said Mark.

▶ **If a quotation is a question or an exclamation, place the question mark or exclamation point inside the closing quotation marks.**

"Who could deny her remarkable contributions ?" asked Carla.

▶ **If quoted words are part of a question or exclamation, place the question mark or exclamation point outside the closing quotation marks.**

Did Mark say, "A computer language was named in her honor "?

 Commas and periods always go inside closing quotation marks. They're too little to stay outside.

Lady Lovelace, a computer science pioneer.

Indirect Quotations

▶ **Do not use quotation marks to set off an indirect quotation.** An indirect quotation is a restatement, in different words, of what someone said. An indirect quotation is often introduced by the word *that*. It does not require a comma.

> DIRECT   Todd said, "The name of one of the first electronic computers was ENIAC."
>
> INDIRECT   Todd said **that** one of the first electronic computers was named ENIAC.

Divided Quotations

A divided quotation is a direct quotation that is separated into two parts, with explanatory words such as *he said* or *she said* between the parts.

▶ **Use quotation marks to enclose both parts of a divided quotation.**

> "ENIAC," said Todd, "was constructed of 18,000 vacuum tubes and nearly filled an entire building."

▶ **Do not capitalize the first word of the second part of a divided quotation unless it begins a new sentence.**

> "If we still used vacuum tubes," explained James, "we would need whole houses for our computers."
>
> "Hmm, that's interesting," answered Todd. "My brother would have no place to put all his CDs."

▶ **Use commas to set off the explanatory words used with a divided quotation.**

> "Well," exclaimed James, "he could always give them to me!"

Quotation Marks in Dialogue

▶ **In dialogue, a new paragraph and a new set of quotation marks signal a change in speakers.**

A dialogue is a conversation between two or more speakers.

> **LITERARY MODEL**
>
> The boy was probably twelve years old, but undersized. He wore overalls and a torn shirt, and was barefooted.
>
> He said, "I can chop some wood today."
>
> I said, "But I have a boy coming from the orphanage."
>
> "I'm the boy."
>
> "You? But you're small."
>
> "Size don't matter, chopping wood," he said.
>
> —Marjorie Kinnan Rawlings, "A Mother in Mannville"

❷ Practice and Apply

CONCEPT CHECK: Punctuating Quotations

Rewrite each sentence, adding quotation marks and other punctuation where needed. If a sentence is correct, write *Correct.*

How Intelligent Is a Robot?

"I've been reading an article about artificial intelligence said Lashawna. "Scientists use it in robots and other computers."

"You mean a robot or a computer can be intelligent? laughed Stacy

"Well, yes, if humans teach it," said Lashawna. For example, they can teach a robot to pick up an egg without breaking it."

"That's fantastic agreed Stacy. What else can robots do?

Scientists are teaching robots to move their heads in response to sounds and to wave their arms to get attention.

"It's amazing!"

➡ **For a SELF-CHECK and more practice, see the EXERCISE BANK, p. 347.**

A. End Marks and Commas Write the words and numbers from the postcard below that should be followed by end marks or commas. Include these punctuation marks in your answers.

Nov 14 2000

Dear Tisha
My family and I are here in Chicago
Illinois visiting my aunt In a little while
we're going to the Museum of
Broadcast Communications I can't wait
Do you believe that it has more than
30,000 television and radio programs in
its library I'm not lying Now I might at
last see the final episode of <u>Samantha</u>
See you later
Julia

Tisha Reynolds
155 Sparrow St
Tulsa OK 74103

Q

B. Punctuation in Dialogue Have you ever written a dialogue with a partner? If not, here's your chance. At the top of a piece of paper, write the following question: How will communication be different in the future?

Write your first response; then let your partner write a response. Continue to take turns, with each partner writing four responses. Make sure to use correct punctuation throughout your dialogue. The example below will help you get started.

> Sam—"In the future, we will be able to see people when we
> talk with them on the telephone."
> Ted—"There will definitely be a way to turn off the picture if
> you don't want your caller to see you."

PUNCTUATION

Semicolons and Colons

LESSON 5

❶ Here's the Idea

A **semicolon** separates elements in a sentence. It is stronger than a comma but not as strong as a period. A **colon** indicates that a list follows. Colons are also used after greetings in business letters and in expressions of time.

Semicolons in Compound Sentences

▶ **Use a semicolon to join parts of a compound sentence without a coordinating conjunction.**

The Pony Express Company was formed in 1860**;** it carried mail between St. Joseph, Missouri, and Sacramento, California.

▶ **Use a semicolon between parts of a compound sentence when the clauses are long and complicated or when they contain commas.**

Pony Express riders were young, strong men**;** and they rode for many hours at a stretch, persisted in bad weather, and avoided fights with settlers.

Semicolons with Items in a Series

▶ **When there are commas within parts of a series, use semicolons to separate the parts.**

The riders were expected to treat the horses, oxen, and other animals well**;** to carry horns to sound their arrival**;** and, above all, to reach their destinations on time.

Colons

▶ **Use a colon to introduce a list of items.**

Pony Express riders wore the same clothing**:** red shirts, slouch hats, jeans, and boots.

Avoid using a colon directly after a verb or a preposition.

INCORRECT The clothing was**:** red shirts and jeans.

INCORRECT At one time, mail was delivered to California by**:** steamships, trains, and stagecoaches.

▶ **Use a colon after the formal greeting in a business letter.**

Dear Dr. Russell **:**   Dear Ms. Wells **:**

For models, see the business letters in the Model Bank.

▶ **Use a colon between hours and minutes in expressions of time.**

The exhausted rider arrived at 11 **:** 35 A.M. He threw the mail pouch to the waiting rider, who galloped off at 11 **:** 36 A.M.

❷ Practice and Apply

CONCEPT CHECK: Semicolons and Colons

Write the words and numbers from the paragraph that should be followed by semicolons or colons. Include these punctuation marks in your answers.

Not Just Ponies

Many animals have carried the mail pigeons, mules, camels, and reindeer are among them. Pigeons are good postal carriers moreover, one of these winged messengers was awarded a medal during World War I. Camels have also carried some U.S. mail they were used on desert routes in the Southwest. Unfortunately, people had several complaints about the camels they smelled, they got angry, and they spit! In Alaska, before airplanes delivered mail, dogsleds often carried letters reindeer were also used. The Havasupai Indian reservation is in Arizona it sits deep in the Grand Canyon. There are only three ways in and out of the canyon on foot, by horseback, or on a mule. Mules make the trip five days each week the journey takes three to five hours each way. Your postal carrier is actually very lucky he or she may get off work by 330 P.M.

➜ For a SELF-CHECK and more practice, see the EXERCISE BANK, p. 348.

PUNCTUATION

Hyphens, Dashes, and Parentheses

❶ Here's the Idea

Hyphens, dashes, and parentheses help make your writing clear by separating or setting off words or parts of words.

Hyphens

▶ **Use a hyphen if part of a word must be carried over from one line to the next.**

1. The word must have at least two syllables to be broken.
RIGHT: com - puter   WRONG: dis - k

2. Separate the word between syllables.
RIGHT: broad - cast   WRONG: broadc - ast

3. You must leave at least two letters on each line.
RIGHT: sig - nal   WRONG: a - bout

▶ **Use hyphens in certain compound words.**

vice - president   self - reliance

▶ **Use hyphens in compound numbers from twenty-one through ninety-nine.**

thirty - three   forty - nine

▶ **Use hyphens in spelled-out fractions.**

three - eighths of an inch   one - third of a cup

Dashes

▶ **Use dashes to show an abrupt break in thought.**

Clara Barton — whose nickname was Angel of the Battlefield — founded the Red Cross.

Parentheses

▶ **Use parentheses to set off material that is loosely related to the rest of the sentence.**

During the Civil War (1861–1865) she helped keep track of dead soldiers in order to help their families.

❷ Practice and Apply

A. CONCEPT CHECK: Hyphens, Dashes, and Parentheses

Read the following paragraphs. Then indicate where hyphens, dashes, and parentheses are needed in each underlined passage. If the underlined text is correct, write *Correct*.

Women's Work

Clara Barton was born during a period **(1)** <u>the early 1800s</u> when women did not live independent lives. She is best remembered for founding the Red Cross when she was about **(2)** <u>fifty nine</u>. During the Civil War **(3)** <u>1861–1865</u>, however, Barton performed another important national service.

First, she started an ambitious project to help **(4)** <u>in-jured soldiers</u> and their families. More soldiers died of disease **(5)** <u>measles, smallpox, and typhoid</u> than died of hostile gunfire. Barton was a rare sight on the battlefield because **(6)** <u>I'm not kidding</u> women were not supposed to travel on their own. She began recording the names of wounded and dead soldiers **(7)** <u>she had nursed many of them</u> to publish in newspapers. Pressure on the U.S. War Department **(8)** <u>including a letter to President Lincoln</u> led to her being given an office for her work. Over time she and her staff were able to find about 22,000 missing soldiers, **(9)** <u>including many in a famous prison</u>.

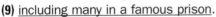

Barton's communication skills served her well in her relief efforts. Today, the Red Cross continues Barton's work, successfully responding to people **(10)** <u>victims of hurricanes, floods, fires, and wars</u> in emergencies.

➡ For a SELF-CHECK and more practice, see the EXERCISE BANK, p. 348.

B. REVISING: Adding Hyphens

Rewrite the following phrases, adding hyphens where needed. If the phrase is correct, write *Correct*.

three hundred points   fourth quarter of the game
tonight's half moon   one half the weight

Apostrophes

LESSON 7

CHAPTER 11

1 Here's the Idea

Apostrophes are used in possessive nouns, contractions, and some plurals.

Apostrophes in Possessives

▶ **Use an apostrophe to form the possessive of any noun, whether singular or plural.**

For a singular noun, add 's even if the word ends in s.
    Jenny**'s** e-mail   Russ**'s** computer

For plural nouns that end in s, add only an apostrophe.
    the robot**s'** programs   the prisoner**s'** escape

For plural nouns that do not end in s, add 's.
    the men**'s** conversation   the women**'s** relay

Apostrophes in Contractions

▶ **Use apostrophes in contractions.**

In a contraction, words are joined and letters are left out. An apostrophe replaces the letter or letters that are missing.

Commonly Used Contractions					
I am	Æ I'm	you are	Æ you're	you will Æ you'll
she is Æ she's	they have	Æ they've	it is	Æ it's
cannot Æ can't	they are	Æ they're	was not Æ wasn't

Don't confuse contractions with possessive pronouns, which do not contain apostrophes.

Contractions versus Possessive Pronouns	
Contraction	**Possessive Pronoun**
it's (*it is* or *it has*)	its (belonging to it—*its claws*)
who's (*who is*)	whose (belonging to whom—*whose home*)
you're (*you are*)	your (belonging to you—*your letter*)
they're (*they are*)	their (belonging to them—*their addresses*)

Apostrophes in Plurals

▶ **Use an apostrophe and s to form the plural of a letter, a numeral, or a word referred to as a word.**

Dot your *i* **'s**.

He scored 9**'s** and 10**'s** in competition.

Replace some of your *said* **'s** with stronger verbs.

❷ Practice and Apply

A. CONCEPT CHECK: Apostrophes

Find and correct the errors in the use of apostrophes.

Calling All Hams

Teenager Richard Paczkowski has a neat job; hes a ham operator and the assistant emergency coordinator of the Amateur Radio Emergency Service. He likes to hear his friend's voices over his two-way radio. Sometimes Richards' job is fun. But occasionally its' involved with danger. Richard lives in Florida; the states' hot summer of 1998 caused an outbreak of wildfires. After the firefighters's work had controlled the fires, many started up again. The Red Cross' shelters needed ham operators. Richard and his 75-member crew worked for many days getting victim's messages to and from shelters. He remembers that the job was'nt easy, especially when a fire approached his own home. Luckily, Richard's home didnt burn.

➡ For a **SELF-CHECK** and more practice, see the **EXERCISE BANK, p. 349.**

B. WRITING: Using Possessives and Contractions

Write the correct forms from the choices in parentheses.

(Whose, Who's) going to help me make signs for the game tonight? We want to let the other team know (they're, their) going to lose badly. We also have to support (Jeannie's, Jeannies') comeback and encourage the team to do (its, it's) best. Come on, folks! (You're, Your) not artists, but you can write cheers!

Punctuating Titles

❶ Here's the Idea

Use quotation marks and italics correctly in titles to show what kind of work or selection you are writing about.

Quotation Marks

▶ **Use quotation marks to set off the titles of short works.**

Quotation Marks for Titles	
Book chapter	"Into the Primitive" from *The Call of the Wild*
Story	"Block Party"
Essay	"Reprise"
Article	"Do Try This at Home"
TV episode	"The City on the Edge of Forever" from *Star Trek*
Song	"America the Beautiful"
Poem	"Speech to the Young/Speech to the Progress-Toward"

Italics and Underlining

▶ **Use italics for titles of longer works and for the names of ships, trains, spacecraft, and airplanes (but not for types of planes).** In handwriting, you show that something should be in italic type by **underlining** it.

Italics or Underlines for Titles and Names			
Book	*Roughing It*	**Epic poem**	*Iliad*
Play	*Ragtime*	**Painting**	*Starry Night*
Magazine	*Life*	**Ship**	U.S.S. *Constitution*
Movie	*The Phantom Menace*	**Train**	*Broadway Limited*
TV series	*Dateline NBC*	**Spacecraft**	*Voyager 1*
Long musical work	*Music for the Royal Fireworks*	**Airplane**	*Flyer*

❷ Practice and Apply

A. CONCEPT CHECK: Punctuating Titles

Read the paragraph and rewrite the titles and vehicle names, using either quotation marks or underlining as appropriate.

He Reached for the Stars
Astronomer Carl Sagan was a scientist, writer, and teacher who died in 1996. The magazine Odyssey published an entire issue on his life and work. Sagan grew up reading science fiction, such as Edgar Rice Burroughs's novel Gods of Mars. He worked on the project that sent the spacecraft Voyager 1 and Voyager 2 to explore the outer solar system. Recordings of Earth songs were sent on the spacecraft, including Chuck Berry's Johnny B. Goode and Louis Armstrong's Melancholy Blues. Sagan produced a television series about the universe, called Cosmos. He wrote the book Pale Blue Dot to teach readers about Earth and other planets and the novel Contact about a human encounter with aliens.

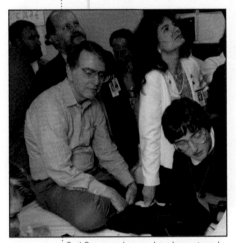
Carl Sagan and co-workers busy at work.

Sagan's appearances on Johnny Carson's Tonight Show thrilled many viewers with the wonders that surround us.

➜ For a SELF-CHECK and more practice, see the EXERCISE BANK, p. 349.

B. MIXED REVIEW: The Critic's Corner

Write a short review of your favorite book, short story, movie, TV show, or magazine article. Include the title of your choice and a few sentences explaining why you enjoy it. At the end, write a quotation from your selection that you find memorable. Make sure to use correct punctuation throughout your review.

PUNCTUATION

Grammar in Fine Arts

Punctuation and Writing About Art

Even when you write about great pieces of fine art, details like punctuation matter. Punctuation is especially important when you refer to titles of works of art, books, or articles. Notice the punctuation in the student model.

The Letter, 1891, by Mary Cassatt

Communication, 1995, by Diane Ong

Art often reflects the lifestyles and technology of its time period. The Letter, by Mary Cassatt, and Communication, by Diane Ong, were created over a hundred years apart. Each shows a woman in the act of communicating; one is writing a letter, and the other is talking on the phone.

In her article about the two paintings, "Letters and Phone Calls in Art," student Marie Moore writes that the two paintings are "different in style, but similar in content." While they show very different moods and very different kinds of communication, the fact is that both show people sharing ideas.

Left: *The Letter* (1891), Mary Cassatt. David David Gallery, Philadelphia/Superstock.
Right: *Communication* (1995), Diana Ong. Superstock.

Practice and Apply

WRITING: Using Punctuation

For a fine-arts project, you might be asked to write a short essay about an artist. Below are examples of typical notes a student might take. Write two or three paragraphs about Cassatt, taking care to correctly punctuate the titles of books, magazines, and works of art. Save your work in your 📁 **Working Portfolio.**

BOOK: Mary Cassatt: Impressionist at Home
AUTHOR: Barbara Stern Shapiro
PUBLISHER: Universe
DATE: 1998
—mostly private, indoor settings
—famous paintings:
    Mother and Child, The Boating Party, Woman Bathing,
    Lady at the Tea Table, The Letter

BOOK: Mary Cassatt, Modern Woman
AUTHOR: Judith A. Barter, et al.
PUBLISHER: Art Institute of Chicago and Harry
            N. Abrams
DATE: 1998
—born 1844 in Pittsburgh, U.S.A.
—died 1926 in Paris, France
—studied at Pennsylvania Academy of Fine
    Arts in Philadelphia, where she met other
    important artists

Contains information about exhibitions of Cassatt's works.
Also contains information about criticism of Cassatt's works

Mixed Review

A. Punctuation Write the words from the following paragraph that should be followed by commas, semicolons, or colons. Include these punctuation marks in your answers.

PROFESSIONAL MODEL

> Chelsea Hernandez of Austin Texas was already a top-notch communicator at the age of fourteen. Every Sunday morning viewers tuned in to watch her on *Kids' Ideas* a program she helped create. Chelsea held three important positions co-director writer, and star. Her show focused on kids and their hobbies, talents and concerns. She said "Kids listen to me because I'm a kid." Good preparation was also important it kept her from being too nervous when she interviewed members of Congress. Chelsea was something of a celebrity in her hometown. She was often asked to sign autographs at the mall and this pleased her. Today she works as a filmmaker and television intern.

B. Punctuation Proofread the following passage and correct errors in the use of punctuation.

> Ramon and Sal met on the library steps after school! Sal asked Ramon if "he had finished his research on communication?"
>
> "I'm only half done," sighed Ramon, because there's just so much to find out. Did you know there are almost 4,000 languages spoken today?" He added, "About 845 of those are spoken in India."
>
> Sal broke in, I know that Chinese is the most common language and is spoken by more than a billion people.
>
> Right, said Ramon. "So what else did you find out?"
>
> Sal told his friend that "several African languages use clicks for some of the sounds." Sal also said that "Canary Islands people use whistles to communicate with their neighbors.

For each numbered item, choose the letter of the best revision.

Television was invented in the <u>early 1900s; but</u> it became
(1)
popular only after World War II. The quality of early television was

not <u>very good, in fact</u>, it was dreadful. The picture <u>skipped; rolled</u>
(2)   (3)
<u>over and</u>, created ghost images. Often a <u>sets'</u> picture and sound
(3)   (4)
disappeared altogether. Early TV producers <u>did'nt</u> want to spend
(5)
money, so production values suffered. Stages had to be well <u>lighted</u>

<u>and hot lights</u> caused problems. Actors sweated so much that they
(6)
dripped sweated into their <u>shoes?</u> <u>Still</u>, there were popular shows,
(7)   (8)
including *The Lone Ranger* and <u>"The Texaco Star Theater."</u> When
(9)
asked what he liked about his invention, Vladimir Zworykin

replied, <u>The off switch</u>.
(10)

1. A. early 1900s but
   B. early 1900s, but
   C. early, 1900s, but
   D. Correct as is

2. A. very good: in fact,
   B. very good. in fact,
   C. very good; in fact,
   D. Correct as is

3. A. skipped, rolled over, and
   B. skipped: rolled over: and
   C. skipped (rolled over) and
   D. Correct as is

4. A. sets
   B. set's
   C. sets's
   D. Correct as is

5. A. didnt'
   B. didn't
   C. did'not
   D. Correct as is

6. A. lighted, and hot lights
   B. lighted - and hot lights
   C. lighted (and hot lights)
   D. Correct as is

7. A. shoes,
   B. shoes;
   C. shoes!
   D. Correct as is

8. A. Still;
   B. Still:
   C. Still-
   D. Correct as is

9. A. *"The Texaco Star Theater"*
   B. The Texaco Star Theater
   C. *The Texaco Star Theater*
   D. Correct as is

10. A. <u>The off switch.</u>
    B. "The off switch."
    C. — The off switch —.
    D. Correct as is

Student Help Desk

Punctuation at a Glance

( ) **Parentheses**

○ **Colon**

! **Exclamation Point**

⬭ **Hyphen**

, **Apostrophe**

⬭ **Dash**

, **Comma**

? **Question Mark**

• **Period**

; **Semicolon**

" " **Quotation Marks**

Punctuating Titles — Long and Short

Italics (longer works)

books, movies, magazines, plays,
TV series, paintings, long musical works,
epic poems

Quotation Marks (shorter works)

stories, essays, songs, poems, book chapters,
episodes of TV series, magazine articles

Punctuation with Commas — Breaks and Interruptions

	Use commas . . .	Examples
Items in a series	to separate items in a series	Do you enjoy watching TV comedies , dramas , or sports?
Adjectives	to separate adjectives	I really like old , funny shows.
Introductory words	after introductory words	In winter , Adam watches football games.
Interrupters	to set off interrupters	Mom and Dad , however , prefer to see documentaries.
Nouns of direct address	to set off nouns of direct address	What's your favorite show , Jenna?

Punctuation with Quotation Marks The Inside Scoop

Always Inside (no matter what)

Period	Alanna said, "I didn't like that movie**.**"
Comma	"I liked the special effects **,**" said Harry.

Sometimes Inside (if they punctuate the part within the quote marks)

Question mark	"Do you have to make a speech **?**" asked Delia.
Exclamation point	"Oh, no, everyone will leave **!**" moaned Sue.

Sometimes Outside (if they punctuate the overall sentence, not just the quote)

Question mark	Did you read Nikki Giovanni's poem "Choices **"?**
Exclamation point	I was surprised by the ending of "A Mother in Mannville **"!**

The Bottom Line

Checklist for Punctuation

Have I . . .

___ ended every sentence with the appropriate end mark?

___ used a comma before the conjunction in a compound sentence?

___ used commas to separate items in a series?

___ used commas correctly in dates, addresses, and letters?

___ used quotation marks before and after a speaker's exact words?

___ used apostrophes correctly?

___ used italics and quotation marks correctly to set off titles?

Diagramming: Sentence Parts

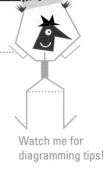

Mad Mapper

Here's the Idea

Diagramming is a way of showing the structure of a sentence. Drawing a diagram can help you see how the parts of a sentence work together to form a complete thought.

Watch me for diagramming tips!

Simple Subjects and Verbs

Write the simple subject and verb on one line. Separate them with a vertical line that crosses the main line.

Journalists investigate.

Journalists	investigate

Compound Subjects and Verbs

For a compound subject or verb, split the main line. Put the conjunction on a dotted line connecting the compound parts.

Compound Subject

Journalists and reporters investigate.

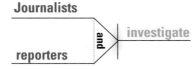

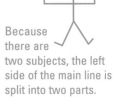

Because there are two subjects, the left side of the main line is split into two parts.

Compound Verb

Journalists investigate and inform.

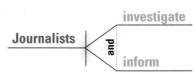

DIAGRAMMING

Compound Subject and Compound Verb

Journalists and reporters investigate and inform.

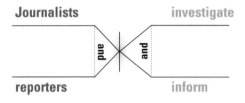

Because there are two subjects and two verbs, both sides of the main line are split into two parts.

A. CONCEPT CHECK: Subjects and Verbs

Diagram these sentences, using what you have learned.

1. News breaks.

2. Reporters and photographers scramble.

3. Editors and copyeditors read and revise.

Adjectives and Adverbs

Write adjectives and adverbs on slanted lines below the words they modify.

Busy reporters scribble very rapidly.

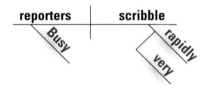

B. CONCEPT CHECK: Adjectives and Adverbs

Diagram these sentences, using what you have learned.

1. Television anchors speak clearly.

2. Anxious directors watch and worry.

3. Successful news broadcasts end very promptly.

Subject Complements

- Write a predicate noun or a predicate adjective on the main line after the verb.
- Separate the subject complement from the verb with a slanted line that does not cross the main line.

Predicate Noun

Television anchors are skillful performers.

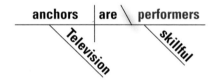

Predicate Adjective

They are usually very articulate.

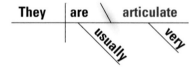

C. CONCEPT CHECK: Subject Complements

Diagram these sentences, using what you have learned.

1. Journalism is not always easy.
2. A journalist must be a forceful person.

Direct Objects

Write a direct object on the main line after the verb.

Many anchors write their own stories.

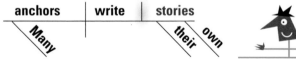

The vertical line between a verb and its direct object does not cross the main line.

Sometimes a sentence has a compound direct object. Write the direct objects on parallel horizontal lines that branch from the main line.

The news director selects the stories and the visual images.

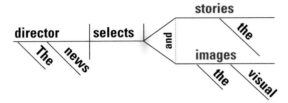

Indirect Objects

Write an indirect object below the verb, on a horizontal line connected to the verb by a slanted line.

The director may give the reporters their assignments.

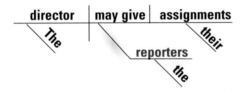

D. CONCEPT CHECK: Direct and Indirect Objects

Diagram these sentences, using what you have learned.

1. A reporter gets a tip.
2. The reporter tells the news director the idea.
3. The director gives the reporter her approval.

E. MIXED REVIEW: Diagramming

Diagram the following sentences.

1. A fierce warehouse fire starts quickly.
2. Reporters and photographers are soon busy.
3. The reporters ask witnesses numerous questions.
4. Camera operators bring their bulky equipment.
5. They rapidly shoot dramatic video footage.
6. They send the station their sensational images.
7. The warehouse soon becomes a ruin.
8. The witnesses remain quite anxious.
9. Later they watch the TV news.
10. They see their own faces!

Diagramming: Phrases

Prepositional Phrases

- Write the preposition on a slanted line below the word that the prepositional phrase modifies.
- Write the object of the preposition on a horizontal line attached to the slanted line and parallel to the main line.
- Write words that modify the object of the preposition on slanted lines below it.

Adjective Prepositional Phrase

The climbers reached the camp at the base of the mountain.

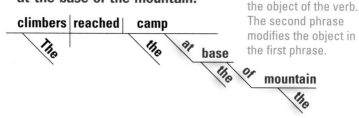

The first phrase modifies the object of the verb. The second phrase modifies the object in the first phrase.

Adverb Prepositional Phrase

They pitched their tents in twenty minutes.

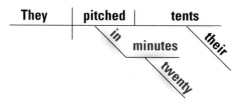

This adverb phrase modifies a verb. Adverb phrases can also modify adjectives and adverbs.

F. CONCEPT CHECK: Prepositional Phrases

Diagram these sentences using, what you have learned.

1. The heavy clouds lifted during the night.
2. The climbers could see to the top of the peak.
3. They began the climb of their lives.

Participles and Participial Phrases

- The participle curves along a bent line below the word it modifies.
- For a participial phrase, diagram direct and indirect objects after the participle in the usual way.
- Diagram any prepositional phrases as usual.
- Write modifiers, such as adverbs and adjectives, on slanted lines below the words they modify.

Fascinated tourists watched the erupting volcano.

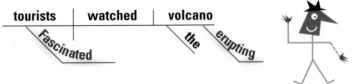

Flowing rapidly down the slope, the lava glowed red.

Past participles and present participles are diagrammed in the same way. Notice how the participles are slightly curved.

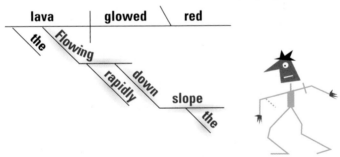

G. CONCEPT CHECK: Participles and Participial Phrases

Diagram these sentences, using what you have learned.

1. Glowing lava flowed swiftly.
2. The lava cooled, hardening into solid rock.
3. Built by many eruptions, the volcano was immense.

Gerunds and Gerund Phrases

- The gerund curves over a line that looks like a step.
- Use a vertical forked line to connect the step to the part of the diagram that corresponds to the role of the phrase in the sentence.
- Diagram the other parts of the sentence in the usual way.

Standing too close could be dangerous.

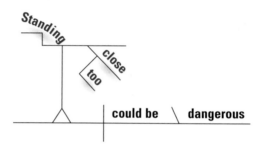 

This gerund phrase is used as a subject. Remember that a gerund phrase can be used in any way a noun can.

Infinitives and Infinitive Phrases

- Write the infinitive on a bent line, with the word *to* on the slanted part and the verb on the horizontal part.
- If the infinitive or infinitive phrase functions as a noun, use a vertical forked line to connect the bent line to the part of the diagram that corresponds to its role in the sentence.
- If the infinitive or infinitive phrase functions as a modifier, place the bent line below the word it modifies.
- Diagram the other parts of the sentence in the usual way.

Infinitive Phrase as a Noun

The explorers decided to visit the distant island.

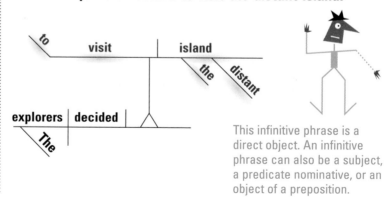

This infinitive phrase is a direct object. An infinitive phrase can also be a subject, a predicate nominative, or an object of a preposition.

Infinitive Phrase as a Modifier

Their decision to sail there was courageous.

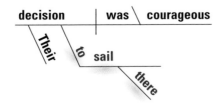

This infinitive phrase acts as an adjective modifying *decision*. An infinitive phrase can also act as an adverb.

H. CONCEPT CHECK: Gerund and Infinitive Phrases

Diagram these sentences, using what you have learned.

1. Their aim was to reach the distant island.
2. They would need to cross dangerous waters.
3. Sailing against the current posed a problem.
4. To cross the inlet would be difficult.
5. They considered abandoning their plans.

I. MIXED REVIEW: Diagramming

Diagram the following sentences.

1. People of all ages enjoy fishing.
2. Catching fish is not always easy.
3. First, you need to find a likely pond.
4. You may find fish hiding under rocks.
5. Hidden fish are not easily seen.
6. Your plan to catch a fish requires the right bait.
7. Some fish like wriggling worms or squirming minnows.
8. The challenge is to find the best lure.
9. Some people like to use flies.
10. They enjoy tying their own flies.

Diagramming: Clauses

Compound Sentences

- Diagram the independent clauses on parallel horizontal lines.
- Connect the verbs in the two clauses by a dotted line with a solid step in it.
- Write the coordinating conjunction on the step.

Visitors talk to the lions at the zoo, but the large cats typically ignore them.

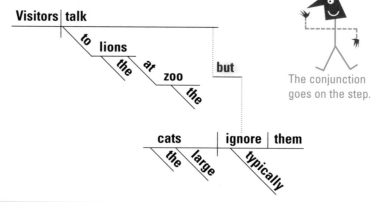

The conjunction goes on the step.

J. CONCEPT CHECK: Compound Sentences

Diagram these sentences, using what you have learned.

1. The lions are in their habitats, and the visitors are safely outside.
2. You can watch the lions eating, but you should not feed them.
3. The animals are not behind bars, yet they do not escape.

Complex Sentences

Adjective and Adverb Clauses
- Diagram the main clause first, and then diagram the dependent clause on its own horizontal line below the main line.
- Use a dotted line to connect the word introducing the clause to the word that it modifies.

Adjective Clauses

The polar bear is a creature that swims very well.

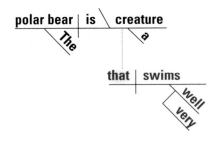

Here the pronoun introducing the clause is the subject of the clause.

Polar bear cubs have faces that people like.

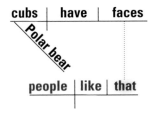

Here the pronoun introducing the clause is the direct object of the verb in the clause.

Adverb Clause

After they took the complete tour, the visitors returned to the bears.

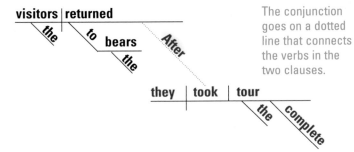

The conjunction goes on a dotted line that connects the verbs in the two clauses.

Noun Clauses

- Diagram the main clause first.
- Figure out what role the dependent clause plays in the sentence.
- Diagram the dependent clause on a separate line that is attached to the main line with a vertical forked line.
- Place the forked line in the diagram according to the role of the noun clause in the sentence.
- Diagram the word introducing the noun clause according to its function in the clause.

Noun Clause Used as a Direct Object

The zookeepers decide what the animals eat.

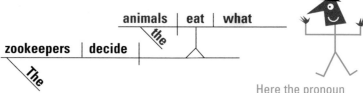

Here the pronoun introducing the noun clause functions as a direct object in the clause.

Noun Clause Used as a Subject

When the animals eat is also their decision.

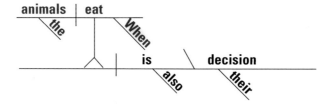

K. CONCEPT CHECK: Complex Sentences

Diagram these sentences, using what you have learned.

1. The habitats include places where the animals can hide.
2. You can guess why the animals hide.
3. After they have had visitors throughout the day, the pandas become shy.

L. MIXED REVIEW: Diagramming

Diagram the following sentences.

1. Modern zoos keep animals in settings that resemble their original homes.
2. Because they offer safe environments, zoos have saved animal lives.
3. A zoo is safe, but it can also be a dull place for animals.
4. Zoos provide whatever amuses the animals.
5. They give apes poles that resemble trees.
6. Polar bears are given chunks of ice, which they can push around.
7. Chimpanzees, who are very smart, poke artificial anthills for food.
8. Zoos even provide waterfalls for animals who like them.
9. You can go with a guide, or you can tour on your own.
10. Whatever you see will probably be worthwhile.

Quick-Fix Editing Machine

You've worked hard on your assignment. Don't let misplaced commas, sentence fragments, and missing details lower your grade. Use this Quick-Fix Editing Guide to help you detect grammatical errors and make your writing more precise.

QUICK FIX

1 Sentence Fragments

What's the problem? Part of a sentence has been left out.

Why does it matter? A fragment doesn't convey a complete thought.

What should you do about it? Find out what is missing and add it.

What's the Problem?

Quick Fix

A. A subject is missing.

Practiced for a whole week.

Add a subject.

My friends and I practiced for a whole week.

B. A predicate is missing.

Auditions in the school auditorium.

Add a predicate.

Auditions **were held** in the school auditorium.

C. Both a subject and a predicate are missing.

For almost a month.

Add a subject and a predicate to make an independent clause.

We rehearsed for almost a month.

D. A dependent clause is treated as if it were a sentence.

Because we all wore costumes.

Combine the fragment with an independent clause.

The performance was exciting because we all wore costumes.

OR

Delete the conjunction.

~~Because~~ **W**e all wore costumes.

For more help, see Chapter 1, pp. 25–27.

Run-On Sentences

What's the problem? Two or more sentences have been written as though they were a single sentence.

Why does it matter? A run-on sentence doesn't show where one idea ends and another begins.

What should you do about it? Find the best way to separate ideas or to show the proper relationship between them.

What's the Problem?

Quick Fix

A. The end mark separating two sentences is missing.

Dolapo raced up the court her defender closed in.

Add an end mark to divide the run-on into two sentences.

Dolapo raced up the court. **H**er defender closed in.

B. Two sentences are separated only by a comma.

Dolapo faked a shot, her defender wasn't fooled.

Add a coordinating conjunction.

Dolapo faked a shot, **but** her defender wasn't fooled.

OR

Change the comma to a semicolon.

Dolapo faked a shot; her defender wasn't fooled.

OR

Replace the comma with an end mark and start a new sentence.

Dolapo faked a shot. **H**er defender wasn't fooled.

OR

Change one of the independent clauses to a dependent clause by adding a subordinating conjunction.

Although Dolapo faked a shot, her defender wasn't fooled.

For more help, see Chapter 1, pp. 25–27.

QUICK FIX

③ Subject-Verb Agreement

What's the problem? A verb does not agree with its subject in number.

Why does it matter? Readers may think your work is careless.

What should you do about it? Identify the subject and use a verb that matches it in number.

What's the Problem?

Quick Fix

A. The first helping verb in a verb phrase does not agree with the subject.

We has been enjoying tea during our stay in London.

Decide whether the subject is singular or plural, and make the helping verb agree with it.

We have been enjoying tea during our stay in London.

B. The contraction doesn't agree with its subject.

Many **Britons doesn't** work at 4:00 P.M. because of teatime.

Use a contraction that agrees with the subject.

Many **Britons don't** work at 4:00 P.M. because of teatime.

C. A singular verb is used with a compound subject that contains *and.*

Many **natives and** an **occasional tourist visits** this fancy tearoom.

Use a plural verb.

Many **natives and** an occasional **tourist visit** this fancy tearoom.

D. A verb doesn't agree with the nearer part of a compound subject containing *or* or *nor.*

Neither the waiters nor the **owner want** any unhappy customers.

Make the verb agree with the nearer part.

Neither the waiters nor the **owner wants** any unhappy customers.

E. A verb doesn't agree with an indefinite-pronoun subject.

Each of the servers **give** customers undivided attention.

Decide whether the pronoun is singular or plural, and make the verb agree with it.

Each of the servers **gives** patrons undivided attention.

For more help, see Chapter 9, pp. 208–221.

QUICK FIX

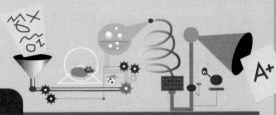

What's the Problem?

Quick Fix

F. A collective noun referring to individuals is treated as singular. The **staff dresses** in formal attire.	Use a plural verb if the collective noun refers to individuals. The **staff dress** in formal attire.
G. A singular subject ending in _s_ or _ics_ is mistaken for a plural. **Politics are** often discussed in the tearoom.	Watch out for these nouns and use singular verbs with them. **Politics is** often discussed in the tearoom.
H. A verb doesn't agree with the true subject of a sentence beginning with _here_ or _there_. **There is** tea, finger sandwiches, and cakes on the menu.	Mentally turn the sentence around so that the subject comes first, and make the verb agree with it. There **are tea, finger sandwiches, and cakes** on the menu.
I. A verb agrees with the object of a preposition rather than with its subject. A tea in some **areas tend** to be a meal.	Mentally block out the prepositional phrase, and make the verb agree with the subject. A **tea** ~~in some areas~~ **tends** to be a meal.
J. A plural verb is used with a period of time or an amount. **Two hours are** all the time we had to enjoy our tea.	Use a singular verb. **Two hours is** all the time we had to enjoy our tea.

For more help, see Chapter 9, pp. 208–221.

QUICK FIX

4 Pronoun Reference Problems

What's the problem? A pronoun does not agree in number, person, or gender with its antecedent, or an antecedent is unclear.

Why does it matter? Lack of agreement or unclear antecedents can confuse your readers.

What should you do about it? Find the antecedent and make the pronoun agree with it, or rewrite the sentence to make the antecedent clear.

What's the Problem?

What's the Problem?	Quick Fix
A. A pronoun doesn't agree in number with its antecedent. A computer user **group** has **their** advantages.	Make the pronoun agree in number with the antecedent. A computer user **group** has **its** advantages.
B. A pronoun doesn't agree in person or in gender with its antecedent. **Ernesto** has discovered **you** can learn valuable tips from others.	Make the pronoun agree with its antecedent. **Ernesto** has discovered **he** can learn valuable tips from others.
C. A pronoun doesn't agree with an indefinite-pronoun antecedent. **Anyone** who owns a computer can increase **their** knowledge by sharing with a group.	Decide whether the indefinite pronoun is singular or plural, and make the pronoun agree with it. **Anyone** who owns a computer can increase **his or her** knowledge by sharing with a group.
D. A pronoun could refer to more than one noun. **Irma** and **Kira** attended a meeting. **She** learned a lot.	Substitute a noun for the pronoun to make the reference clear. **Irma** and **Kira** attended a meeting. **Kira** learned a lot.
E. A pronoun agrees with a word or a phrase that comes between it and its antecedent. **Kira,** like many **people,** may not know a lot about **their** computer.	Mentally block out the word or phrase and change the pronoun so that it agrees with its antecedent. **Kira,** ~~like many people,~~ may not know a lot about **her** computer.

For more help, see Chapter 3, pp. 73–83.

⑤ Incorrect Pronoun Case

What's the problem? A pronoun is in the wrong case.

Why does it matter? Readers may think your work is careless, especially if you are writing a school paper or formal letter.

What should you do about it? Identify how the pronoun is being used, and replace it with the correct form.

What's the Problem?

Quick Fix

A. A pronoun that follows a linking verb is in the wrong case.

The most experienced computer user **is her.**

Always use the subject case after a linking verb.

The most experienced computer user **is she.**

B. A pronoun used as an object is in the wrong case.

Kira **showed** Kent and **I** some shortcuts.

Always use an object pronoun as a direct object, an indirect object, or the object of a preposition.

Kira **showed** Kent and **me** some shortcuts.

C. A contraction is used instead of a possessive pronoun.

You're computer skills have really improved.

Use a possessive pronoun.

Your computer skills have really improved.

D. A pronoun in a compound subject is in the wrong case.

A few members and **me** talked about software problems.

Always use the subject case when a pronoun is used as part of a compound subject.

A few members and **I** talked about software problems.

E. A pronoun followed by an identifying noun is in the wrong case.

A software company asked **we members** to test a new game.

Mentally block out the identifying noun to test for the correct case.

A software company asked **us** ~~members~~ to test a new game.

For more help, see Chapter 3, pp. 61–83.

6 *Who* and *Whom*

What's the problem? The pronoun *who* or *whom* is used incorrectly.

Why does it matter? When writers use *who* or *whom* correctly, readers are more likely to take their ideas seriously.

What should you do about it? Decide how the pronoun functions in the sentence, and then choose the correct form.

What's the Problem?

What's the Problem?	Quick Fix
A. *Whom* is incorrectly used as a subject pronoun. **Whom knows** the origin of origami?	Use *who* as a subject pronoun. **Who knows** the origin of origami?
B. *Whom* is incorrectly used as a predicate pronoun. The expert on origami **is whom?**	Use *who* as a predicate pronoun. The expert on origami **is who?**
C. *Who* is incorrectly used as a direct object. **Who can** we **ask** about these paper sculptures?	Use *whom* as a direct object. **Whom can** we **ask** about these paper sculptures?
D. *Who* is incorrectly used as the object of a preposition. These instructions are **for who?**	Use *whom* as the object of a preposition. These instructions are **for whom?**
E. *Who* is incorrectly used as an indirect object. You **asked who** these questions?	Use *whom* as an indirect object. You **asked whom** these questions?
F. *Who's* is incorrectly used as the possessive pronoun *whose.* **Who's sculpture** is most likely to win first prize?	Use *whose* to show possession. **Whose sculpture** is most likely to win first prize?

For more help, see Chapter 3, pp. 70–72.

What's the problem? The wrong form of an adjective or adverb is used in making a comparison.

Why does it matter? Comparisons that are not worded correctly can be confusing.

What should you do about it? Use a form that makes the comparison clear.

What's the Problem?

Quick Fix

What's the Problem?	Quick Fix
A. Both -er and more or -est and most are used in making a comparison.	Delete one of the forms from the sentence.
Long ago, chariot races in Rome were **more dangerouser** than any modern auto race.	Long ago, chariot races in Rome were **more dangerouser** than any modern auto race.
The best driver was not the one who raced **most fastest.**	The best driver was not the one who raced **most fastest.**
B. A comparative form is used where a superlative form is needed.	Use the superlative form when comparing more than two things.
The best driver was the one who was **more** successful at forcing other drivers to crash.	The best driver was the one who was **most** successful at forcing other drivers to crash.
C. A superlative form is used where a comparative form is needed.	Use the comparative form when comparing two things.
However, crowds cheered **most** loudly for land battles than for chariot races.	However, crowds cheered **more** loudly for land battles than for chariot races.

For more help, see Chapter 5, pp. 137–139.

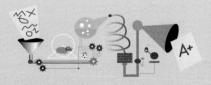

QUICK FIX

8 Verb Forms and Tenses

What's the problem? The wrong form or tense of a verb is used.

Why does it matter? Readers may regard your work as careless or find it confusing.

What should you do about it? Change the verb to the correct form or tense.

What's the Problem?

Quick Fix

What's the Problem?	Quick Fix
A. The wrong form of a verb is used with a helping verb. Many towns **have grew** with the expansion of railroads.	Always use a participle form with a helping verb. Many towns **have grown** with the expansion of railroads.
B. A helping verb is missing. In the late 1800s, herds of cattle **raised** in Texas.	Add a helping verb. In the late 1800s, herds of cattle **were raised** in Texas.
C. A past participle is used incorrectly. Cowhands **gone** to the end of the rail lines with their cattle.	To write about the past, use the past form of a verb. Cowhands **went** to the end of the rail lines with their cattle. **OR** Change the verb to the past perfect form by adding a helping verb. Cowhands **had gone** to the end of the rail lines with their cattle.
D. Different tenses are used in the same sentence even though no change in time has occurred. Cow towns **sprang** up around the rail lines, and more **appear** farther west as the railroads **did.**	Use the same tense throughout the sentence. Cow towns **sprang** up around the rail lines, and more **appeared** farther west as the railroads **did.**

For more help, see Chapter 4, pp. 100–114.

Missing or Misplaced Commas

What's the problem? Commas are missing or are used incorrectly.

Why does it matter? Incorrect use of commas can make sentences difficult to follow.

What should you do about it? Figure out where commas are needed, and add or omit them as necessary.

What's the Problem?

Quick Fix

A. A comma is missing from a compound sentence.

The cover of this book is torn and the pages are missing.

Add a comma before the coordinating conjunction.

The cover of this book is torn, and the pages are missing.

B. A comma is incorrectly placed after a closing quotation mark.

"I'll have to take this book back to the library", said Tristan.

Always put a comma before a closing quotation mark.

"I'll have to take this book back to the library," said Tristan.

C. A comma is missing before the conjunction in a series.

Ivan, LaToya and Keiko will meet him there after school.

Add a comma.

Ivan, LaToya, and Keiko will meet him there after school.

D. A comma is missing after an introductory word, phrase, or clause.

Fortunately Tristan proved that he did not damage the book.

Add a comma after an introductory word, phrase, or clause.

Fortunately, Tristan proved that he did not damage the book.

E. Commas are missing around an appositive or a clause that is not essential to the meaning of the sentence.

The librarian Tristan's aunt assured us that the book will be repaired immediately.

Add commas to set off the appositive or clause.

The librarian, Tristan's aunt, assured us that the book will be repaired immediately.

For more help, see Chapter 11, pp. 253–255.

10 Improving Weak Sentences

What's the problem? A sentence repeats ideas or contains too many ideas.

Why does it matter? Repetitive or overloaded sentences can bore readers and weaken the message.

What should you do about it? Make sure that every sentence contains a clearly focused idea.

What's the Problem?

Quick Fix

A. An idea is repeated.

Thursday was garbage collection day, **so the garbage would be picked up.**

Eliminate the repeated idea.

Thursday was garbage collection day. ~~so the garbage would be picked up.~~

B. A single sentence contains too many loosely connected ideas.

I heard a strange noise and looked outside, and the wind was so strong, and many garbage cans toppled over, and the whole block was covered with debris.

Divide the sentence into two or more sentences, using conjunctions such as *and, but,* or *when* to show relationships between ideas.

I looked outside **when** I heard a strange noise. The strong wind had toppled many garbage cans, **and** the whole block was covered with debris.

C. Too much information is crammed into one sentence.

Luckily, it was a holiday and many people were at home so everyone cleaned up the mess, and Ms. Ramirez made hot chocolate for all the neighbors, who really had fun working together.

Divide the sentence into two or more sentences, using conjunctions such as *and, but, when, although,* and *because* to show relationships between ideas.

Luckily, many people were at home **because** it was a holiday. **While** everyone cleaned up the mess, Ms. Ramirez made hot chocolate for all the neighbors. We really had fun working together.

⑪ Avoiding Wordiness

What's the problem? A sentence contains unnecessary words.

Why does it matter? The meaning of wordy sentences can be unclear to readers.

What should you do about it? Use words that are precise and eliminate extra words.

What's the Problem?

Quick Fix

A. An idea is unnecessarily expressed in two ways.

At 3:00 P.M. **in the afternoon,** the townspeople discovered that their worst fear was true.

Delete the unnecessary words.

At 3:00 P.M. ~~in the afternoon~~, the townspeople discovered that their worst fear was true.

B. A simple idea is expressed in too many words.

Because of the fact that there had been little snow that winter, the water level in the reservoir was low.

Simplify the expression.

Because ~~of the fact that~~ there had been little snow that winter, the water level in the reservoir was low.

C. A sentence contains words that do not add to its meaning.

The point is that young people were upset because the pool, **which was** a source of jobs for teenagers, had to be closed.

Delete the unnecessary words.

~~The point is that~~ Young people were upset because the pool, ~~which was~~ a source of jobs for teenagers, had to be closed.

12 Varying Sentence Structure

What's the problem? Too many sentences begin in the same way, or one type of sentence is overused.

Why does it matter? Lack of variety in sentences makes writing dull and choppy.

What should you do about it? Rearrange the phrases in some of the sentences, and use different types of sentences for variety and impact.

What's the Problem?

Quick Fix

A. Too many sentences in a paragraph start the same way.

The microprocessor was developed in 1971. **The microprocessor** is a tiny computer chip. It has had a big impact on the computer industry. **Video games** appeared when smaller computers became possible. **Video games** became popular quickly, especially among teenagers.

Rearrange words or phrases in some of the sentences.

Developed in 1971, the microprocessor is a tiny computer chip. It has had a big impact on the computer industry. Video games appeared when smaller computers became possible. **Especially among teenagers,** video games became popular quickly.

B. Too many declarative sentences are used.

Video games are fun because they have realistic graphics and interesting sound effects. Winning requires certain skills. A player must have good coordination and quick reflexes; however, a player's greatest challenge is concentration.

Add variety by rewriting one sentence as a command, a question, or an exclamation.

Video games are fun because they have realistic graphics and interesting sound effects. **What skills does a player need to win?** Good coordination and quick reflexes are important; however, a player's greatest challenge is concentration.

13 Varying Sentence Length

What's the problem? A piece of writing contains too many short, repetitive sentences.

Why does it matter? The use of too many short, repetitive sentences makes writing choppy and monotonous.

What should you do about it? Combine or reword sentences to create sentences of varying lengths.

What's the Problem?

Too many short sentences are used.

The National Weather Service issued a warning. The warning was about a storm. Torrential rains had struck towns. The towns were along the coast. Now the storm was turning. Its turn was sudden. It was turning inland. Many travelers were stranded. This happened when the airport had to close. The closing was temporary. The National Weather Service urged people to evacuate the area. Many people stayed at home. It rained for several days. There was flooding. People had to be rescued.

Quick Fix

Combine sentences that add only one detail about the subject with other sentences.

The National Weather Service issued a **storm** warning. Torrential rains had struck towns **along the coast. Suddenly** the storm turned **inland.**

OR

Use conjunctions such as *or, and*, or *but* to combine related sentences.

The airport had to close temporarily, **and** many travelers were stranded.

OR

Use words such as *while* or *although* to form a complex sentence.

Although the National Weather Service urged people to evacuate the area, many people stayed at home.

OR

Combine the sentences to form a compound-complex sentence.

After it rained for several days, there was flooding, **and** people had to be rescued.

For more help, see Chapter 8, pp. 192–199.

QUICK FIX

14 Adding Supporting Details

What's the problem? Not enough details are given for readers to fully understand the topic.

Why does it matter? Unexplained terms and unsupported claims can weaken a piece of writing.

What should you do about it? Add information and details that will make statements clear.

What's the Problem?

What's the Problem?	Quick Fix
A. An important word is not explained or defined. Computer **chips** are made from quartz rock.	Explain or define the word. **Engineers can now fit computer circuitry into tiny squares called chips,** composed of material that comes from quartz rock.
B. No details are given. An early electronic digital computer was built in 1946.	**Add details that will help readers understand the significance of the topic.** An early electronic digital computer was built in 1946. **It was huge compared with computers of today. At first, only scientists used computers, but now people use them at home, school, and work.**
C. No supporting facts are given. Computer chips are used in many things.	Add supporting facts. Computer chips are used in **watches, cars, games, telephones, and many household appliances.**
D. No reason is given for an opinion. Our lives would be quite different without computer chips.	Add a reason. Our lives would be quite different without computer chips. **Computer chips have helped us automate processes and achieve other technological gains.**

15 Avoiding Clichés and Slang

What's the problem? A piece of formal writing contains clichés or slang expressions.

Why does it matter? Clichés do not convey fresh images to readers. Slang is not appropriate in formal writing.

What should you do about it? Replace the clichés and slang with clear, fresh expressions.

What's the Problem?

Quick Fix

A. A sentence contains a cliché.

After their tournament victory, the members of the women's volleyball team **were as happy as larks.**

Replace the cliché with a fresh description or explanation.

After their tournament victory, the members of the women's volleyball team **frantically cheered, laughed, and hugged one another. They were like students on graduation day, full of joy and relief all at once.**

B. A sentence contains inappropriate slang.

The explanation he gave is **whack.**

Replace the slang with more appropriate language.

The explanation he gave is **not acceptable.**

QUICK FIX

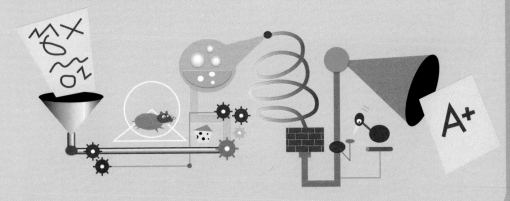

16 Using Precise Words

What's the problem? Nouns, modifiers, and verbs are not precise.

Why does it matter? Writers who use vague or general words don't give readers an accurate picture of their topic.

What should you do about it? Replace vague words with precise and vivid ones.

What's the Problem?

Quick Fix

A. Nouns and pronouns are too general.

The **people** walked into that **passageway during the day** without **some supplies**.

Use specific words.

The **hikers** walked into that **canyon at noon** without **water**.

B. Modifiers are too general.

As they marched, the **hot** sun actually felt **good** on their backs. **Later,** the **hot** weather felt **bad**.

Use vivid adjectives and adverbs.

As they marched, the **radiant** sun actually felt **comforting** on their backs. **Two hours later,** the **steamy** weather felt **oppressive**.

C. Verbs tell about the action rather than show it.

The group **sat** on some rocks to rest. Without water, their throats **were** full of dry, dusty canyon air. They **got nervous** when a thunderstorm **came**.

Use vivid verbs to show the action.

The group **sprawled** on some rocks to rest. Without water, their throats **were parched** from dry, dusty canyon air. They **panicked** when a thunderstorm **approached**.

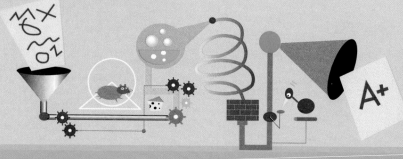

17 Using Figurative Language

What's the problem? A piece of writing is dull or unimaginative.

Why does it matter? Dull writing bores readers because it doesn't help them form mental pictures of what is being described.

What should you do about it? Add figures of speech to make writing lively and to create pictures in readers' minds.

What's the Problem?

A description is dull and lifeless.

The principal was the first one to get the message about a movie. She flashed the news to the teachers. However, a student must have overheard the teachers talking about the announcement, because by the afternoon, everyone seemed to have the information.

Of course, by then the story was exaggerated.

There were so many different stories. Were we really going to be in a movie?

Quick Fix

Add a simile.

The principal was the first one to get the message about a movie. **Like a child waving a new toy,** she flashed the news to the teachers. However, a student must have overheard the teachers talking about the announcement, because by the afternoon, everyone seemed to have the information.

OR

Add a metaphor.

Of course, by then the story was **a wildfire that could not be contained.**

OR

Use personification.

The burning excitement fueled **rumors that skipped and darted down the hallways and into the classrooms.** Were we really going to be in a movie?

18 Paragraphing

What's the problem? A paragraph contains too many ideas.

Why does it matter? A long paragraph discourages readers from continuing.

What should you do about it? Break the paragraph into shorter paragraphs. Start a new paragraph whenever a new idea is presented or the time, place, or speaker changes.

QUICK FIX

What's the Problem?

Too many ideas are contained in one paragraph.

I'll never forget the first time I saw a rattlesnake. Willie and I were camping in the mountains when we decided to go for a hike on a trail heading up the rocky side of a hill. As I stepped across a rock along the trail, I noticed something in the way. I leaped into the air and jumped backward in one fluid motion. "Arrgh!," I cried. "I think it's a snake." "Ha! I bet this is one of your tricks," Willie snickered. After the longest moment of my life, we heard a hiss and a rattling sound at the same time. We froze as we watched the snake slither into the bushes. We were more cautious about where we stepped after that harrowing experience.

Quick Fix

I'll never forget the first time I saw a rattlesnake. Willie and I were camping in the mountains when we decided to go for a hike on a trail heading up the rocky side of a hill.

Start a new paragraph to introduce a new idea.

As I stepped across a rock along the trail, I noticed something in the way. I leaped into the air and jumped backward in one fluid motion.

Start a new paragraph whenever the speaker changes.

"Arrgh!," I cried. "I think it's a snake."

"Ha! I bet this is one of your tricks," Willie snickered.

Start a new paragraph when the time or place changes.

After the longest moment of my life, we heard a hiss and a rattling sound at the same time. We froze as we watched the snake slither into the bushes. We were more cautious about where we stepped after that harrowing experience.

What's the Problem?

An essay is treated as one long paragraph.

When laptop computers were first introduced in 1981, it took a while for their popularity to build. At that time, they were bulky and still relied on an outlet for power. They were mostly used by businesspeople, who could take their work with them. In the 1990s, two important innovations improved laptop technology; as a result, sales skyrocketed. The first was improved battery capability. Lighter and more efficient lithium batteries replaced the older and heavier lead-acid batteries. Second, better liquid-crystal displays made laptops more user-friendly. Earlier laptop screens were black and white and were likely to produce shadows and blurriness. New technology allowed laptop screens to show clearer and sharper images and also display accurate color visuals. Finally, internal modems were placed in laptop computers. This made it possible for users to connect to the Internet away from home. These innovations have made laptops just as popular and easy to use as their desktop counterparts. Laptop computers have finally lived up to their initial promise of being truly portable and usable anywhere.

Quick Fix

When laptop computers were first introduced in 1981, it took a while for their popularity to build. At that time, they were bulky and still relied on an outlet for power. They were mostly used by businesspeople, who could take their work with them.

Start a new paragraph to introduce the first main idea.

In the 1990s, two important innovations improved laptop technology; as a result, sales skyrocketed. The first was improved battery capability. Lighter and more efficient lithium batteries replaced the older and heavier lead-acid batteries.

Start a new paragraph to introduce a new idea.

Second, better liquid-crystal displays made laptops more user-friendly. Earlier laptop screens were black and white and were likely to produce shadows and blurriness. New technology allowed laptop screens to show clearer and sharper images and also display accurate color visuals.

Set off the conclusion in its own paragraph.

These innovations have made laptops just as popular and easy to use as their desktop counterparts. Laptop computers have finally lived up to their initial promise of being truly portable and usable anywhere.

Student Resources

Exercise Bank

Boost your grammar fitness! Use the circled arrows ➜ to find the answers to the Self-Check items. In addition, you can complete exercises in this section to get extra practice in a skill you've just learned.

1 The Sentence and Its Parts

1. Complete Subjects and Predicates (links to exercise on p. 7)

➜ **1.** complete subject (CS): *Species of plants and animals;* complete predicate (CP): *are disappearing near cities*
2. CS: *Urban sprawl;* CP: *harms their habitats*

On a sheet of paper, label one column "Complete Subjects" and another "Complete Predicates." For each sentence write the complete subject and complete predicate in the proper columns.

1. The goal of settlement houses is the improvement of neighborhoods.
2. Their services include recreational and educational activities.
3. Various types of counseling are also offered at settlement houses.
4. The first settlement house was founded in London in 1884.
5. Neighborhood Guild opened in New York two years later.
6. Hull House was one of the most famous settlement houses.
7. Jane Addams helped found this Chicago institution in 1889.
8. People of many different nationalities sought help at Hull House.
9. Addams worked tirelessly for social reform.
10. Her efforts won her the Nobel Peace Prize in 1931.

2. Simple Subjects (links to exercise A, p. 9)

➜ **1.** Industrial Revolution   **2.** industries

Write the simple subject of each sentence.

1. Early humans wandered from place to place.
2. Farming families began settling in villages about 11,000 years ago.
3. The first cities developed several thousand years later.
4. Technological advances allowed cities to grow.
5. Ancient Rome had nearly a million residents at its height.
6. Most cities were fairly small during the Middle Ages.
7. Modern industry created dramatic changes in urban life.
8. Large factories needed many workers.

9. The populations of older cities increased rapidly.
10. Other industrial cities sprang up in open areas.

3. Simple Predicates, or Verbs (links to exercise A, p. 11)

➡ **1.** is   **2.** hold

Write the simple predicate, or verb, of each sentence.

1. The Aztecs founded the city of Tenochtitlán in the 1300s.
2. This site became Mexico City after the Spanish conquest.
3. Mexico City is the capital of Mexico.
4. The city has a population of over 9 million.
5. Another 7 million people live in the metropolitan area.
6. Mexico City lies on an ancient lake bed.
7. Residents enjoy a mild climate.
8. The high altitude creates breathing problems for some people.
9. Splendid public buildings grace the center of Mexico City.
10. The city dominates Mexico's political, cultural, and economic activities.

4. Verb Phrases (links to exercise on p. 13)

➡ **1.** have allowed   **2.** can cause

Write the verb phrase found in each sentence below.

1. The United States has been called a "throwaway society."
2. The average American is throwing out over three pounds of waste per day.
3. City dwellers may be even more wasteful.
4. For example, New Yorkers are discarding nearly seven pounds per person.
5. Landfills have been filling up throughout the country.
6. New locations for landfills are becoming hard to find.
7. Some cities are burning their excess waste.
8. However, incinerators can cause air pollution.
9. Recycling might be the best solution.
10. Americans also should reduce their level of waste production.

5. Compound Sentence Parts (links to exercise A, p. 15)

➡ **1.** compound subject: *Juneau, cities*
   5. compound verb: *survived, profited*

Write and identify the compound subject (CS) or compound verb (CV) in each sentence.

1. Cities and towns may take years to recover from a natural disaster.
2. Powerful hurricanes have killed and destroyed on a vast scale.
3. High winds and heavy rains make these storms dangerous.
4. Weather balloons, radar, and satellites help meteorologists track hurricanes.
5. Seismologists study and measure earthquakes.
6. Sections of Earth's crust shift and break during these events.
7. The shaking of the ground can damage or topple buildings.
8. Architects and engineers can create earthquake-resistant structures.
9. Well-designed homes, schools, and office buildings may save many lives.
10. However, no precautions or safety measures can eliminate the danger of earthquakes.

6. Kinds of Sentences (links to exercise A, p. 17)

→ **1.** INT **2.** D

Identify each of the following sentences as declarative (D), interrogative (INT), exclamatory (E), or imperative (IMP).

1. How much time do you spend in your local mall?
2. Shopping malls have become the social centers of many cities and towns.
3. Consider the different forms of entertainment in malls.
4. Does your local mall have movie theaters and game arcades?
5. Many malls also offer live entertainment, such as concerts.
6. Of course, shopping is the main activity in malls.
7. One mall in Canada has over 800 stores!
8. Imagine how long it would take to visit all of them.
9. There is even a mall just for kids, in Michigan.
10. A restaurant in the food court serves 50 types of peanut butter and jelly sandwiches!

7. Subjects in Unusual Order (links to exercise A, p. 20)

→ **1.** subject: *you;* verb phrase: *Have heard*
   2. subject: *amusement park;* verb: *lies*

Make two columns on a separate sheet of paper, and write the simple subject and verb (or verb phrase) of each sentence in the appropriately labeled column.

1. Would you like a trip to the past?
2. Visit the historic town of Williamsburg, Virginia.
3. Between the James and York rivers lies this popular tourist attraction.
4. Here is a brief description.
5. Within the town are over 80 homes and other buildings from the 1700s.
6. There are also more than 400 reconstructed buildings.
7. Along the streets stroll actors in colonial costumes.
8. Inside some buildings are demonstrations of crafts.
9. Are you planning a trip to Williamsburg?
10. Read a brochure or travel book for more information.

8. Complements: Subject Complements (links to exercise A, p. 22)

➡ **1.** Windy City—PN   **4.** high—PA

Write the subject complement found in each sentence, and identify it as a predicate noun (PN) or predicate adjective (PA).

1. New Orleans is a city in Louisiana.
2. It was the birthplace of jazz.
3. Preservation Hall is famous for its jazz concerts.
4. The restaurants of New Orleans are another attraction.
5. The Cajun dishes taste spicy.
6. The city seems especially exciting during the annual Mardi Gras festival.
7. The architecture of New Orleans is a blend of old and new.
8. The historic French Quarter neighborhood is picturesque.
9. New Orleans is a major seaport.
10. The city is also a center for business and industry.

9. Complements: Objects of Verbs (links to exercise on p. 24)

➡ **1.** cities, IO; connection, DO   **2.** system, DO

Write the objects in these sentences, identifying each as a direct object (DO) or an indirect object (IO).

1. Most city dwellers cherish their urban parks.
2. These open spaces add variety to a city.
3. They give residents opportunities for recreation.
4. Chicago's Lincoln Park hugs the shore of Lake Michigan.
5. The park's free zoo teaches children lessons about nature.
6. Fairmount Park in Philadelphia provides tours of its seven colonial mansions.

7. Many filmmakers have shot scenes in Central Park.
8. The park offers visitors splendid views of New York City.
9. San Francisco's Golden Gate Park includes a Japanese teahouse.
10. The staff serves customers tea in the traditional Japanese way.

10. Fragments and Run-Ons (links to exercise A, p. 27)

➡ **1.** RO   **2.** F

Identify the following items as fragments (F), run-ons (RO), or complete sentences (CS).

1. Beijing is home to one of three great Chinese cooking styles, this style is called Beijing or Mandarin cuisine.
2. The food generally mild.
3. Wheat an important ingredient in many recipes.
4. Noodle dishes popular in Beijing cuisine.
5. Stuffed buns and filled dumplings are served as snacks or meals.
6. Beijing duck a famous dish.
7. This delicious meal takes a long time to prepare, it is served in three separate courses.
8. Chefs in Shanghai base their meals on rice rather than wheat.
9. Many Shanghai dishes feature seafood, the city is close to the sea.
10. Shanghai recipes often have interesting names, such as hairy crab and lion's head casserole.

2 Nouns

1. Kinds of Nouns (links to exercise A, p. 38)

➡ **1.** astronauts, food, tubes: common
   2. Astronauts, tray, forks, spoons: common; Space Shuttle Program: proper

List the nouns found in each sentence, and identify them as common or proper. Then write three collective nouns from your list.

1. The Soviet Union launched the first satellite into orbit in 1957.
2. Yuri Gagarin of the Soviet Union became the first person to orbit Earth four years later.
3. President John F. Kennedy then challenged the United States to put an astronaut on the moon.
4. Teams of scientists worked to develop a suitable spacecraft.
5. The project to land astronauts on the moon was named *Apollo.*
6. American astronauts finally reached the moon in July 1969.

7. Neil Armstrong was the first person to stand on the moon.
8. As he stepped onto the surface, Armstrong said, "That's one small step for man, one giant leap for mankind."
9. Many Americans expressed pride in this historic achievement.
10. Soviet and American crews worked closely together on some later missions.

2. Singular and Plural Nouns (links to exercise A, p. 40)

➡ **1.** quantities   **2.** amounts

Rewrite the nouns in parentheses in their plural forms.

1. Sally Ride made (headline) in 1983 when she became the first American woman in space.
2. Yet a Russian woman had beaten her there by two (decade).
3. Valentina Vladimirovna Tereshkova's life was similar to the (life) of other ordinary Soviet citizens.
4. As a teenager, she worked in (factory) that produced tires and textiles.
5. However, at night she took (class) to continue her education.
6. She began making parachute (jump) in her spare time.
7. She showed (flash) of courage and strength while pursuing her goal of becoming a cosmonaut.
8. Soviet officals finally admitted her and four other (woman) into the training program.
9. She orbited Earth for nearly three (day) during her historic mission in 1963.
10. Russians regarded her as one of the country's (hero) when she returned home safely.

3. Possessive Nouns (links to exercise A, p. 43)

➡ **1.** *Astronomy's,* singular   **2.** *Babylonians',* plural

Write the possessive form of each noun in parentheses. Then label each possessive noun *singular* or *plural.*

1. Maria Mitchell was (America) first professional woman astronomer.
2. She inherited her (parents) passion for education.
3. As a teenager she began participating in her (father) astronomical studies.
4. One day she looked through his telescope and noticed a (star) unusual position.
5. (Mitchell) observations convinced her that the star was really a comet.

6. She received a gold medal from (Denmark) king in 1848 for her discovery.
7. She was the first female member of the American Academy of Arts and Sciences, one of the (country) oldest educational societies.
8. Vassar College eventually hired her as a professor and director of the (school) observatory.
9. Her research at the observatory included the study of (planets) surfaces.
10. Mitchell also became an important spokesperson for the advancement of (women) rights.

4. Compound Nouns (links to exercise A, p. 45)

→ 1. *mountaintop;* singular
2. *headaches,* plural; *sea level,* singular

Write each compound noun in these sentences, and label it *singular* or *plural*.

1. NASA launched a spacecraft to increase our understanding of Mars.
2. It landed with the aid of parachutes, rockets, and airbags.
3. Then it bounced like a basketball for two and a half minutes.
4. It finally came to a successful touchdown.
5. A small vehicle rolled out of a doorway onto the Martian surface.
6. The vehicle examined rocks and collected data according to a planned timetable for exploration.
7. Scientists at NASA headquarters gave silly names like Barnacle Bill and Flat Top to the rocks that were found.
8. Anchorpersons told television viewers about these discoveries on evening newscasts.
9. NASA received praise for the mission in many newspapers.
10. My great-grandmother finds space exploration fascinating.

5. Nouns as Subjects and Complements (links to exercise on p. 47)

→ 1. subject; complement   2. subject

Identify each underlined noun as a subject or complement.

1. The <u>Hubble Space Telescope</u> (HST) is the first <u>telescope</u> based in space.
2. It avoids the <u>distortions</u> of Earth's atmosphere by orbiting the planet.
3. <u>NASA</u> launched <u>HST</u> into orbit in 1990.

4. <u>Astronomers</u> soon discovered a <u>flaw</u> in the telescope's mirror.
5. The <u>flaw</u> prevented the <u>telescope</u> from focusing properly.
6. <u>NASA</u> sent <u>HST</u> a <u>repair crew</u> in 1993.
7. The <u>crew</u> captured <u>HST</u> as it orbited the earth.
8. They installed corrective <u>mirrors</u> on the telescope.
9. <u>HST</u> then began to send <u>astronomers</u> astonishingly clear <u>images</u>.
10. <u>HST</u> is now a great <u>success</u> instead of a failure.

6. Nouns in Phrases (links to exercise on p. 49)

➡ **1.** appositive   **2.** appositive

Identify each underlined noun as an object of a preposition or as an appositive.

1. Some of the most important space missions were accomplished without <u>astronauts</u>.
2. They were carried out by space probes, unmanned <u>spacecraft</u> that transmit information.
3. Space probes can be sent into <u>areas</u> too dangerous for humans.
4. They have provided much of our information about <u>planets</u>.
5. Venus and Mars, the <u>planets</u> nearest Earth, are frequent targets of space probes.
6. The probe *Mariner 2* reached Venus in 1962.
7. *Mariner 4,* the first <u>probe</u> to explore Mars, sent back important pictures of the planet.
8. *Magellan* spent four years taking photographs as it orbited the planet <u>Venus</u>.
9. It completed its mission by plunging into Venus's <u>atmosphere</u>.
10. *Magellan* and the other probes often performed beyond <u>expectations</u>.

③ Pronouns

1. What Is a Pronoun? (links to exercise A, p. 59)

➡ **1.** her   **2.** She, they

List the personal pronoun(s) in each sentence.

1. Have you ever gone on a backpacking trip?
2. Backpackers need to consider safety aspects when planning their trips.
3. They need to know what to do in an emergency.
4. One experienced backpacker explained his most important rule: to avoid dangerous situations.

5. Whenever I go backpacking, I always take the latest weather report with me.
6. Careful backpackers never ignore any threatening weather heading toward them.
7. Electrical storms, snowstorms, or flash floods can cause you serious problems.
8. We need to know how to build sturdy temporary shelters in case our trip is interrupted by dangerous weather.
9. In my opinion, surviving in snow is the greatest weather challenge a backpacker can face.
10. Safe backpacking is one of the most exciting activities in my life, and it could also be a big part of yours.

2. Subject Pronouns (links to exercise on p. 62)

➡ **1.** I   **3.** They

Write the correct form of the pronoun to complete each sentence. Choose from the words given in parentheses.

1. My friends and (I, me) enjoy reading novels about young people who survive dangerous situations.
2. (We, Us) especially enjoyed *Hatchet* by Gary Paulsen.
3. In the novel, Brian Robeson's small plane crashes, and (he, him) is forced to survive by himself in the Canadian wilderness.
4. The pilot of Brian's plane dies, and the only survivor is (he, him).
5. For more than 50 days, (he, him) must use his skills to find food, build shelter, and keep safe.
6. Another terrific novel about survival is *Julie of the Wolves* by Jean Craighead George; (she, her) has written many popular books.
7. Miyax, also called Julie, is an Inuit, or Eskimo, girl; (she, her) struggles to survive a cross-country journey through the harsh Alaskan forests.
8. The only human for many miles around is (she, her).
9. Miyax befriends a pack of wolves, and (they, them) become like brothers to her.
10. It is (they, them) who help Miyax survive her ordeal in the Arctic wilderness.

3. Object Pronouns (links to exercise on p. 64)

➡ **1.** *me,* object   **3.** *him,* object

Write the correct pronoun to complete each sentence. Label each pronoun subject (S) or object (O).

1. About 50,000 noticeable earthquakes occur each year somewhere on earth, but only about 100 of (they, them) are strong enough to cause serious damage.
2. On January 17, 1995, residents of the Kobe-Osaka region of Japan awoke when the ground shook beneath (they, them).
3. The earthquake claimed about 6,000 lives and damaged thousands of buildings; at least 100,000 of (them, they) were destroyed.
4. The extent of the damage shocked (we, us) and other people around the world.
5. Kobe is the world's sixth-busiest port, serving many of Japan's ships. (They, Them) came almost to a halt following the quake.
6. To my friends and (I, me), the response of the Japanese people to the disaster was amazing.
7. In the six months following the Kobe earthquake, the Japanese people built 40,000 temporary houses; more than 300,000 homeless people used (they, them) for shelter.
8. Today, the people of Kobe have rebuilt much of their city, but the memory of that terrible morning will be with (they, them) forever.
9. When the next major earthquake strikes, will (we, us) be prepared?
10. What important lessons can the Kobe earthquake, and the tremendous relief efforts of the Japanese people, teach (we, us) about surviving disasters?

4. Possessive Pronouns (links to exercise A, p. 67)

➡ **2.** their   **3.** its

Write the correct pronoun or contraction for each sentence.

1. Caves are one fascinating element of this natural world of (ours, our's).
2. Caves can be formed by the sea, lava, glaciers, or the wearing away of underground rock; depending on (their, they're) origins, caves have different characteristics.
3. Is exploring a cave (you're, your) idea of fun?
4. The exploration of caves has (it's, its) own name—(it's, its) called spelunking.
5. If (you're, your) thinking of becoming a spelunker, it's important to learn the proper safety techniques.
6. (It's, Its) not dangerous to explore a cave if you follow the safety rules and use good judgment.
7. If people don't pay attention in a cave, (their, they're) more likely to fall down or get lost.

8. Rescuing an injured person from a cave can be quite difficult, especially if (its, it's) passageways are narrow and crooked.

9. You can sometimes find (you're, your) way out of a cave by following underground water downstream to the mouth of the cave.

10. Many caves have strong echoes; any shout you hear could be (your's, yours)!

5. Reflexive and Intensive Pronouns (links to exercise on p. 69)

➜ **1.** himself, (R)   **3.** herself, (I)

Write the reflexive or intensive pronoun in each sentence. Then identify it as reflexive (R) or intensive (I).

1. Have you ever asked yourself how you might deal with a disability?

2. Basketball player Mahmoud Abdul-Rauf has found the strength within himself to succeed, in spite of a disorder.

3. He suffers from Tourette's syndrome, a nerve disease that causes him to twitch and shout in spite of himself.

4. A star with the NBA's Denver Nuggets in the mid-1990s, Abdul-Rauf inspired many people who have struggled themselves with disabilities.

5. People with this condition sometimes isolate themselves from others because the disorder causes such embarrassment.

6. Abdul-Rauf believes that the disorder itself has made him into a better person and athlete.

7. It has caused him to push himself and practice harder.

8. He dedicated himself to overcoming the condition and becoming the best basketball player he could be.

9. The player's faith and dedication are qualities we ourselves can admire and try to imitate.

10. I myself have seen Abdul-Rauf play many times on television.

6. Interrogatives and Demonstratives (links to exercise A, p. 72)

➜ **3.** That   **4.** whom

For each sentence, choose the correct pronoun from the words in parentheses.

1. (This, That) is the story of how I survived the fishing trip during my week at summer camp.

2. (Whose, Who's) bright idea was it to collect earthworms for the fishing trip?

3. Of course, you need bait to go fishing, but (who, what) is the best bait?
4. Our counselor said red wigglers and night crawlers were good earthworms to use for (this, these).
5. Of course, there are always (those, these) who hate to handle worms.
6. (Who, Whom) was responsible for holding the flashlight while I tried to grab the red wigglers with my bare hands?
7. (This, That) was about the worst job I've ever had— digging in the dirt and trying to hold the squirming mess of worms.
8. (Who, Which) was the longest worm we caught? It must have been six inches long.
9. After all my trouble, guess (whom, who) didn't catch a single fish the next day?
10. (What, Which) do you mean, I didn't try hard enough?

7. Pronoun-Antecedent Agreement (links to exercise A, p. 75)

➡ **1.** their (cultures)   **3.** She (Rose Robinson)

Write the pronouns in these sentences, along with their antecedents.

1. Over the years, the people of the Sea Islands of Georgia and South Carolina have kept alive their ancestral culture and language.
2. Enslaved Africans, brought to the islands during colonial times, mixed their West African languages with English.
3. Before the Civil War, the Sea Islands were known for their rice and cotton plantations.
4. After the war, many of them were given to freed slaves.
5. The culture that developed on the islands is known as Gullah. It has its roots in the cultures of West Africa.
6. The Gullah language is still a mixture, containing almost 6,000 African words; most of them are personal names.
7. You probably have several Gullah words in your own vocabulary.
8. The words *gumbo, voodoo, goober,* and *jukebox* come from Gullah. They are familiar, aren't they?
9. Students of languages are fascinated when they encounter a mixed language like Gullah.
10. When people visit the Sea Islands, they see evidence of a culture's survival and development over centuries.

8. Indefinite-Pronoun Agreement (links to exercise A, p. 78)

➡ **1.** he or she   **3.** them

Write the pronoun that agrees with the indefinite-pronoun antecedent.

1. Has anyone ever read about prehistoric cave paintings in (their, his or her) trips to the library?
2. No one who has ever seen prehistoric cave paintings will forget the powerful impression they make on (them, him or her).
3. Many have written about (his, their) impressions of prehistoric paintings of horses, deer, bears, bison, and aurochs, an ancient breed of cattle.
4. One of the horses in a cave in Chauvet, France, tosses (their, its) mane proudly while others watch.
5. Several are so skillfully painted that it looks as if (it, they) could stampede right off the cave walls!
6. Some of the animals are shown making (its, their) way across the cave walls in large herds.
7. Another raises (its, their) head to challenge a rival in battle.
8. All of the prehistoric artists who left (his, their) drawings on the cave walls are unknown.
9. None of the artists were able to sign (his or her, their) names to the paintings because written language had not yet been developed.
10. However, each has left (his or her, their) mark through the beauty and power of the paintings that have survived for more than 30,000 years.

9. Pronoun Problems (links to exercise A, p. 80)

➡ **1.** we

Choose the better noun or pronoun from the words in parentheses.

1. There is a special animal that (we, us) Americans have always admired as a symbol of the West and its wide-open spaces.
2. The American bison, or buffalo, gives (we, us) animal lovers a thrill because of its great size, majesty, and interesting habits.
3. Last year, a scientist talked to (we, us) students about the near extinction and comeback of the bison herds on the Great Plains.
4. During the last century, millions of American bison roamed the Great Plains. (They, The Great Plains) stretched from the Mississippi River to the Rocky Mountains.
5. Native Americans of the Great Plains and other areas of the West depended on the bison herds for food, clothing, and shelter. (They, the Native Americans) even used the bison's bones to make tools.

6. There may have been 60 million bison spread across the region before the European settlers came to the West. (They, The bison) lived together in gigantic herds.

7. But European hunters slaughtered (them, the bison), often for sport and target practice.

8. By 1900, animal conservationists were alarmed that fewer than a thousand bison were left in North America. With the help of President Theodore Roosevelt, they created successful programs to ensure (their, the bison's) survival.

9. If anyone enjoys learning about interesting animals and their struggle for survival, it's (we, us) members of the school environmental club.

10. The bison makes (we, us) lovers of the old West think about times past.

10. More Pronoun Problems (links to exercise A, p. 82)

➡ **1.** me   **2.** him

For each sentence, write the correct pronoun from the choice given in parentheses.

1. When our teacher asked Jason and (I, me) to do a presentation on an explorer, we chose the Frenchwoman Alexandra David-Néel.

2. David-Néel, the daughter of French parents, made (her, their) way into the forbidden Tibetan city of Lhasa, becoming the first Western woman to do so.

3. Jason and (I, me) read about David-Néel's great interest in Buddhism, the religion of Tibet and other countries in Asia.

4. David-Néel, who spent much time away from home, still enjoyed a strong and lasting relationship with (she, her) husband.

5. In 1912, David-Néel met the Dalai Lama, leader of the world's Buddhists; she and (he, him) became friends.

6. While living and studying in a Buddhist monastery in the Himalayan kingdom of Sikkim, she met a boy named Aphur Yongden, who became (her, his) adopted son.

7. (He, Him) and David-Néel explored Tibet and its capital, Lhasa, which was forbidden to Westerners.

8. One winter, freezing temperatures forced Aphur and (she, her) to seek refuge in a mountain cave, where they had a dinner of shoe-leather soup!

9. Disguised as a Tibetan peasant, (she, her) and Aphur spent two months exploring the secret city.

10. The current Dalai Lama, the 14th leader to hold the title, and many of (his, their) followers live in India, far away from the city of Lhasa.

4 Verbs

1. What Is a Verb? (links to exercise A, p. 94)

➡ **1.** has ridden   **3.** is

Write the verb or verb phrase found in each of the following sentences. Then write *A* if it is an action verb or *L* if it is a linking verb.

1. People have slid down icy hillsides for thousands of years.
2. Since 1914, one form of sliding down hills has been a championship sport.
3. The sport's name is luge.
4. To some people, luge appears similar to bobsledding.
5. Both sports occur on a rounded, icy track built on the side of a hill.
6. However, many important differences separate the two sports.
7. In luge, the sled is a small platform with steel runners.
8. In some ways, luge seems similar to riding down an icy hill on a cafeteria tray!
9. The luge racer lies faceup on the luge, with feet forward.
10. In competitions such as the Winter Olympics, top speeds can approach 90 miles an hour!

2. Action Verbs and Objects (links to exercise A, p. 97)

➡ **1.** feat, DO   **3.** himself, IO; vehicle, DO

The following sentences contain 7 direct objects and 4 indirect objects. For each sentence, write and label each direct object (DO) and each indirect object (IO). Then, write *T* if the verb is transitive or *I* if it is intransitive.

1. One of the most famous automobile races in the world occurs around Memorial Day each year.
2. Since 1911, the Indianapolis 500 has given spectators thrills.
3. The 33 fastest cars and drivers compete in the race each year.
4. Hundreds of thousands of fans cheer the drivers during the race.
5. The race begins with the announcement for drivers to start their engines.
6. Television shows people around the world the spectacular auto race.
7. Could you send me a list of the drivers in this year's race?
8. Indy cars use special tires for better control.
9. A black-and-white checkered flag signals the end of the race.
10. Race officials traditionally give the winner of the race a bottle of milk.

3. Linking Verbs and Predicate Words (links to exercise on p. 99)

➡ **1.** was, mild (PA)   **3.** felt, calm (PA)

Each sentence in the following paragraph contains a linking verb. Write the linking verb and the subject complement. Then write *PN* if the subject complement is a predicate noun. Write *PA* if the subject complement is a predicate adjective.

For many people, the Tournament of Roses Parade is the highlight of New Year's Day. This parade first became popular in the 1890s. Parade watchers in Pasadena, California, and TV viewers around the world grow excited as the parade approaches. The more than 60 gorgeous floats are probably the parade's biggest attraction. Their roses, camellias, carnations, and other flowers smell divine. The music of the numerous marching bands sounds cheerful. The beautifully decorated horses and riders look very elegant. Riding on a float at the end of the parade, the Rose Queen is often a college student from the Los Angeles area. The volunteers who work hard every year to create the parade must feel extremely proud. Memories of the beautiful floats remain strong for years.

4. Principal Parts of Verbs (links to exercise on p. 101)

➡ **1.** past   **2.** present

Identify each underlined principal part as the present, the present participle, the past, or the past participle.

1. During the 1950s and 1960s, African Americans <u>struggled</u> for equal rights.
2. In many Southern states, waiting rooms and restaurants in bus stations <u>segregated</u> African Americans.
3. In 1961, 70,000 "Freedom Riders" of all races <u>challenged</u> segregation in these bus stations and on buses.
4. By traveling throughout the South on buses and risking arrest, the Freedom Riders <u>focused</u> attention on segregation and injustice.
5. The bravery of the Freedom Riders has <u>inspired</u> many Americans.
6. In September 1961, a government commission <u>ruled</u> that all interstate buses and stations must be integrated.
7. Thanks to young people like the Freedom Riders, many Americans are <u>benefiting</u> from the civil rights campaigns of the 1960s.
8. Since the successful Freedom Rides of 1961, American minorities have <u>gained</u> many rights, as well as new responsibilities.
9. Today, all Americans <u>enjoy</u> equal rights under the law.
10. However, the campaign to make equal rights a reality for all Americans is <u>continuing</u>.

5. Irregular Verbs (links to exercise on p. 104)

➡ **1.** won **2.** gave

Write the correct form of the verb in parentheses.

1. Peter Cooper (builded, built) the first American railroad locomotive.
2. Cooper (began, beginned) his career as a builder and designer of horse-drawn carriages.
3. But Cooper soon (feeled, felt) that a railroad could compete with the newly opened Erie Canal and carry freight to the growing western states.
4. *Tom Thumb* was the name Cooper (gave, give) to the small but powerful locomotive he built.
5. In 1830, *Tom Thumb* (taked, took) 40 passengers on a historic ride through the hilly Maryland countryside at the breathtaking speed of 10 miles an hour.
6. Several other inventions of Cooper's have also (did, done) much to shape modern life.
7. For example, most Americans have (make, made) use of a washing machine to do laundry.
8. The New York City educational institution he founded, Cooper Union, has probably (become, became) the inventor's best-known gift to the nation.
9. Many people have (gone, went) to free classes in art and science at Cooper Union.
10. Late in his life, Peter Cooper (write, wrote), "The object of life is to do good."

6. Simple Tenses (links to exercise A, p. 107)

➡ **1.** past **2.** present

Identify the tense of each underlined verb as present, past, future, present progressive, past progressive, or future progressive.

1. Nellie Bly <u>became</u> one of the most famous reporters in American newspaper history.
2. In 1889, many people <u>were reading</u> Jules Verne's popular novel, *Around the World in Eighty Days.*
3. The novel's main character, Phileas Fogg, <u>journeys</u> around the world in exactly 80 days.
4. Nellie Bly's newspaper, the *New York World,* <u>sent</u> its star reporter on a round-the-world journey just like Phileas Fogg's.
5. Newspaper readers <u>were wondering</u> breathlessly if Bly would match Fogg's time.

RESOURCES

6. "Nellie <u>will go</u> around the world in 80 days!" claimed her enthusiastic supporters.
7. "No," answered others. "She <u>is attempting</u> a feat that is impossible."
8. In early 1890, readers cried, "Nellie <u>will be arriving</u> in New York soon!"
9. The world-famous traveler <u>finished</u> her journey in 72 days, 6 hours, more than a week faster than Phileas Fogg.
10. Perhaps you <u>are wondering</u> how long such a journey would take today.

7. Perfect Tenses (links to exercise A, p. 110)

➡ 1. *had compared,* past perfect
2. *will have experienced,* future perfect

Write each verb in the following paragraphs. Identify the two examples each of the present perfect, past perfect, and future perfect tenses.

The sport of rodeo has entertained people for more than a hundred years. Because riding and roping have always been necessary skills for cowboys on the Western ranges, cowboys had developed skills demanded in rodeo events today.

During the early 20th century, the adventurous cowboy Bill Pickett had wrestled a steer to the ground by biting its lip! From this feat developed the rodeo event called steer wrestling. The five standard events in a modern rodeo are calf roping, bull riding, steer wrestling, saddle bronc riding, and bareback bronc riding. A cowboy or cowgirl who begins to practice for any rodeo event will have accepted a major challenge.

Even today's audiences, notorious for their short attention spans, enjoy the entertainment a rodeo provides. The bronc riding events may be the most spectacular. A rider must remain on a bucking horse for eight to ten seconds, holding on with only one hand. Anyone staying on the bronco this long will have accomplished quite a feat!

8. Using Verb Tenses (links to exercise A, p. 114)

➡ 1. patrol   2. have ridden

For each sentence, write the correct verb form in parentheses. Then identify the form as present, past, or future and as simple, perfect, or progressive.

1. Thousands of people (have dreamed, will be dreaming) of traveling into space and exploring our solar system.
2. Maybe you too (long, had longed) to take a ride aboard the space shuttle or another spacecraft when you are older.
3. By the time Sally Ride entered Stanford University, she (will give, had given) up her goal of playing professional tennis.
4. She (earned, earn) a Ph.D. in physics in 1978.
5. Before 1978, the National Aeronautics and Space Administration, known as NASA, (is not considering, was not considering) women as mission specialists.
6. "Sally Ride (Will Be, Has Been) America's First Female in Space" read the newspaper headlines in 1983 before she was sent into space.
7. Sally Ride flew two missions on the space shuttle after she (had qualified, will have qualified) as America's first woman astronaut.
8. Some scientists predict that people (took, will be taking) space flights often in the coming centuries.
9. Perhaps many women (fly, will have flown) into space by the middle of the 21st century.
10. (Are you thinking, Will you think) you'd like to follow in Sally Ride's footsteps?

9. Troublesome Verb Pairs (links to exercise A, p. 117)

➡ **1.** Let   **2.** sits

Choose the correct verb in parentheses for each of the following sentences.

1. Have you ever had the chance to (set, sit) on a camel's hump?
2. Camels used as transportation in the Arabian Desert can often be seen (lying, laying) in the shade.
3. Years ago, large camel caravans (left, let) trading cities loaded with goods to cross the desert.
4. A driver riding on a camel might (raise, rise) more than ten feet above the ground.
5. An Arabian camel, which has one hump, can (raise, rise) its speed to nearly ten miles an hour.
6. (Leave, Let) me tell you about the day we went to the zoo to see the new camel exhibit.
7. I had (lain, laid) my book about camels next to my bed so I'd be sure to remember to take it with me.
8. At the zoo, I (sat, set) the book on the railing while we watched the camels walk around.

9. One camel (rose, raised) its head to look at my book.
10. Then it leaned over the railing and took a bite out of my book, (letting, leaving) me with half a camel book!

5 Adjectives and Adverbs

1. What Is an Adjective? (links to exercise on p. 128)

→ **1.** terrific, power
2. circular, winds; strong, tornadoes; more, damage; other, storms; similar, size

Write each adjective in these sentences, along with the noun or pronoun it modifies. Do not include articles.

1. In 1900, a severe hurricane in Galveston, Texas, caused many deaths.
2. When the ferocious storm hit, it was a complete surprise.
3. The average Galvestonian expected a regular hurricane with minor flooding and little damage.
4. But Galveston lay on a small island along the southern shore of Texas.
5. The high point in the city was only nine feet above the sea.
6. The constant winds of the unusual hurricane pushed the heavy water into mountainous waves.
7. This frightening phenomenon is known as a storm surge.
8. Waves of 20 feet and shrieking winds destroyed the unfortunate city.
9. About 6,000 people died.
10. Galvestonians rebuilt the city behind tall walls to protect it from the Gulf of Mexico.

2. Predicate Adjectives (links to exercise A, p. 130)

→ **1.** brave, Anna Edson Taylor **2.** certain, She

Write each predicate adjective in these sentences, along with the noun or pronoun it modifies.

1. Joshua Norton, a merchant who moved to San Francisco during the gold rush, was rich.
2. He became indispensable to companies and individuals.
3. Norton grew so successful that people referred to him as an empire builder.
4. The businessman was friendly, and people began calling him the Emperor.

5. Norton dismissed this, insisting that the country's democracy remained strong.
6. Then Norton lost his money and became poor.
7. He appeared insane, declaring himself emperor and dressing in an officer's uniform.
8. Instead of mocking him, the kind residents of San Francisco were happy to honor him.
9. They felt glad to see Norton with his two dogs, Bummer and Lazarus.
10. When Norton died, the *San Francisco Chronicle* announced, "The king is dead."

3. Other Words Used as Adjectives (links to exercise A, p. 133)

➡ **1.** your, fingerprints; their, marks   **2.** skin, ridges; their, surface

Write each noun or pronoun that is used as an adjective, followed by the noun or pronoun that it modifies.

1. DNA determines the hair color and other characteristics of you and your friends.
2. DNA is found in every blood cell and skin cell in our bodies.
3. Your DNA is unique to you, unless you have an identical twin.
4. If I commit a crime, my DNA may be found at the scene, not yours.
5. Detectives appreciate this fact, because it makes their jobs somewhat easier.
6. Crime labs can always analyze DNA from body tissue.
7. Sometimes the labs can analyze DNA from sweat stains and saliva on cigarette butts.
8. These samples are put through a complex process to form an identification for each person.
9. Millions of these DNA "fingerprints" are entered in a national database.
10. This kind of evidence has freed some innocent crime suspects and convicted many others.

4. What Is an Adverb? (links to exercise A, p. 136)

➡ **1.** professionally, climb (verb)   **2.** quite, extraordinary (adjective)

Write each adverb and the word or words it modifies. Then identify the modified word as a verb, an adjective, or an adverb. There may be more than one adverb in a sentence.

1. Makonnen David Blake Hannah, a high school student, often dreams about computers.
2. He wants to see computers everywhere in Jamaica.
3. Hannah has the very long title of youth technology consultant to Jamaica's minister of commerce and technology.
4. You may have already guessed that Hannah is a computer genius.
5. He lives on the Caribbean island, and he serves there as the youngest government advisor in Jamaica's history.
6. He talks passionately to schoolkids about computers.
7. He quite regularly reports to the technology minister about computer issues.
8. Hannah learned computers early.
9. Today he often designs computer software.
10. He is particularly happy to surf, both on the Web and off the Caribbean shore.

5. Making Comparisons (links to exercise A, p. 139)

➡ **1.** most fascinating   **2.** wetter

For each sentence, choose the correct comparative or superlative form from the choice in parentheses.

1. In 1994, people saw what may have been the (more spectacular, most spectacular) event of the century.
2. In 1992, Comet Shoemaker-Levy 9 passed Jupiter (more closely, more closer) than it had done before.
3. Jupiter's massive gravity shattered the huge comet into 21 pieces that were (smaller, smallest) than the original.
4. Using the (best, better) data available, astronomers determined that the comet's pieces would collide with Jupiter during their next flyby in 1994.
5. In mid-July, the (more powerful, most powerful) telescopes in the world were turned on Jupiter.
6. People without telescopes could see the event (more better, better) on their televisions than with the naked eye.
7. The (worse, worst) predictions of all said there would be nothing to see, while the (most positive, positivest) ones said the collision would be the greatest show not on Earth.
8. The first comet piece hit Jupiter (harder, more hardly) than anything viewed before.
9. The impacts were seen (more clearly, clearlier) than anyone had believed possible.
10. For a week, people watched the impact sites, which appeared (darker, more darker) than the rest of Jupiter's surface.

6. Adjective or Adverb? (links to exercise on p. 141)

→ **1.** good, adjective **2.** badly, adverb; really, adverb

For each sentence, choose the correct modifier from those given in parentheses. Identify each word you choose as an adjective or an adverb.

1. The "magnet lady" has a (real, really) thing for magnets.
2. Her name is (real, really) Louise Greenfarb.
3. She began her collection of over 26,000 magnets because she wanted to do (good, well) by her children.
4. When her young children got magnets as prizes in toy machines, Greenfarb thought this was a (bad, badly) thing.
5. What if they choked on these (real, really) small objects?
6. So Greenfarb chose (good, well) by sticking the magnets to her refrigerator.
7. Her collection (real, really) grew, and soon she started collecting magnets from all over the world.
8. She did so (good, well) that she was written up in the newspapers and eventually set a Guinness world record.
9. "The magnets are a (real, really) conversation piece," she says.
10. Greenfarb's magnet collection is the largest on record in the world—not (bad, badly) for a (good, well) mother.

7. Avoiding Double Negatives (links to exercise A, p. 143)

→ **1.** can **3.** is

Write the word in parentheses that is correct for each sentence.

1. You (can, can't) hardly have an anteater as a pet.
2. You (would, wouldn't) never be able to feed this animal, because it eats mostly ants and termites.
3. I (can, can't) scarcely believe that an anteater could eat 30,000 ants a day.
4. No animal (has, hasn't) a longer tongue than an anteater.
5. I (can't, can't hardly) believe that its tongue may be two feet long!
6. Anteaters don't have (any, no) teeth to chew their food.
7. You (will, won't) never mistake an anteater for another animal, because of its long, slender muzzle.
8. Anteaters don't live (anywhere, nowhere) but in southern Mexico and Central and South America.
9. Baby anteaters don't (ever, never) leave their mothers during their first year of life.

10. There isn't (nothing, anything) more threatening to anteaters than the humans who destroy the forests and grasslands where anteaters live.

6 Prepositions, Conjunctions, and Interjections

1. What Is a Preposition? (links to exercise on p. 154)

➜ **1.** in, outer space   **2.** with; instructions, rules

Write the preposition and the object or objects of the preposition in each sentence.

1. The word *robot* was coined by playwright Karel Čapek.
2. Čapek introduced *robot* in his 1921 play *R.U.R.*
3. In the early 1800s, Mary Shelley wrote *Frankenstein.*
4. Frankenstein's creation was an android composed of human parts.
5. Stories about robots and androids are still popular.
6. There is a difference between androids and robots.
7. An android is made with actual human parts or parts that resemble human parts.
8. A robot is a machine made from hardware.
9. According to the precise definition, the *Star Wars* character C-3PO is technically a robot.
10. Real computer-driven robots are all around us.

2. Using Prepositional Phrases (links to exercise A, p. 157)

➜ **1.** around the world, manufacturers   **2.** In factories, work

Write the prepositional phrase and the word it modifies for each of the following sentences.

1. Scientists create robots for new tasks and experiments.
2. A robot surgeon, or robodoc, can drill a perfect cavity in a bone.
3. This helps human doctors fit an implant precisely into the bone.
4. Robots that are powered by the sun can locate unexploded land mines.
5. Robots equipped with artificial intelligence explore the ocean floor.
6. These robots gather data beneath the icy surface.
7. A six-foot-long lunar rover is an expert explorer of the moon's rough terrain.
8. A robotic helicopter, Cypher, pilots itself through takeoff and landing.
9. A computer operator controls this new breed of autonomous flier.

10. Some futurists speculate that robots may replace humans as Earth's dominant creatures.

3. Conjunctions (links to exercise A, p. 160)

➜ **1.** and; Cog, Kismet
   2. but; The robot Cog has an upper body, it doesn't have any legs

For each sentence, write the coordinating or correlative conjunction and the words or groups of words that it joins.

1. First, study computer programming, for you must write a program that gives the robot its instructions.
2. Do you want an expensive or an inexpensive robot?
3. You can use a garbage can and wheels for its body.
4. Neither arms nor legs are needed for a hobby robot.
5. Three wheels set in a triangular pattern can propel the robot either forward, backward, or sideways.
6. The wheels are controlled by the brain and a stepper motor.
7. The robot's brain is the computer power source, and it is housed in the body.
8. The power source can be lead-acid batteries, but they are heavy.
9. Nickel-cadmium batteries are better than lead-acid, yet they are very expensive.
10. Many robots are equipped with sonar sensors, for these devices detect obstacles.

7   Verbals and Verbal Phrases

1. Gerunds and Gerund Phrases (links to exercise A, p. 171)

➜ **1.** creating the Gothic novel *Frankenstein*
   2. Completing *Frankenstein* at 19

Write the gerund or gerund phrase in each sentence, and identify it as a subject, a predicate noun, a direct object, or an object of a preposition. If a sentence does not contain a gerund, write *None*.

1. It was time for sleeping.
2. But tossing in bed was all that 14-year-old Jenny could do.
3. Why won't that dog stop barking, she thought?
4. Even the clock's ticking annoyed her.
5. Jenny tried reading for a while.
6. Soon she was poring over a story by Edgar Allan Poe.
7. Reading scary stories is not a good way to invite sleep.

8. The beating of Jenny's heart grew louder than the ticking clock!
9. She began noticing shadows that weren't there before!
10. Next time, she'll try counting sheep.

2. Participles and Participial Phrases (links to exercise A, p. 174)

→ **1.** frightening, story
3. annoyed by Ichabod's flirtations, Brom Bones

Write the participles or participial phrases in the following sentences. Give the word or words that each phrase modifies.

1. The bubonic plague, also called the Black Death, was once a terrible killer.
2. Its grim rampage during the Middle Ages is a horrifying story.
3. Killing two-thirds of some populations, the bubonic plague swept through Europe in the 1300s.
4. An estimated 30,000 people died in London alone.
5. Victims, suffering terribly, ran high fevers.
6. A tongue turned yellow or brown was a telltale sign of the disease.
7. Known for its awful speed, the plague killed its victims within five days.
8. The dreaded disease was spread by fleas.
9. The fleas picked up the plague germs from infected rats.
10. Cities in the Middle Ages, lacking good sanitation, were easy targets for the spread of disease.

3. Infinitives and Infinitive Phrases (links to exercise A, p. 177)

→ **1.** to scare an entire nation with an imaginary story
2. to broadcast a radio play about a Martian invasion

Identify the infinitive phrase found in each sentence, and tell whether it acts as a noun, adjective, or adverb. If a sentence doesn't have an infinitive phrase, write *none*.

1. *The Island of Lost Souls* was made to entertain moviegoers in the 1930s.
2. In the movie, a mad scientist tries to turn animals into humans.
3. To accomplish this feat, he performs painful operations on the animals.
4. The doctor teaches his animal people to be gentle.
5. They are totally unaware of their ability to be violent.
6. Only the doctor has the power to be cruel, they believe.
7. Then the scientist tells one of his ape men to commit a murder.
8. Realizing they are able to revolt, the animals attack the scientist.
9. They take him to his own operating room.

10. Is this film a warning to be kind to animals?

8 Sentence Structure

1. What Is a Clause? (links to exercise A, p. 187)

→ **1.** independent   **2.** dependent

Identify each underlined group of words as an independent clause or a dependent clause.

1. <u>Enrico is the head chef at Ristorante Roma</u>.
2. He arrives at the restaurant <u>before his assistants show up</u>.
3. <u>While Enrico puts on his chef's apron</u>, he reviews the menu.
4. Before he approves the menu, <u>he checks the quality and freshness of the ingredients</u>.
5. <u>While Enrico works</u>, his assistant chefs arrive at the restaurant.
6. <u>Because the scallops are not satisfactory</u>, Enrico crosses them off the menu.
7. <u>Enrico replaces the scallops with shrimp</u> because they look very fresh.
8. Then he creates a dish of shrimp with pasta <u>that includes a light cream sauce</u>.
9. <u>When he's done</u>, he invites the other chefs to sample the dish.
10. <u>He does this</u> so that the staff knows what is being served.

2. Simple and Compound Sentences (links to exercise A, p. 190)

→ **3.** simple   **4.** simple

Identify each sentence as simple or compound.

1. Frank Webber is in the eighth grade and is proud of his perfect attendance record.
2. He woke up with a sore throat on Tuesday, and he soon felt feverish.
3. Frank's mother told him to stay in bed; Frank protested without success.
4. His mother called the school nurse and reported his illness.
5. Frank buried his head in his pillow; his perfect attendance record was ruined.
6. Frank's dog tried to cheer him up.
7. His little brother Kevin wanted to play a game.
8. Frank's mother quickly banished Kevin from Frank's room, and she told him to stay away until Frank felt better.
9. The dog snuggled on the end of Frank's bed.

10. Frank sank into a deep sleep and dreamed of next year's perfect attendance record.

3. Complex Sentences (links to exercise on p. 193)

➜ **4.** Aunty Misery, <u>who lives alone</u>, is teased by children.
5. <u>When these children yell insults at the old woman</u>, Mr. Hernandez makes his voice squeaky and high-pitched.

Write these sentences on a sheet of paper. Underline each independent clause once and each dependent clause twice.

1. When Dr. Poulas first started her dental practice, very few women were in the field.
2. Many people are afraid of going to the dentist because they fear the experience will be painful.
3. Dr. Poulas, who practices in a large city, lives near her office and walks to work.
4. Before seeing her first patient, she reviews his case.
5. Since Billy Walters's last check-up was a year ago, Dr. Poulas expects Billy to have one or two cavities.
6. Dr. Poulas calls Billy into the room where she will examine his teeth.
7. Billy has brushed and flossed every day so that his teeth would stay healthy.
8. Because of Billy's efforts, he has no cavities.
9. Billy smiles when Dr. Poulas finishes cleaning his teeth.
10. As Billy leaves, Dr. Poulas gives him a new toothbrush as a gift.

4. Kinds of Dependent Clauses (links to exercise A, p. 197)

➜ **1.** Rex is a yellow Labrador retriever <u>who loves to chase squirrels</u>. adjective clause
2. <u>As soon as he sees a squirrel</u>, he yelps with delight. adverb clause

Write these sentences on a sheet of paper. Underline each dependent clause, and identify it as an adjective clause, an adverb clause, or a noun clause.

1. Katrina approached the parallel bars, which loomed above her, and took a deep breath.
2. Katrina's coach, Mr. Franklin, told her to begin whenever she was ready.
3. Mr. Franklin was the coach whom Katrina always depended on for encouragement and support.
4. Katrina brushed aside whatever fears had lodged in her mind.

5. Katrina grabbed the first bar as if she'd done it a million times.

6. She tried out moves that Mr. Franklin had taught her last week.

7. That Mr. Franklin was impressed was obvious.

8. Mr. Franklin's words of encouragement were what she remembered while twisting from one bar to the next.

9. When the set was nearly finished, Katrina somersaulted off the top bar.

10. Mr. Franklin shouted his praise before she even landed on the mat.

5. Mixed Review (links to exercise A, p. 199)

➜ **3.** complex   **4.** complex

Identify each sentence as compound, complex, or compound-complex.

1. When he opened the town post office Friday morning, Mr. Biggley had a line of customers waiting for him.

2. Mr. and Mrs. Cousins, Mrs. Garcia, and the Nickerson kids waited patiently while Mr. Biggley wrestled with the rusty lock.

3. Mr. and Mrs. Cousins needed their pension checks, and Mrs. Garcia wished to mail a parcel.

4. Allie and Ben Nickerson, who lived with their grandmother, often visited the post office to see the latest stamps; both of the children were avid stamp collectors.

5. After Mr. Biggley tended to the other customers, he pulled out the latest sheets of stamps, and they all looked at the new selections.

6. Allie and Ben bought a few new stamps so that they could add them to their collections.

7. Mr. Biggley rang up the sale, and he handed Ben and Allie their new stamps.

8. While Ben and Allie looked at their stamps once again, the bell above the door rang, and Ms. Prescott, who was the new English teacher, entered the shop.

9. Ms. Prescott wished everyone good morning, and the Nickerson kids swiftly ran out of the post office.

10. Since Ms. Prescott was a new customer, Mr. Biggley introduced himself, and hoping to make a good impression, he straightened his postmaster's hat.

9 Subject-Verb Agreement

1. Agreement in Number (links to exercise A, p. 210)

→ **1.** is **3.** spoil

For each sentence, write the form of the verb that agrees with the subject. Choose from the words in parentheses.

1. Personality types (has, have) been studied for centuries.
2. However, classification (is, are) difficult.
3. Scientists often (refers, refer) to two personality types, Type A and Type B.
4. A Type A person (seems, seem) competitive.
5. A Type A person also (behaves, behave) impatiently.
6. Typically, a Type A individual (doesn't, don't) relax.
7. On the other hand, Type B individuals (has, have) an easygoing, relaxed temperament.
8. Your friends probably (has, have) displayed either Type A or Type B traits.
9. Some people (possesses, possess) a combination of both types.
10. Research (suggests, suggest) that people with a Type A personality may be at higher risk for heart disease.

2. Compound Subjects (links to exercise A, p. 212)

→ **1.** Correct **2.** attracts

Proofread each of the following sentences to find the mistakes in subject-verb agreement. Then rewrite the sentences correctly. If a sentence contains no error, write *Correct*.

1. External pressure and internal pressure sometimes affect athletic performance.
2. Fear and anger is experienced by most athletes.
3. Competition and success requires emotional control.
4. Neither trainers nor a fitness instructor teach an athlete how to deal with mental mistakes.
5. Many athletes and their coaches consult sports psychologists.
6. Some problems and solutions seems easy.
7. Team players or solo athletes learns how to think rationally.
8. Emotional control and focus results in a competitive edge.
9. These skills and techniques help others besides athletes.
10. Even school or work demand a degree of self-control.

3. Agreement Problems in Sentences (links to exercise A, p. 215)

→ **1.** Do   **4.** are

Write the form of the verb that agrees with the subject of each sentence. Choose from the verbs in parentheses.

1. (Has, Have) you seen the classic movie *The Three Faces of Eve?*
2. Multiple personality disorder (is, are) the subject of the film.
3. Severe traumas (is, are) often a cause of this disorder.
4. People with this rare condition (develops, develop) two or more distinct personalities.
5. There (is, are) periods of time when one personality takes full control.
6. (Does, Do) the different personalities know about one another?
7. The personalities of a person with this disorder (reflects, reflect) different traits and emotions.
8. There (is, are) usually a dominant, or central, personality.
9. An individual with multiple personalities (refers, refer) to himself or herself as "we."
10. To merge all of the personalities gradually (is, are) the goal of treatment.

4. Indefinite Pronouns as Subjects (links to exercise A, p. 218)

→ **2.** Correct   **3.** has explained

Proofread each of the following sentences. Then rewrite the sentences in which the verb does not agree with its subject. If a sentence is correct, write *Correct.*

1. Everyone value the opinions and lifestyles of others.
2. Some of the movie stars, athletes, and models who are popular today serve as role models.
3. But none of these celebrities affects you directly.
4. Few actually meets you in person.
5. Maybe someone in your school or community inspire you.
6. Some of your friends and classmates exert a powerful influence on your personality.
7. No one learn how to behave properly without positive role models.
8. Most of your behavior has been learned through modeling.
9. Several of your family members is significant role models.
10. Something in their actions keep you on the right track.

5. Problem Subjects (links to exercise A, p. 221)

→ **1.** is   **3.** is

Find the mistakes in subject-verb agreement in the following sentences. Then write the correct verb to agree with each subject.

1. My brother's college class study the human personality.
2. The faculty often disagrees on the topics to teach.
3. About 15 pounds are the weight of all the course books.
4. *The Ego and the Id* by Sigmund Freud describe parts of the personality.
5. Twenty-five pages are the length of each reading assignment for the class.
6. Economics prevent some students from taking a course field trip.
7. Two-thirds of the students plans to major in psychology.
8. Mathematics are useful in analyzing psychological data.
9. *Psychology Today* publish interesting articles.
10. Two weeks are how much time it takes to write the final paper.

10 Capitalization

1. People and Cultures (links to exercise on p. 232)

➡ 1. Giovanni, Caselli   2. Helios

For each sentence, find the words that should be capitalized but aren't. Write the words, giving them the proper capitalization.

1. When philo of Byzantium created his list of wonders, he included the Hanging Gardens of Babylon.
2. Unlike the wonders that were built to pay tribute to greek gods, the Hanging Gardens were built to show a king's love for his wife.
3. The Hanging Gardens were built around 600 B.C. on the orders of king nebuchadnezzar.
4. A powerful king, nebuchadnezzar conquered the Egyptians, the elamites, the Syrians, and the carians.
5. The only group of people the king did not try to defeat were the medes.
6. Instead, he united with the medes and married princess amytis.
7. Amytis had never lived anywhere but in the green, hilly persian land, which she missed when she moved to her new home.
8. The king built the beautiful terraced gardens to remind princess amytis of her homeland.
9. These babylonian gardens were a luxurious oasis in the Mesopotamian desert.
10. The Hanging Gardens still existed at the time of alexander the great, over 200 years later, and for generations after that.

2. First Words and Titles (links to exercise A, p. 235)

→ **1.** What **2.** It

Write the words that should be capitalized in each sentence. If there are no errors, write the word *correct*.

1. last summer my grandparents and I visited our family in Italy.
2. While we were visiting Pisa, my grandfather asked, "did you know that the Leaning Tower has been tipping inch by inch for 800 years?"
3. "why is it tipping?" I asked. "how far has it tipped?"
4. "the land beneath the tower," he explained, "is a mixture of sand, clay, and water."
5. "imagine placing 8,000 cars," he continued, "one on top of the other on soil that is as soft as sand."
6. "Today the Leaning Tower leans about 17 feet," he added, "but I read somewhere about an effort to stop it from tipping over."
7. "good!" I exclaimed. "i hope they can save it."
8. The PBS television show *Nova* aired a program called "fall of the Leaning Tower," about rescue efforts.
9. The program poses the question "can the Leaning Tower be saved through human intervention?"
10. A person interested in learning more about the Leaning Tower can use the following outline:
    I. Leaning Tower of Pisa
       A. construction of the Leaning Tower
          1. when built
          2. flaws in construction
       B. attempts to save the Leaning Tower
          1. restoring the building
          2. restoring the land

3. Places and Transportation (links to exercise A, p. 238)

→ **2.** Eiffel, Tower

For each sentence, write the words that should be capitalized. Do not write words that are already capitalized.

1. Dr. Arnold Wollschlaeger's research for his new book *Modern Wonders of the World: Bridges* began in the united states and continued in europe.
2. From his home in the midwest, Dr. Wollschlaeger took the *zephyr* to the west coast.

3. When he arrived in San francisco, california, his first subject of research was the famed Golden Gate bridge.
4. The Golden Gate bridge, San francisco's deep-orange symbol since 1937, is one of the world's longest suspension bridges.
5. Dr. Wollschlaeger's next stop was london, england.
6. In london he boarded a bus called *the shropshire.*
7. The bus took him to the Iron bridge over the severn river.
8. Dr. Wollschlaeger continued his journey through the Channel tunnel and on to switzerland.
9. The subject of his research in switzerland was the kapellbrücke (Chapel bridge), which was europe's oldest wooden bridge.
10. Satisfied with his research, Dr. Wollschlaeger headed back to north america to begin his writing.

4. Organizations and Other Subjects (links to exercise A, p. 241)

→ **1.** Springhill, Middle, School

Write the words that should be capitalized in each sentence. Do not write words that are already capitalized.

1. Before the christmas holiday, I had to turn in a research paper about a famous discovery.
2. Most of the people in my social studies II class had already selected their topics when I decided to write about Mount Everest.
3. Mount Everest was named after Sir George Everest, who had supervised the Great trigonometrical survey of India.
4. On may 29, 1953, at 11:30 a.m., Edmund Hillary and Tenzing Norgay became the first men to reach the summit of Mount Everest.
5. The expedition that they had been a part of was run by the Royal geographical society.
6. Their expedition had left Kathmandu, Nepal, on march 10, 1953, and had approached the mountain from the south side—the side previously thought unclimbable.
7. Hillary had previously made five expeditions on Himalayan peaks after world war II.
8. Since that friday, may 29, 1953, hundreds of climbers have attempted the dangerous feat of climbing Mount Everest.
9. For my research paper, I interviewed Phil Abernathy, co-owner of the right stuff.
10. Phil promised to tell me about his adventurous experience on Mount Everest if I purchased a woodland backpack.

11 Punctuation

1. Periods and Other End Marks (links to exercise A, p. 252)

➡ **1.** history?   **2.** armies.

Write the words in the paragraph that should be followed by periods, question marks, or exclamation points. Include these end marks in your answers.

The Inca people lived in the Andes Mts of South America. Runners carried messages from the capital to distant towns They relied on the roads to make their journey bearable. Do you believe that their road system covered thousands of miles A team of messengers could travel 150 miles in a day Amazing Can you imagine the fitness of these messengers In addition to having quick feet, they needed quick memories Messages were not written down but recited by messengers Such exhausting work Aren't you glad that you don't have to memorize messages

2. Commas in Sentences (links to exercise on p. 255)

➡ **1.** 1988   **3.** Fessenden

Write the words and numbers in the paragraph that should be followed by commas.

What happens folks, when a radio broadcast communicates the wrong message? On Halloween, 1938 Orson Welles's *Mercury Theater of the Air* had its regular broadcast. Welles a brilliant actor and director aired a play based on *The War of the Worlds* a science fiction novel by H. G. Wells. The play tells the story of a Martian invasion of New Jersey. Listeners heard explosions screams and strange noises coming over the airwaves. Unfortunately many listeners missed the announcements that the show was make-believe. Hundreds of people panicked understandably and fled their homes. Many were treated for shock and possible heart attacks at hospitals.

3. Commas: Dates, Addresses, and Letters (links to exercise A, p. 257)

➡ **1.** Providence   **2.** 22

Write the words and numbers in the letter that should be followed by commas.

177 S. Pinelog Trail
Casper WY 82601
Oct. 22 2004

Dear Maya

Did you know that Paul Revere wasn't the only person to ride through the countryside warning colonists of British troops? It's true! On the night of April 26 1777 Sybil Ludington, a 16-year-old girl from Fredericksburg New York rode through Putnam County. Two thousand redcoats had landed in Westport Connecticut and marched inland. They raided Danbury, burned homes, and wrecked provisions. Sybil, the daughter of the area's commander, helped her father by carrying the news on horseback to the soldiers. In the end, the colonists defeated the British at Ridgefield Connecticut. It's amazing to discover what a major role a young person played in American history.

Your friend

Tori

4. Punctuating Quotations (links to exercise on p. 260)

➜ **1.** intelligence," **2.** Correct

Rewrite each sentence, adding quotation marks and other punctuation where needed. If a sentence is correct, write *Correct.*

1. "When did Alexander Graham Bell invent the telephone?" asked Nancy.
2. "I think it was about 1870," said Jack thoughtfully, "but I know it was over a century ago."
3. "Well, you'd be good on a quiz show! laughed Nancy. Now, who made the first phone call?
4. Jack told his sister that Bell tested his invention by calling his assistant, Mr. Watson.
5. Jack also added, Bell used the words *Hoy* and *Ahoy* as greetings, and Thomas Edison was the first person who used the greeting *Hello*

5. Semicolons and Colons (links to exercise on p. 263)

➡ **1.** mail: **2.** carriers;

Write the words from the paragraph that should be followed by semicolons or colons. Include these punctuation marks in your answers.

Several well-known people worked for the post office two of them even became president. Benjamin Franklin is called the Father of the United States Postal Service moreover, he seems to deserve the title. Franklin improved the service in three ways he found better routes, making mail delivery faster he allowed newspapers to be sent free, helping to spread the news and he increased the money collected by the postal system. Abraham Lincoln was postmaster of New Salem, Illinois, for three years he carried the mail in his hat. Harry Truman also served as postmaster he became president in 1945. Writer William Faulkner was once a postmaster, but people made several complaints against Faulkner he was rude, he refused to sort the mail, and he played cards when he should have been working. John Thompson was not known to the rest of the country however, the miners in the Sierra Nevada Mountains loved him. Thompson delivered the mail on skis through the high mountain drifts his nickname was Snowshoe Thompson.

6. Hyphens, Dashes, and Parentheses (links to exercise A, p. 265)

➡ **1.** (the early 1800s)   **2.** fifty-nine

Read the following passage for punctuation errors. Copy the underlined text, inserting hyphens, dashes, and parentheses where necessary. If the underlined text is correct, write *Correct*.

Colonial women in America were expected **(1)** <u>by all of society</u> to keep their homes clean and to stay out of politics. But as the colonies moved toward rebellion, some women began **(2)** <u>writing</u> about their anti-British feelings. Mercy Otis Warren wrote plays that made fun of Loyalists **(3)** <u>people who supported the British cause</u>. Warren was close to many politicians **(4)** <u>—her brother, James Otis, was a leader in the fight for independence—</u>and she never hesitated to speak her opinion. A defender of colonial freedom and women's rights, Warren died at the age of **(5)** <u>eighty six</u>. Phillis Wheatley also wrote in support of the colonial **(6)** <u>Patriot</u> viewpoint. When she was only **(7)** <u>twenty one</u> she wrote the poem "To the Right Honorable William, Earl of Dartmouth." This work compared the status of the colonies to that of a slave **(8)** <u>she herself was enslaved</u>. Mary Katherine Goddard, a publisher of a Baltimore newspaper, always sought to provide readers with the truth. Eventually, the Second Continental Congress

(9) <u>showing good judgment</u> chose her to produce **(10)** <u>co-pies</u> of the Declaration of Independence for distribution.

7. Apostrophes (links to exercise A, p. 267)

➜ **1.** he's   **2.** friends'

Find and correct the errors in the use of apostrophes.

Elizabeth Chapman is only 14, and already shes' an award-winning author. Her essay in an international contest won first place for it's description of living with cerebral palsy. Cerebral palsy affects a persons' muscles but not his or her mind. Elizabeth would like readers to change they're view of people who are physically challenged. She wrote, ". . . [people] act like just because I cant' walk, I cant hear either." She hopes her writing will help people understand what its like to have a physical disability. Elizabeths' learning to write by using computer software that is voice activated. A keyboards' demands tire her out. She hopes to have her first novel published soon. After all, whose going to stop her?

8. Punctuating Titles (links to exercise A, p. 269)

➜ **1.** <u>Odyssey</u>   **2.** <u>Gods of Mars</u>

Read the paragraph, and rewrite the titles and vehicle names, using either quotation marks or underlining as appropriate.

Our class played a quiz-show game. One person would make a riddle out of the title of a book, TV show, song, or other entertainment, and the first person to guess it correctly won a point. I guessed two movies—Jurassic Park and Star Wars—but I missed the movie Titanic. Sam is good with music, so he quickly guessed This Land Is Your Land and Heartbreak Hotel. I forgot the names of the spacecraft that photographed Venus and Mars. Shirl guessed Magellan and Viking correctly. I fooled Ken with a question about the Lusitania, the ship sunk by the Germans, and also with a riddle about the short story To Build a Fire. Manny finally won when he named the longest-running television news magazine. He guessed 60 Minutes.

Quick-Fix Spelling Machine

QUICK–FIX SPELLING MACHINE: PLURALS OF NOUNS

SINGULAR	RULE	PLURAL
skateboard painting ticket	Add -s to most nouns.	skateboards paintings tickets

WATCH OUT The exceptions to this rule are nouns whose plurals are formed in special ways, such as *man* (*men*), *woman* (*women*), and *child* (*children*).

SINGULAR	RULE	PLURAL
hiss dish ditch box buzz	Add -es to nouns that end in *s, sh, ch, x,* or *z.*	hisses dishes ditches boxes buzzes
auto igloo radio	Add -s to most nouns that end in *o.*	autos igloos radios
potato tomato mosquito	Add -es to a few nouns that end in *o.*	potatoes tomatoes mosquitoes
flurry deputy battery dairy	For most nouns ending in *y,* change the *y* to *i* and add -es.	flurries deputies batteries dairies
alley play turkey	Just add -s when a vowel comes before the *y.*	alleys plays turkeys
calf thief wife leaf knife	For most nouns ending in *f* or *fe,* change the *f* to *v* and add -es or -s.	calves thieves wives leaves knives
belief muff safe	Just add -s to a few nouns that end in *f* or *fe.*	beliefs muffs safes
series sheep species aircraft	Keep the same spelling for some nouns.	series sheep species aircraft

QUICK-FIX SPELLING MACHINE: POSSESSIVES

NOUN	RULE	POSSESSIVE
moon	Add an apostrophe and -s to singular nouns.	moon's light
student		student's locker
club		club's president
restaurant		restaurant's menus
school		school's teachers
bank		bank's assets
college		college's facilities
dog		dog's fur
garden		garden's scents
catalog		catalog's merchandise
museum		museum's exhibit
flower		flower's fragrance
book		book's cover
holiday		holiday's traditions
turkey		turkey's drumstick

WATCH OUT The exception to this rule is that the *s* after the apostrophe is dropped after *Jesus', Moses',* and certain names in classical mythology. Dropping the -*s* makes these possessive forms easier to pronounce.

NOUN	RULE	POSSESSIVE
x-rays	Add an apostrophe to plural nouns that end in -s.	x-rays' envelopes
organizations		organizations' budgets
teams		teams' coaches
buildings		buildings' windows
cities		cities' mayors
airports		airports' schedules
babies		babies' toys
groceries		groceries' prices
violets		violets' buds
necklaces		necklaces' clasps
butterflies		butterflies' wings

NOUN	RULE	POSSESSIVE
deer	Add an apostrophe and -s to plural nouns not ending in -s.	deer's hooves
oxen		oxen's load
salmon		salmon's gills
stepchildren		stepchildren's names
herd		herd's cattle
sheep		sheep's wool
mice		mice's nests
people		people's languages

QUICK–FIX SPELLING MACHINE: WORDS ENDING IN SILENT e

WORD	RULE	CHANGE
home engage hope tune shame state	Keep the silent *e* when a suffix beginning with a consonant is added to a word that ends in a silent *e*.	homeless engagement hopeful tuneless shameful statement

WATCH OUT Some words that are exceptions include *truly, awful, argument, ninth,* and *wholly.*

WORD	RULE	CHANGE
peace courage manage salvage outrage charge	Keep the silent *e* when a suffix beginning with *a* or *o* is added to a silent *e* word if the *e* follows a soft *c* or *g*.	peaceable courageous manageably salvageable outrageous chargeable
agree woe	Keep the silent *e* when a suffix beginning with a vowel is added to a word ending in *ee* or *oe*.	agreeable woeful
flake elevate haze institute shake create	Drop the silent *e* from the base word when you add a suffix beginning with *y* or a vowel.	flaky elevation hazy institution shaky creative

QUICK-FIX SPELLING MACHINE: WORDS ENDING IN y

WORD	RULE	CHANGE
happy thirty merry greedy sneaky deputy	Change the *y* to *i* to add a suffix to a word ending in *y* if the *y* follows a consonant.	happiness thirtieth merriest greedily sneakier deputies
rally marry tally fry	Keep the *y* when adding *-ing* to a word ending in *y* if the *y* follows a consonant.	rallying marrying tallying frying
joy pay boy	Keep the *y* when adding a suffix to a word ending in a vowel and *y*.	joyous payable boyish

QUICK-FIX SPELLING MACHINE: WORDS ENDING IN A CONSONANT

WORD	RULE	CHANGE
mat slip hit dim	If a one-syllable word ends in a consonant preceded by a vowel, double the final consonant before adding a suffix beginning with a vowel.	matting slipped hitter dimmest
heap steal scoot meat	If a one-syllable word ends in a consonant preceded by two vowels, do not double the final consonant.	heaped stealing scooted meaty
transfer admit allot permit	Double the final consonant in a word of more than one syllable only if the word is accented on the last syllable.	transferring admitted allotting permitting

SPELLING

QUICK-FIX SPELLING MACHINE: ADVERBS

ADJECTIVE	RULE	ADVERB
sudden bad rapid	Add *-ly*.	suddenly badly rapidly
true	Drop *e;* add *-ly*.	truly
angry heavy steady	Change *y* to *i;* add *-ly*.	angrily heavily steadily

QUICK-FIX SPELLING MACHINE: COMPOUNDS

	SINGULAR	RULE	PLURAL
One word	dishcloth supermarket airport	Add *-s* to most words.	dishcloths supermarkets airports
Two or more words	feather bed atomic bomb attorney general	Make the main noun plural. The main noun is the noun that is modified.	feather beds atomic bombs attorneys general
Hyphenated words	son-in-law half-dollar vice-president	Make the main noun plural.	sons-in-law half-dollars vice-presidents

QUICK-FIX SPELLING MACHINE: OPEN AND CLOSED SYLLABLES

An *open syllable* ends in one vowel and has a long vowel sound.	baby labor fable cedar	ba by la bor fa ble ce dar
A *closed syllable* ends in a consonant and has a short vowel sound.	ladder mischief problem plunder	lad der mis chief prob lem plun der

QUICK–FIX SPELLING MACHINE: CONTRACTIONS

WORDS	RULE	CONTRACTION
I am	Combine a personal	I'm
you are	pronoun with a verb by	you're
he is	adding an apostrophe in	he's
she is	place of the missing	she's
it is	letters.	it's
we are		we're
they are		they're
I would		I'd
you would		you'd
he would		he'd
she would		she'd
we would		we'd
they would		they'd
I will		I'll
you will		you'll
he will		he'll
she will		she'll
it will		it'll
we will		we'll
they will		they'll
I have		I've
you have		you've
we have		we've
they have		they've
I had		I'd
you had		you'd
he had		he'd
she had		she'd
we had		we'd
they had		they'd
do not	Otherwise, combine two	don't
where is	words into one by adding	where's
there is	an apostrophe in place of	there's
could not	the missing letters.	couldn't
would not		wouldn't
should not		shouldn't
is not		isn't
was not		wasn't
who is		who's

SPELLING

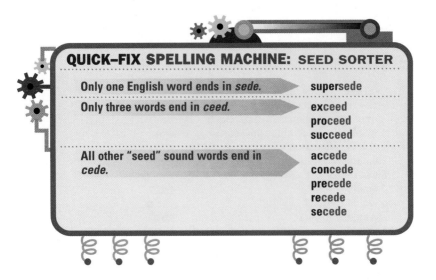

QUICK-FIX SPELLING MACHINE: SEED SORTER

Only one English word ends in *sede*. → super**sede**

Only three words end in *ceed*. → ex**ceed**
pro**ceed**
suc**ceed**

All other "seed" sound words end in *cede*. → ac**cede**
con**cede**
pre**cede**
re**cede**
se**cede**

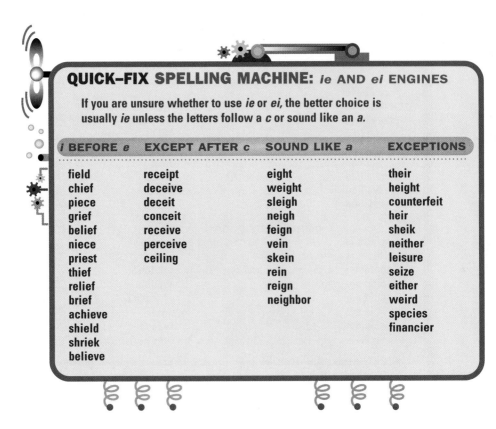

QUICK-FIX SPELLING MACHINE: *ie* AND *ei* ENGINES

If you are unsure whether to use *ie* or *ei*, the better choice is usually *ie* unless the letters follow a *c* or sound like an *a*.

i BEFORE *e*	EXCEPT AFTER *c*	SOUND LIKE *a*	EXCEPTIONS
field	receipt	eight	their
chief	deceive	weight	height
piece	deceit	sleigh	counterfeit
grief	conceit	neigh	heir
belief	receive	feign	sheik
niece	perceive	vein	neither
priest	ceiling	skein	leisure
thief		rein	seize
relief		reign	either
brief		neighbor	weird
achieve			species
shield			financier
shriek			
believe			

QUICK–FIX SPELLING MACHINE: BORROWED WORDS

Over the centuries, as English speakers increased their contact with people from other lands, English speakers "borrowed" words from other languages. The English language began to grow in new directions and acquired new richness and flavor.

Spelling follows certain patterns in every language. For example, some letter patterns in French, Spanish, and Italian appear in words commonly used in English.

PATTERN	WORD

Some borrowed words keep their original spellings and pronunciations.

In many words taken from the French, the final *t* is silent.	ballet beret buffet
In both English and French, the soft *g* is usually followed by *e, i,* or *y*.	mirage region energy
The hard *g* is followed by *a, o,* or *u*.	vague
Many words taken from the Dutch language have *oo* in their spellings.	cookie snoop hook caboose
Many words borrowed from Spanish end in *o*.	taco tornado rodeo bronco
Many words that were plural in Italian end in *i*.	spaghetti macaroni ravioli

Some words from other languages were changed to fit English rules of pronunciation and spelling.

Many words in Native American languages contain sound combinations unlike those in English words. English speakers found these words useful but difficult to pronounce, so they used more familiar sounds and letter combinations.	topaghan = toboggan tamahaac = tomahawk pakani = pecan squa = squaw wampumpeag = wampum qajaq = kayak

Commonly Misspelled Words

A
abbreviate
accidentally
achievement
analyze
anonymous
answer
apologize
appearance
appreciate
appropriate
argument
awkward

B
beautiful
because
beginning
believe
bicycle
brief
bulletin
business

C
calendar
campaign
candidate
caught
certain
changeable
characteristic
clothes
column

committee
courageous
courteous
criticize
curiosity

D
decision
definitely
dependent
description
desirable
despair
desperate
development
dictionary
different
disappear
disappoint
discipline
dissatisfied

E
eighth
eligible
eliminate
embarrass
enthusiastic
especially
essay
exaggerate
exceed
existence
experience

F
familiar
fascinating
favorite
February
foreign
fourth
fragile

G
generally
government
grammar
guarantee
guard

H
height
humorous

I
immediately
independent
irritable

J, K, L
judgment
knowledge
laboratory
library
license
lightning

literature
loneliness

M
mathematics
minimum
mischievous

N
necessary
nickel
ninety
noticeable
nuclear
nuisance

O
obstacle
occasionally
once
opinion
opportunity
outrageous

P
parallel
particularly
people
permanent
persuade
pleasant
pneumonia

possess
possibility
prejudice
principal
privilege
probably
pursue
psychology

R

realize
receipt
receive
recognize
recommend
reference
rehearse
repetition
restaurant
rhythm
ridiculous

S

sandwich
schedule
scissors
separate
sergeant
similar
sincerely
souvenir
specifically
strategy
success
surprise
syllable
sympathy
symptom

T

temperature
thorough
throughout
tomorrow
traffic
tragedy
transferred
truly
Tuesday
twelfth

U

unnecessary
usable

V

vacuum
vicinity
village

W

weird

Commonly Confused Words

Good writers master words that are easy to misuse and misspell. Study the following words, noting how their meanings differ.

accept, except | *Accept* means "to agree to something" or "to receive something willingly." *Except* usually means "not including."
Did the teacher *accept* **your report?**
Everyone smiled for the photographer *except* **Jody.**

advice, advise | *Advice* is a noun that means "counsel given to someone." *Advise* is a verb that means "to give counsel."
Jim should take some of his own *advice.*
The mechanic *advised* **me to get new brakes for my car.**

affect, effect | *Affect* means "to move or influence" or "to wear or to pretend to have." *Effect* as a verb means "to bring about." As a noun, *effect* means "the result of an action."
The news from South Africa *affected* **him deeply.**
The band's singer *affects* **a British accent.**
The students tried to *effect* **a change in school policy.**
What *effect* **did the acidic soil produce in the plants?**

all ready, already | *All ready* means "all are ready" or "completely prepared." *Already* means "previously."
The students were *all ready* **for the field trip.**
We had *already* **pitched our tent before it started raining.**

all right | *All right* is the correct spelling. *Alright* is nonstandard and should not be used.

a lot | *A lot* may be used in informal writing. *Alot* is incorrect.

borrow, lend | *Borrow* means "to receive something on loan." *Lend* means "to give out temporarily."
Please *lend* **me your book.**
He *borrowed* **five dollars from his sister.**

bring, take | *Bring* refers to movement toward or with. *Take* refers to movement away from.
I'll *bring* **you a glass of water.**
Would you please *take* **these apples to Pam and John?**

can, may | *Can* means "to be able; to have the power to do something." *May* means "to have permission to do something." *May* can also mean "possibly will."

We *may* not use pesticides on our community garden.
Pesticides *may* not be necessary, anyway.
Vegetables *can* grow nicely without pesticides.

capital, capitol, the Capitol	*Capital* means "excellent," "most serious," or "most important." It also means "seat of government." A *capitol* is a building in which a state legislature meets. *The Capitol* is the building in Washington, D.C., in which the U.S. Congress meets. **Proper nouns begin with *capital* letters.** **Is Madison the *capital* of Wisconsin?** **Protesters rallied at the state *capitol*.** **A subway connects the Senate and House wings of *the Capitol*.**
desert, dessert	*Desert* (des´ ert) means "a dry, sandy, barren region." *Desert* (de sert´) means "to abandon." *Dessert* (des sert´) refers to a sweet, such as cake. **The Sahara in North Africa is the world's largest *desert*.** **The night guard did not *desert* his post.** **Alison's favorite *dessert* is chocolate cake.**
fewer, less	*Fewer* refers to numbers of things that can be counted. *Less* refers to amount, degree, or value. ***Fewer* than ten students camped out.** **We made *less* money this year on the walkathon than last year.**
good, well	*Good* is always an adjective. *Well* is usually an adverb that modifies an action verb. *Well* can also be an adjective meaning "in good health." **Dana felt *good* when she finished painting her room.** **Angela ran *well* in yesterday's race.** **I felt *well* when I left my house.**
its, it's	*Its* is a possessive pronoun. *It's* is a contraction of *it is* or *it has*. **Sanibel Island is known for *its* beautiful beaches.** ***It's* great weather for a picnic.**
lay, lie	*Lay* is a verb that means "to place." It takes a direct object. *Lie* is a verb that means "to be in a certain place." *Lie*, or its past form *lay*, never takes a direct object. **The carpenter will *lay* the planks on the bench.** **My cat likes to *lie* under the bed.**

lead, led   *Lead* can be a noun that refers to a heavy metal or a verb that means "to show the way." *Led* is the past tense form of the verb.
Lead is used in nuclear reactors.
Raul always *leads* his team onto the field.
She *led* the class as president of the student council.

learn, teach   *Learn* means "to gain knowledge." *Teach* means "to instruct."
Enrique is *learning* about black holes in space.
Marva *teaches* astronomy at a college in the city.

leave, let   *Leave* means "to go away from" or "to allow to remain." *Leave* can be transitive or intransitive. *Let* is usually used with another verb. It means "to allow to."
Don't *leave* the refrigerator open.
She *leaves* for Scotland tomorrow.
The Cyclops wouldn't *let* Odysseus' men *leave* the cave.

like   *Like* used as a conjunction before a clause is incorrect. Use *as* or *as if*.
Ramon talked *as if* he had a cold.

lose, loose   *Lose* means "to mislay or suffer the loss of." *Loose* means "free" or "not fastened."
That tire will *lose* air unless you patch it.
My little brother has three *loose* teeth.

passed, past   *Passed* is the past tense of *pass* and means "went by." *Past* is an adjective that means "of a former time." *Past* is also a noun that means "time gone by."
We *passed* through the Florida Keys during our vacation.
My *past* experiences have taught me to set my alarm.
Ebenezer Scrooge is a character who relives his *past*.

peace, piece   *Peace* means "a state of calm or quiet." *Piece* means "a section or part of something."
Sitting still can bring a sense of *peace*.
Here's another *piece* of the puzzle.

principal, principle   *Principal* means "of chief or central importance" and refers to the head of a school. *Principle* means "a basic truth, standard, or rule of behavior."
Lack of customers is the *principal* reason for closing the store.
The *principal* of our school awarded the trophy.
One of my *principles* is to be honest with others.

raise, rise	*Raise* means "to lift" or "to make something go up." It takes a direct object. *Rise* means "to go upward." It does not take a direct object. **The maintenance workers *raise* the flag each morning.** **The city's population is expected to *rise* steadily.**
set, sit	*Set* means "to place" and takes a direct object. *Sit* means "to occupy a seat or a place" and does not take a direct object. **He *set* the box down outside the shed.** **We *sit* in the last row of the upper balcony.**
stationary, stationery	*Stationary* means "fixed or unmoving." *Stationery* means "fine paper for writing letters." **The wheel pivots, but the seat is *stationary*.** **Rex wrote on special *stationery* imprinted with his name.**
than, then	*Than* is used to introduce the second part of a comparison. *Then* means "next in order." **Ramon is stronger *than* Mark.** **Cut the grass and *then* trim the hedges.**
their, there, they're	*Their* means "belonging to them." *There* means "in that place." *They're* is the contraction for *they are*. **All the campers returned to *their* cabins.** **I keep my card collection *there* in those folders.** **Lisa and Beth run daily; *they're* on the track team.**
to, too, two	*To* means "toward" or "in the direction of." *Too* means "also" or "very." *Two* is the number 2. **We went *to* the mall.** **It's *too* risky riding without a helmet.** ***Two* amusement parks are offering reduced rates for admission.**
whose, who's	*Whose* is the possessive form of *who*. *Who's* is a contraction of *who is* or *who has*. ***Whose* parents will drive us to the movies?** ***Who's* going to the recycling center?**
your, you're	*Your* is the possessive form of *you*. *You're* is a contraction of *you are*. **What was *your* record in the fifty-yard dash?** ***You're* one of the winners of the essay contest.**

Index

Coordinating conjunctions, 158
  common, 158, 189
  between independent clauses, 189,
    204
Correlative conjunctions, 159

D

Dashes, 264
Dates
  capitalization in, 240
  commas in, 256–257
Days, capitalization of, 240
Declarative sentences, 16
  periods in, 16, 250
  subject position in, 18
Definite article, 127
Deities, capitalization of, 231
Demonstrative pronouns, 71–72
  as adjectives, 131
  here and *there* never used with, 72
Dependent clauses, 186–188
  adjective clauses, 194, 204, 205,
    285
  adverb clauses, 194–195, 204,
    205, 285
  in complex sentences, 192
  in compound-complex sentences, 198
  introductory words for, 186
  kinds of, 194–197
  noun, 195–196, 205, 286
Description
  adjectives for, 126, 132
  compound-complex sentences for,
    198
  conjunctions in, 159
  objects of verbs for, 24
Details
  adjectives for supplying, 128, 129
  dependent clauses for adding, 196
  nouns in phrases providing, 49
  subject complements for providing,
    22
Diagramming sentences, 276–287
  adjective clauses, 285
  adjectives, 277
  adverb clauses, 285
  adverbs, 277
  clauses, 284–286
  complex sentences, 285–286
  compound sentences, 284
  compound subjects and verbs,
    276–277
  direct objects, 278–279
  gerunds and gerund phrases, 282
  indirect objects, 279

infinitives and infinitive phrases,
  282–283
noun clauses, 286
participles and participial phrases,
  281
phrases, 280–283
predicate adjectives, 278
predicate nouns, 278
prepositional phrases, 280
simple subjects and verbs, 276
subject complements, 278
Dialogue
  for imitating speech, 16
Direct address, commas with nouns of,
  254, 274
Directions, capitalization of, 237
Direct objects, 23
  action verbs and, 95
  adverbs looking like, 96
  as complements, 46
  diagramming, 278–279
  function of, 33
  gerunds as, 170
  noun clauses as, 195, 196, 286
  nouns as, 55
  object pronouns as, 63, 70, 88,
    295, 296
  specific nouns as, 96
  transitive verbs with, 96
Direct quotations
  capitalization of first words of, 233
  punctuation of, 258
Divided quotations
  capitalization of first words of, 233,
    259
  punctuation of, 259
Divisions of the world, capitalization of,
  236
Do, as helping verb, 12, 93
Documents, capitalization of historical,
  239
Doesn't, subject-verb agreement with,
  209
Don't, subject-verb agreement with, 209
Double comparisons, 138, 149
Double negatives, 142–143, 149

E

Earth, capitalization of, 236
East, capitalization of, 237
Editing and proofreading
  clichés, 305
  commas, 299
  comparisons, 297
  figurative language, 307
  fixing errors, 290–299

INDEX

I, J, K

I, capitalization of, 231
  in compound subjects, 81
  and *me,* 64, 82
Imperative sentences, 16
  exclamation points in, 16
  periods in, 16, 250
  subject position in, 18
Indefinite articles, 127
Indefinite pronouns
  as adjectives, 131
  personal-pronoun agreement with,
    76–78
  singular and plural, 76–78,
    216
  subject-verb agreement with,
    216–218, 226
Independent clauses, 186–188
  in complex sentences, 192
  in compound-complex sentences,
    198
  in compound sentences, 189
  joining, 189, 204
  in simple sentences, 189
Indirect objects, 23
  action verbs and, 95
  as complements, 46
  diagramming, 279
  function of, 33
  noun clauses as, 195, 196
  nouns as, 55
  object pronouns as, 63, 88
  verbs that often take, 95
  whom for, 70
Indirect questions, periods with, 250
Indirect quotations, punctuation of, 259
Infinitive phrases, 175–177
  diagramming, 282–283
  prepositional phrases distinguished
    from, 176, 182
  using, 175, 183
Infinitives, 175–177
  diagramming, 282
Information
  complements for adding, 47
Initials
  capitalization of, 230
  periods with, 251
Institutions, capitalization of, 239
Intensifiers, 134–135
Intensive pronouns, 68–69
  for stressing a point, 69
Interjections, 161
  exclamation points with, 251
  functions of, 166, 167
Interrogative pronouns, 70–72

Interrogative sentences, 16. *See also*
  Questions
  question marks with, 16, 250
Interrupters, commas with, 254, 274
Intransitive verbs, 96
Introductory words and phrases,
  commas after, 254, 274
Inverted sentences, 18–19
  subject-verb agreement in, 213
Irregular verbs, 102–104
  memorizing principal parts of, 103
Islands, capitalization of, 236
Italics
  for titles and names, 268, 274
  underlining and, 268

L

Landforms, capitalization of, 236
Landmarks, capitalization of, 237
Languages, capitalization of, 232
Lay, lie, 115, 361
Leave, let, 116, 362
Letters (documents)
  capitalization of parts of, 234, 247
  colon after greeting in business,
    262, 263
  commas in parts of, 256–257
Letters (of the alphabet)
  apostrophes in plurals of, 267
  in outlines, 251
Lie, lay, 115, 361
Linking verbs, 92–93, 122
  common linking verbs, 21, 61, 92, 98
  predicate adjectives following, 129
  and predicate words, 98–99
  replacing with action verbs, 94
  as simple predicates, 10
  subject complements following, 21,
    33, 98–99, 129
  subject pronouns following, 61
Lists
  colons to introduce items in, 262
  periods after numbers or letters in,
    251
Little, comparative and superlative of,
  138

M

Magazines
  capitalization of titles, 234
  italics for titles, 268
Main verbs, in verb phrases, 12–13
Masculine gender, 74
Me
  in compound objects, 81
  and *I,* 64, 82

Q

Question marks, 250
  with interrogative sentences, 16, 250
  with quotation marks, 258, 275
Questions
  indirect, 250
  interrogative pronouns for introducing, 70
  interrogative sentences, 16, 250
  subject position in, 18
  subject-verb agreement in, 213, 227
Quotation marks
  commas inside of, 258, 275
  in dialogue, 260
  in direct quotations, 258
  in divided quotations, 259
  exclamation points with, 258, 275
  periods inside of, 258, 275
  punctuation with, 258, 275
  question marks with, 258, 275
  for titles of works, 268, 274
Quotations
  capitalization of first words of, 233
  direct, 233, 258
  divided, 233, 259
  indirect, 259
  punctuating, 258–261

R

Races, capitalization of, 232
Raise, rise, 116, 363
Real, as an adjective, 140, 148
Really, as an adverb, 140, 148
Reflexive pronouns, 68–69
Regions, capitalization of, 236, 237
Regular verbs, 100, 122
Relative pronouns
  adjective clauses introduced by, 194
  common relative pronouns, 194
Religious terms, capitalization of, 231
Rise, raise, 116, 363
Roads, capitalization of, 236
Run-on sentences, 26–27
  fixing, 26, 291

S

Sacred days, capitalization of, 231
Sacred writings, capitalization of, 231
School subjects, capitalization of, 240
-self or *-selves,* 68, 88
Semicolons, 262
  in compound sentences, 189, 204, 262
  in series, 262

Sentence fragments, 25
  dependent clauses as, 187
  fixing, 26, 290
Sentences, 4–33. *See also* Predicates; Sentence structure; Subjects (of sentences)
  basic parts of, 6, 32
  choppy, 190
  commas in, 253–255
  complete, 6
  declarative, 16, 18, 250
  diagramming, 276–287
  exclamatory, 16, 251
  fragments, 25, 26, 187, 290
  imperative, 16, 18, 250
  interrogative, 16, 250
  inverted, 18–19, 213
  kinds of, 16–17, 33
  run-ons, 26–27, 291
Sentence structure, 184–205
  compound, 189–191, 204, 253, 262, 284
  complex, 192–193, 204, 285–286
  compound-complex, 198–199
  simple, 189–191
Series
  commas in, 253, 274
  semicolons in, 262
Set, sit, 115, 363
She, in compound subjects, 81
Ships
  capitalization of names, 237
  italics for names, 268
Short story
  capitalization of titles, 234
  quotation marks for titles, 268
Simple predicates, 10–11
  identifying, 32
Simple sentences, 189–191
Simple subjects, 8–9
  diagramming, 276
  identifying, 32
Simple tenses, 105–107. *See also* Future tense; Past tense; Present tense
Simple verbs, diagramming, 276
Singular nouns, 39–41
  apostrophes in possessives, 266
  subject-verb agreement with nouns ending in s, 219, 226
Singular pronouns
  demonstrative, 72
  indefinite, 76–78, 216
  object, 63
  personal, 58–59
Sit, set, 115, 363
Some, as singular or plural, 217

X, Y, Z

Acknowledgments

For Literature and Text

Brandt & Hochman Literary Agents: Excerpt from "The Third Wish," from *Not What You Expected: A Collection of Short Stories* by Joan Aiken. Copyright © 1974 by Joan Aiken. Reprinted by permission of Brandt & Hochman Literary Agents, Inc.

Henry Holt: Excerpts from "The Clown," from *Real Ponies Don't Go Oink!* by Patrick F. McManus. Copyright © 1974, 1981, 1985, 1989, 1990, 1991 by Patrick F. McManus. Reprinted with the permission of Henry Holt and Company, LLC.

Marian Reiner: Stanza from "Simile: Willow and Ginkgo" from *A Sky Full of Poems* by Eve Merriam. Copyright © 1964, 1970, 1973 by Eve Merriam. Reprinted by permission of Marian Reiner.

Jewell Parker Rhodes: Excerpt from "Block Party" by Jewell Parker Rhodes. Copyright © 1993 by Jewell Parker Rhodes. Reprinted by permission of the author.

Scribner: Excerpts from "A Mother in Mannville," from When the *Whippoorwill* by Marjorie Kinnan Rawlings. Copyright © 1936, 1940 by Marjorie Kinnan Rawlings; copyright renewed © 1964, 1968 by Norton Baskin. Reprinted with the permission of Scribner, a division of Simon & Schuster.

Time: Excerpt from "Fallen Rider" by Gregory Cerio, from *People Weekly,* June 12, 1995. Copyright © 1995 by Time, Inc. Reprinted by permission of Time, Inc. All rights reserved.

Table of Contents

v, vi Illustrations by Todd Graveline; **viii** © Jacob Taposchaner/Getty Images; **ix** Illustration by Todd Graveline; **x** © Getty Images; **xi, xii, xiii, 1** Illustrations by Todd Graveline.

Illustrations by Todd Graveline

8, 32, 33, 39, 47, 55, 68, 72, 89, 105, 123, 149, 152, 166, 167, 182, 183, 189, 204, 205, 210, 227, 246, 247, 263, 275, 276, 288, 290.

Art Credits

COVER © Ryan Aldrich/McDougal Littell

CHAPTER 1 **2–3** © Getty Images; **4 top** © Ron Chapple/FPG International/PNI; **bottom left** © Corbis; **bottom center** © T. J. Florian/PhotoNetwork/PNI; **bottom right** © Mark Gibson/Corbis; **9** Photo by Dennis Kitchen Studio, Inc.; **17** © Tony Brown, Eye Ubiquitous/Corbis; **19** © Charles E. Rotkin/Corbis; **25** © Michael T. Sedam/Corbis; **28** © Chinese Girl, Emil Orlik, oil on canvas, Christie's Images/SuperStock.

CHAPTER 2 **34** © Jerry Schad/Photo Researchers, Inc.; **36, 38** NASA; **41 left** © Chris Butler/Science Photo Library/Photo Researchers, Inc.; **right** NASA; **43** NASA; **46** © Getty Images; **50** NASA; **52** Photo courtesy of U.S. Space Camp®.

CHAPTER 3 **56** Photofest; **60** © Myrleen Ferguson/PhotoEdit; **61, 66** © Getty Images; **84** AP/Wide World Photos.

CHAPTER 4 **90** © Carol Bernson/Black Star/PNI; **92** © Bernard Boutrit/Woodfin Camp/PNI; **97** AP/Wide World Photos; **99** Corbis/Bettmann; **101, 104, 107** AP/Wide World Photos/NASA; **108** © Tom Bean/Corbis; **111** © Kevin Schafer, Martha Hill/All Stock/PNI; **112** © Peter Bianchi/NGS Image Collection; **120** AP/Wide World Photos.

CHAPTER 5 **124 background** Charles Michael Murray/Corbis; **foreground** © Getty Images; **126** AP/Wide World Photos; **130 left, right** © Getty Images; **132** *Dinner at Haddo House* (1884), Alfred Edward Emslie, National Portrait Gallery, London, www.npg.org.uk; **139 left, center, right** © Getty Images; **143** © Dave Watts/Natural Selection; **144** Max Seabaugh/MAX; **145** © Getty Images; **148** © Earl Kowall/Corbis.

CHAPTER 6   **150** Photofest; **154** © Lowell Georgia/Corbis; **156** © Ed Kashi/Phototake/PNI; **157** © Richard Pasley/Stock Boston/PNI; **158** © Sam Ogden Photography; **161** The 5th Wave reprinted with permission of Rich Tennant; **162 left, right** NASA; **163 inset** © Getty Images.

CHAPTER 7   **168** © Corbis/Bettmann; **173** Photo by Meighan Depke; **175** © Getty Images; **179** Wallpaper design for Swan, Rush and Iris, Walter Crane (1845–1915), Victoria & Albert Museum, London, UK/Bridgeman Art Library, London/New York.

CHAPTER 8   **184** © Arne Hodalic/Corbis; **188** © Gunter Marx/Corbis; **195** © Galen Rowell/Corbis; **197** © Kevin R. Morris/Corbis; **201** © Charles Harris, Pittsburg Courier/Corbis; **202** © Getty Images.

CHAPTER 9   **206 background, 212** Photo by Sharon Hoogstraten; **206 foreground** © Getty Images; **213 top** © Stephen Shaver/AFP/Getty Images; **bottom** © Vince Bucci/AFP/Getty Images; **216, 218** © Alison Wright/Corbis; Detail of Pointer with Pheasant (1700s), Anonymous. Benelli Collection, Florence. © Scala/Art Resource, New York.

CHAPTER 10   **228 background** © Hilarie Kavanagh/Getty Images; **top right** The Granger Collection, New York; **bottom right** Victoria & Albert Museum, London/Art Resource, NY; **230** © Chris Hellier/Corbis; **232** The Granger Collection, New York; **233** © Phyllis Picardi; **234** Owen Franken/Corbis; **235** © David Ryan/Photo 20-20/PNI; **236** © Getty Images; **238** © Giraudon/Art Resource, NY; **242** Scala/Art Resource, NY; **243 bottom left** © Adam Woolfit/Corbis; **bottom center** © Brian Vikander/Corbis; **bottom right** © Richard T. Nowitz/Corbis; **244** © Magellan Geographix/PNI.

CHAPTER 11   **248** © Bill Bachmann/Stock Boston; **252** © Getty Images; **253** © Corbis/Bettmann; **257** Copyright © 1999 Zits Partnership. Reprinted with special permission of King Features Syndicate; **258** Mary Evans Picture Library; **265** © Steve Shelton/Black Star/PNI; **269** © Roger Ressmeyer/Corbis; **270 left** © David David Gallery, Philadelphia/SuperStock; **right** © Diana Ong/SuperStock.

The editors have made every effort to trace the ownership of all copyrighted material found in this book and to make full acknowledgment for its use. Omissions brought to our attention will be corrected in a subsequent edition.